Contents

Introduction

We often look to the New Testament to learn about spiritual disciplines—those spiritual practices that set us apart for God and draw us closer to Him. But there is much we can learn from the Old Testament about timeless practices of faith. In this study of First and Second Kings, we will examine the holy habits of the prophets and kings who were set apart by their close walk with God. Each week we will explore the central story of one of these intriguing men of God and the specific practice he observed, as well as what the Bible teaches about this practice. As we journey together, we will discover what we can learn from

> Solomon's experience of being consecrated,
> Elijah's practice of listening to God,
> Elijah and Elisha's practice of mentoring,
> Elisha and Naaman's example of practicing humility,
> Hezekiah's practice of worshiping God alone, and
> Josiah's practice of discovering God's Word.

Each of these men was trying to follow God while carrying out his calling on earth. As we consider their examples, we will discover that even prophets and kings struggled and grew in their faith through spiritual practices, and we will learn how these same practices can help us to draw closer to God and follow His unique purposes for us in His kingdom. We'll see that being set apart is not only for our own good but also for the good of others, as they come to see God in and through us.

Getting Started

For each week of our study there are five readings. Each of these readings includes the following elements:

Read God's Word A portion of the Bible story for the week, occasionally with other Scripture readings.

Reflect and Respond A guided reflection and study of the Scripture with space for recording your responses.

Talk with God A sample prayer to guide you into a personal time of prayer.

Act on It Ideas to help you act on what you have read.

Extra Insight Additional "bonus" insights or facts to enhance your study.

You will be able to complete each reading in about 20–30 minutes. (Be sure to have a pen or pencil and your Bible ready.) Completing these readings each week will help to prepare you for the discussion and activities of the group session.

Once a week you will gather with your group to watch a video in which I share additional insights into the stories and their application for our lives. I encourage you to discuss what you're learning and to share how God is working in your own life. You will find that sharing with one another will enable you to recognize God's activity in your life even more clearly and help you to encourage and pray for one another.

Before you begin this journey, give God permission to work in your heart and life. Offer yourself to Him and express your desire to be set apart as chosen, royal, and holy for the sake of His kingdom. May God richly bless you as you study His Word and discover how to become more like Him.

Blessings,

Week 1
Solomon
Set Apart by Consecration

Apart from fairy-tale movies and occasional stories of British royalty, our experience of coronation is limited. That moment when an existing king or queen passes on the crown to the appointed successor—the pomp and circumstance and ceremony—is tied to a fairy-tale image in most of our minds. Kings and queens are established as named leaders of a monarchy—that's coronation. But it's not consecration.

Consecration is two-way set-apartness. We are set apart *by* God for His purposes and His glory. But we also *set ourselves* apart, handing over all the parts of our lives to God—all surrendered to God for God's purposes. The word *consecration* is related to the word *sacred*. Being set apart or consecrated is a sacred and holy act.

King Solomon doesn't just have the fairy-tale coronation ceremony, one in which his father, King David, passes down the crown and they live happily ever after. He is consecrated, set apart for a holy and sacred purpose. But he will not thrive as king by relying only on his earthly crown. It is his consecration, his set-apart-by-God-ness, that makes him a great king. When he follows God's wisdom and leads by surrendering to God, he thrives. When he seeks God's wisdom first and lives a life different from the culture of idolatry around him, he finds success. But when he becomes overly enamored with the power of the crown, his story takes a turn.

I hope that you have experienced a consecration in your life—a time when another person dedicated you to God, prayed over you, and spoke words of faith into your life. But at some point, we have to consecrate ourselves to God—to hand over all the parts of our lives to God. We have to say to God, "I want to live a set apart life that glorifies you."

This week we're jumping right into Solomon's consecration story to discover more about what it means to be set apart by God and to set ourselves apart to be used by God.

Day 1: Set Apart as King

Read God's Word

¹ *When King David was very old, he could not keep warm even when they put covers over him.* ² *So his attendants said to him, "Let us look for a young virgin to serve the king and take care of him. She can lie beside him so that our lord the king may keep warm."*

³ *Then they searched throughout Israel for a beautiful young woman and found Abishag, a Shunammite, and brought her to the king.* ⁴ *The woman was very beautiful; she took care of the king and waited on him, but the king had no sexual relations with her.*

⁵ *Now Adonijah, whose mother was Haggith, put himself forward and said, "I will be king." So he got chariots and horses ready, with fifty men to run ahead of him.* ⁶ *(His father had never rebuked him by asking, "Why do you behave as you do?" He was also very handsome and was born next after Absalom.)*

. . .

²⁸ *Then King David said, "Call in Bathsheba." So she came into the king's presence and stood before him.*

²⁹ *The king then took an oath: "As surely as the LORD lives, who has delivered me out of every trouble,* ³⁰ *I will surely carry out this very day what I swore to you by the LORD, the God of Israel: Solomon your son shall be king after me, and he will sit on my throne in my place."*

³¹ *Then Bathsheba bowed down with her face to the ground, prostrating herself before the king, and said, "May my lord King David live forever!"*

³² *King David said, "Call in Zadok the priest, Nathan the prophet and Benaiah son of Jehoiada." When they came before the king,* ³³ *he said to them: "Take your lord's servants with you and have Solomon my son mount my own mule and take him down to Gihon.* ³⁴ *There have Zadok the priest and Nathan the prophet anoint him king over Israel. Blow the trumpet and shout, 'Long live King Solomon!'* ³⁵ *Then you are to go up with him, and he is to come and sit on my throne and reign in my place. I have appointed him ruler over Israel and Judah."*

. . .

³⁸ *So Zadok the priest, Nathan the prophet, Benaiah son of Jehoiada, the Kerethites and the Pelethites went down and had Solomon mount King David's mule, and they escorted him to Gihon.* ³⁹ *Zadok the priest took the horn of oil from the sacred tent and anointed Solomon. Then they sounded the trumpet and all the people shouted, "Long live King Solomon!"* ⁴⁰ *And all the people went up after him, playing pipes and rejoicing greatly, so that the ground shook with the sound.*

1 Kings 1:1-6; 28-35, 38-40

Reflect and Respond

If you have spent any time at all in the checkout line at the grocery store, then most likely you have noticed that our culture has a fascination with royalty. If you are old enough to remember Princess Diana, you'll remember the coverage of her life from the moment she came on the scene until her tragic death. And just a few years ago we became enamored with Catherine (Kate) Middleton, who married Diana's son Prince William. For some reason, the concept of royalty captures our attention and keeps us coming back for more. The idea that a human being was at some point in his or her lineage set apart and called "royal" is fairytale-like and stirs our imagination.

Early in the Scriptures we read that God would rather not introduce the pattern of kings. Instead, God would lead His people and speak through judges and prophets. But the people wanted a king. Other nations had kings and palaces and courts; it was all so fascinating! Even God's people were consumed with the idea of royalty—so much so that they begged God to give them a king. They couldn't be satisfied with the Creator of the Universe leading through chosen prophets and judges. They wanted something more—more ornate, more official, more royal. They wanted a king. Finally, God relented and gave them their king, but He alone would determine the first king. God would set apart a chosen man to become the first king and, for better or worse, the history of God's people would be made by the actions and leadership of a line of kings.

As the book of First Kings begins, you can sense the excitement about who will be the next king after the great King David dies. If you've ever wondered how a king became a king, you'll get an idea here in Chapter 1.

King David, widely held as the greatest king ever to rule Israel, was in his last days. Once known as a great and strong ruler, David's heyday was clearly behind him. He was so frail and chilled that his advisors brought him a young girl to serve as a human space heater (1 Kings 1:1-2). While he was still technically king, David was so out of the loop on the happenings in his own country (and his own family) that his key advisor Nathan and wife Bathsheba had to cook up a scheme to inform him that Adonijah, his oldest living son, had seized the throne, declaring himself king without his father's blessing (1 Kings 1:11-27).

If David hadn't realized it before, it became clear to him that his days on this earth as king of Israel were coming to an end. And if he wanted to have any input into who would succeed him as king, he would need to act now. The future of the nation was no longer in his hands but in the hands of its forthcoming leaders, and the decision about who would be the next king was one that would forever shape the nation that David loved.

The Books of First and Second Kings are particularly interested in leadership. You don't need to look much further than the books' titles to find that they will reveal the important place that kings play in the history of God's people.

Extra Insight
First and Second Kings were originally written as one book, on one scroll, in Hebrew. When the text was translated into Greek, which made it longer, it was separated into two books.[1]

A good king meant good days ahead for the people of Israel. "As goes the leader, so goes the nation," according to the old saying. For Israel, the leaders were prophets and kings, powerful people whose own personal lives paved the way to a good or bad future for their followers.

The Books of First and Second Kings are primarily interested in whether a leader chose to follow and worship the One True God or fall into the temptation of allowing the worship of false gods and idols. The integrity of the king was ultimately connected to the fate of the people, and First and Second Kings are explicit about the fact that the leader's relationship to God is the most important thing about him.

Whatever they accomplish in their reign—whatever cities they build, wars they fight, civic accomplishments they have—these are of no consequence if the leader in question compromises his faith in God. A judgment of his reign is summarized in the first few sentences about each king.

Read the introductions to a handful of the kings in First and Second Kings. Next to each name, write how this king measured up in the Bible's judgment of his reign:

2 Kings 8:16-18 – Jehoram: *was is wicked as King ahabe ase he married one of ahabs daughters*

1 Kings 15:1-3 – Abijah: *committed same sins as his father and was not faithful to God*

1 Kings 15:9-11 – Asa: *did what was pleasing in the Lords sight. his heart remained faithful to his Lord throughout his life*

2 Kings 18:1-3 – Hezekiah: *did what was pleasing to God - he trusted God + remained faithful to God*

2 Kings 22:1-2 – Josiah: *did what was pleasing to God & followed example of King David*

As you can see from just a few examples, full devotion to God was the first and most important qualification for being a good ruler of God's people. Because of this, the takeover of the throne by David's oldest surviving son, Adonijah, sent a clear message about what kind of king he would be. Here was a leader who grabbed power for himself without concern for his father's will—or even for the fact that his father, the king, was still alive when he named himself king.

A wise mentor in ministry once gave me instructions about meeting new people in the first days and weeks as pastor of a church: "Watch out for the people who walk into your office and declare to you, 'I'm a leader. I'm important. I'm in charge of things here.' But look for the people who have their sleeves rolled up and are serving, making ministry happen. Those are your leaders."

Who are the leaders in your world who quietly make ministry happen?

In contrast to his older brother Adonijah's selfish takeover, Solomon received the throne because he was chosen by his father. Leadership is a gift. The roles we have that allow us to influence others are always a gift—both from the leaders who have influenced us and for the people over whom we have charge.

Consider the immediate transformation that Solomon went through in that moment when his father named him king. While he was already royalty by virtue of being born the son of a king, he went from being just one of many royal sons (1 Chronicles 3:9 lists nineteen sons and one daughter born to David) to ruler of the nation.

To drive home the impact of Solomon's royal conversion, the book of First Kings mentions him ten times before David's instructions to make him the next king, and every single time he is mentioned only in relationship to someone else:

1. his brother Solomon (1:10)
2. Solomon's mother (1:11)
3. your son Solomon (1:12)
4. your son Solomon (1:13)
5. your son Solomon (1:17)
6. your servant Solomon (1:19)
7. my son Solomon (1:21)
8. your servant Solomon (1:26)
9. your son Solomon (1:30)
10. my son Solomon (1:33)

It's as if no one even recognizes Solomon's name except in relationship to someone who was already important. He is a royal nobody.

But when David gives instructions for Solomon to be named king over Israel, there is no name attached to give Solomon status. He now carries the rank of royal leadership.

Write below the words David instructs to be declared over Solomon when he is named king in 1 Kings 1:34. *Long live King Solomon*

This is the stuff fairy tales are made of. Cinderella finds herself transformed from maid to princess. The frog prince goes from the swamp to the throne with just a kiss. If the number of fairy-tale books and movies sold is any indication, rising to the rank of royalty is something that many people fantasize about.

Being set apart as king meant that Solomon would have incredible privilege, wealth, and power. Who wouldn't want to live in a palace with servants and robes and food fit for a king? But along with royal privilege comes the royal responsibility for the nation that he would serve.

Extra Insight
After her mention in the first chapter of First Kings, the next time Bathsheba is named in the book she is given status only in relationship to her son and is called "Solomon's mother" (see 1 Kings 2:13). This signifies the elevation of Solomon's status.[1]

The Book of First Peter tells us that the same thing has happened to you and to me. We were nobodies, with no status. And then God chose us to become royalty, with great privilege and great responsibility.

But you are a chosen people, a royal priesthood, a holy nation, God's special possession, that you may declare the praises of him who called you out of darkness into his wonderful light. Once you were not a people, but now you are the people of God; once you had not received mercy, but now you have received mercy.

1 Peter 2:9-10

Chosen. Royal. Holy. These words go together. They could have been written about Solomon, but they weren't. They are about you. They are declarations of who you are in Christ.

Below, write your name three times in the blanks on the left. Then in the blanks on the right, write the words *chosen*, *royal*, and *holy*. Read each statement out loud, taking in the impact of its meaning.

Sheryl is chosen.

Sheryl is royal.

Sheryl is holy.

When we read it in connection to ourselves, *holy* is possibly the hardest word on this list to swallow. We tend to identify this word either with those who are so good that they seem to live on a different spiritual plane or with those who act "holier than thou."

Being set apart is not something that means we see ourselves as better than others. On the contrary, it is only God's Spirit living in us that marks us and makes us different from those around us, and it is our brokenness and sinfulness that drive us to seek a new way, a new life in Christ. In his book *Called to Be Holy*, John Oswalt writes, "When the holy character of God is seen in broken, fallible people it is apparent that something supernatural has taken place in them. And this becomes a sign of hope to the world that their sinful condition can be addressed as well."[2] The prophet Ezekiel talks about this when he says, "Then the nations will know that I am the LORD, declares the Sovereign LORD, when I show myself holy through you before their eyes" (Ezekiel 36:23).

The king was set apart to rule, not for his own sake but for the sake of his followers and his kingdom. Likewise, being set apart is something that happens *in* us *for* others. When we display the character of God, people around us are drawn to know Him.

> Being set apart is something that happens *in* us *for* others.

In the coming weeks, we will explore what it means for God to set us apart as chosen, royal, and holy, and how this draws others to God. For now, let it begin to sink in: God chose you. He loves you. Once you were nobody, but now you are His. This privilege is greater than any earthly palace can provide.

Talk with God

Almighty God, thank You for giving me the interest and desire to study Your Word. Please reveal Yourself and Your love for me through this study. Help me to understand, beginning today, that I am chosen by You, that I am royalty because of You, that I am holy and precious in Your eyes. Set me apart, Lord, for Your kingdom purposes, not only in my life but also in the lives of others. Amen.

Act on It

Solomon was "chosen" to be king by his father. In your life, who has noticed special gifts and abilities in you and called them out? Has someone told you through words or actions that you are special and can do something worthwhile with your life? Say a prayer of thanks for the faith these persons had in you. You may want to write each one a note of thanks or tell someone about them and the positive influence they had on you.

Day 2: Marked

Read God's Word

 ³² *King David said, "Call in Zadok the priest, Nathan the prophet and Benaiah son of Jehoiada." When they came before the king,* ³³ *he said to them: "Take your lord's servants with you and have Solomon my son mount my own mule and take him down to Gihon.* ³⁴ *There have Zadok the priest and Nathan the prophet anoint him king over Israel. Blow the trumpet and shout, 'Long live King Solomon!'* ³⁵ *Then you are to go up with him, and he is to come and sit on my throne and reign in my place. I have appointed him ruler over Israel and Judah."*

Jesus did this

1 Kings 1:32-35

> ²² *Then the L*ORD *said to Moses,* ²³ *"Take the following fine spices: 500 shekels of liquid myrrh, half as much (that is, 250 shekels) of fragrant cinnamon, 250 shekels of fragrant calamus,* ²⁴ *500 shekels of cassia—all according to the sanctuary shekel—and a hin of olive oil.* ²⁵ *Make these into a sacred anointing oil, a fragrant blend, the work of a perfumer. It will be the sacred anointing oil.* ²⁶ *Then use it to anoint the tent of meeting, the ark of the covenant law,* ²⁷ *the table and all its articles, the lampstand and its accessories, the altar of incense,* ²⁸ *the altar of burnt offering and all its utensils, and the basin with its stand.* ²⁹ *You shall consecrate them so they will be most holy, and whatever touches them will be holy.*
>
> ³⁰ *"Anoint Aaron and his sons and consecrate them so they may serve me as priests.* ³¹ *Say to the Israelites, 'This is to be my sacred anointing oil for the generations to come.* ³² *Do not pour it on anyone else's body and do not make any other oil using the same formula. It is sacred, and you are to consider it sacred.* ³³ *Whoever makes perfume like it and puts it on anyone other than a priest must be cut off from their people.'"*

Exodus 30:22-33

We are a people who are set apart, called to be different than the world around us, marked for a purpose greater than we could dream of.

Reflect and Respond

When I was nine years old, I went away to summer camp for the first time. Judging from the whirlwind of preparation that overtook our household in the weeks before I left, you would have thought I was going to another continent. In the midst of all the piles of supplies gathered in our living room, one indispensable piece of the camp-readiness equipment was the black permanent marker we used to mark my things. According to my mom's instructions, everything to be packed for camp was immediately marked with permanent marker. T-shirts, sandals, bug spray, even toothpaste—all were inscribed with my name.

I thought this ritual of marking things a little silly at first (*Even the bottle of sunscreen?*) and then a bit embarrassing (*Really? Even my underwear?*). But then I arrived in a cabin of twelve girls and two counselors and saw just how necessary this practice had been. From day one the cabin was in utter chaos: our trunks and suitcases spilling out into the middle of the room, and all the clothes our mothers had neatly packed and folded now strewn about. With multiple identical Rainbow Brite T-shirts thrown over various bunk beds, how were we to know whose was whose? I found myself relieved that I could always spot mine—the black permanent marker on the tag had done its job.

Marked. Set apart from the others. Ownership declared.

These are actions meant not only for camping supplies but for people as well. Again and again in Scripture, God declares that we are a people who are set apart, called to be different than the world around us, marked for a purpose greater than we could dream of.

This is the kind of legacy David longs to give his son Solomon. David's intentions for Solomon to be set apart from those around him go beyond the role of kingship; they involve David's longing for his son to be fully devoted to God.

As part of Solomon's coronation, David commands that Solomon be anointed by both a priest and a prophet. These men, Zadok and Nathan, are two of David's most important spiritual leaders. We tend to think of kings as having the ultimate authority over their subjects, but even kings need spiritual leaders. Perhaps David was communicating to his son that he would need guidance from these men and those who would follow them in their roles. Take note of which prophet David chooses to anoint his son—his old friend Nathan.

David himself was appointed as king (since he was not born into a royal family) and then anointed by the prophet Samuel (1 Samuel 16:1-13). David was a stranger to the prophet Samuel at the time, having been selected with specific guidance from God. In contrast, the prophet Nathan has known Solomon all his life, even since before he was born.

The history of the relationship between Solomon's mother and father, David and Bathsheba, is infamous, and Nathan played a part in the scandalous story. David committed adultery with Bathsheba, and when she became pregnant, David had her husband murdered to cover up David's sins.

Read Nathan's scathing rebuke of David for adultery and murder in 2 Samuel 12:1-15.

Who has the authority in this conversation? The king or the prophet?

Nathan the prophet who was sent by God to talk to David the king

As Nathan confronted David with the error of his ways, this conversation must have been deeply emotional and difficult for David. Proverbs 27:6 says, "Wounds from a friend can be trusted." Sometimes it takes someone very close to us to tell us a difficult truth.

When has someone close to you spoken difficult words of truth, enabling you to hear them from a trusted source?

We can tell that David and Nathan maintained an especially close relationship, not only because David chose Nathan to anoint his son Solomon as king but also because David and Bathsheba even named one of their sons born after the scandal "Nathan"—probably as an homage to the truth-telling prophet (1 Chronicles 3:5). So, when he anointed Solomon as the new king, Nathan was acting as both a prophet and a deeply trusted advisor and friend of Solomon's father, one who had been part of their family history—both good and bad—since before Solomon's birth.

We see the practice of anointing throughout the Scriptures. Anointing is a deep and ancient symbol of being set apart, marked by God as a sign of His grace for a special act.

Read 1 Kings 19:15-16. Who are the three people God calls Elijah to anoint in this passage, and for what roles? *Hazael to be king of Aram, Jehu to be king of Israel & Elisha as prophet to replace Elijah*

Anointing was used to mark prophets, priests, and kings as set apart for a special calling. Once they had been anointed, they would be recognized by those around them as being different from their peers. The sheen of oil would wear off, but their lives and identities were altered forever by that experience.

Having grown up in a nation that prides itself on the principle of the separation of church and state, it's hard for me to picture a king, the leader of a nation, being given authority and permission to lead by a priest and a prophet. When I struggle with that picture, it makes me realize again how different our own culture is from that of ancient Israel. The king was not just a political leader or figurehead. Solomon's spiritual lineage and his continued dedication to worship God alone was just as important as any civil or military role he played as the nation's leader. In fact, the success or failure of his reign would rise and fall not on his military victories or financial gain but on his commitment to remaining set apart—marked to be different in the purity of his dedication to God.

Reread Exodus 30:22-33 (page 14). What objects and people are being anointed in this passage? *Tent of meeting, ark of the covenant law, table & all its articles, lampstand & its accessories, altar of incense, altar of burnt offering & all its utensils, & basin with stand and Aaron & his sons*

What explicit instructions and prohibitions are given about the scent of the oil used? *Do not pour it on anyone else's body (but Aaron & sons) & do not make any other oil using same formula & it is sacred*

Our sense of smell can evoke powerful emotions and memories. You may be able to recall a scent that immediately brings to mind a specific person from your past, an era of your history, or an event. Over the years, I've attended or served churches that are always filled with lilies on Easter morning. Those lilies are so connected to my Easter tradition that now I can practically smell them as I prepare for Easter services. And if I'm around lilies at any other time of year, I automatically think of Easter and the resurrection of Christ.

God's instructions about the use of this scent in the Tabernacle meant the place of worship and the people who led worship there would carry with them a scent that set them apart as different from anyone else. I'm sure that the scent used evoked images and memories of the Tabernacle in those who smelled it. These objects of worship and the people who led worship in that special place would always carry that scent—one that became known as the fragrance of God's presence. The scent rubbed off on people and gave others a clue that they had been with God. But it also wore off eventually. Worshipers needed to return again and again to experience and receive that special scent of the presence of God.

Being anointed means being set apart. It means walking in an aroma of God's presence. It means being marked as one who belongs to the Almighty. And it's not only for prophets, priests, and kings; it's also for you. You are anointed in Christ:

> *Now it is God who makes both us and you stand firm in Christ. He anointed us, set his seal of ownership on us, and put his Spirit in our hearts as a deposit, guaranteeing what is to come.*
>
> 2 Corinthians 1:21-22

The first time I read this passage after learning more about anointing, I got chills. The idea that God has anointed me and placed a seal of ownership on me brings such a feeling of belonging and having a special part in the Kingdom. It also reminds me that, like the worshipers in the Tabernacle, I need to return again and again to the means of God's grace—things such as prayer, reading of Scripture, and gathering to worship with other believers—so that the scent of God's presence saturates my being and rubs off on those I come into contact with.

What are some practices that saturate you with the presence of God?

Bible Study, Church service, reading upper room or Jesus Calling, Music Communion & praying

When you encounter someone who exudes God's presence, what do you notice about this person? *Mary Lee - her kindness towards others, her caring.*

The name *Messiah,* the precious title of our Lord Jesus, literally means "Anointed One." He is the One who exudes mercy and grace. Take time to be with Him today, to rest in His presence, and to let Him know you love Him. Remember that you are anointed and sealed. He has put His deposit down on your life by giving His own life. You are His.

Extra Insight
Anointing comes from the root *chrisas*, which is where we get our word for Christ—meaning the Anointed One. When we give our lives to Christ and he abides in us, we become one with the Anointed One. We are "christed." Anointing also sets us apart for something. In Jesus' first sermon, He proclaimed that the Spirit of the Lord was upon him because [the Spirit] anointed him to proclaim good news to the poor (Luke 4). Followers of Jesus are anointed for that same work as well.[3]

Talk with God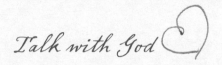

Holy Anointed One, Messiah, remind us again that You have anointed us for a purpose. Make us hungry to spend time in Your presence. And when we come into contact with other people, may they notice that the aroma of grace is all around us. Amen.

Act on It

Invite a small group of spiritual friends to join in a prayer of anointing over one other. You can buy special bottles of anointing oil, or you can set aside a small dish with olive oil in it. Friends can take turns anointing one another, or have a designated leader anoint each person in the group. Dip your finger in the oil, mark the symbol of a cross on your friend's forehead, and say the words, "I anoint you in the name of the Father, the Son, and the Holy Spirit. You are marked. You are His." Follow with specific prayers for that person's needs and for blessings.

Day 3: The Wisdom of Solomon

Read God's Word

[3] *Solomon showed his love for the LORD by walking according to the instructions given him by his father David, except that he offered sacrifices and burned incense on the high places.*

[4] *The king went to Gibeon to offer sacrifices, for that was the most important high place, and Solomon offered a thousand burnt offerings on that altar.* [5] *At Gibeon the Lord appeared to Solomon during the night in a dream, and God said, "Ask for whatever you want me to give you."*

[6] *Solomon answered, "You have shown great kindness to your servant, my father David, because he was faithful to you and righteous and upright in heart. You have continued this great kindness to him and have given him a son to sit on his throne this very day.*

[7] *"Now, LORD my God, you have made your servant king in place of my father David. But I am only a little child and do not know how to carry out my duties.* [8] *Your servant is here among the people you have chosen, a great people, too numerous to count or number.* [9] *So give your servant a discerning heart to*

govern your people and to distinguish between right and wrong. For who is able to govern this great people of yours?"

¹⁰ The Lord was pleased that Solomon had asked for this. ¹¹ So God said to him, "Since you have asked for this and not for long life or wealth for yourself, nor have asked for the death of your enemies but for discernment in administering justice, ¹² I will do what you have asked. I will give you a wise and discerning heart, so that there will never have been anyone like you, nor will there ever be. ¹³ Moreover, I will give you what you have not asked for—both wealth and honor—so that in your lifetime you will have no equal among kings. ¹⁴ And if you walk in obedience to me and keep my decrees and commands as David your father did, I will give you a long life." ¹⁵ Then Solomon awoke—and he realized it had been a dream.

He returned to Jerusalem, stood before the ark of the Lord's covenant and sacrificed burnt offerings and fellowship offerings. Then he gave a feast for all his court.

1 Kings 3:3-15

Reflect and Respond

In most of the churches I've attended since childhood, it seems there is one beloved pastor or staff person from the past that people talk about with particular fondness. Even if it has been years since that leader has been gone and many others have served the church since then, people continue to reminisce about the glory days when that person was there.

Of all the kings of Israel, everyone agreed that David was the best. He was the king that people talked about for generations after his reign, the king who was the standard by which all other kings would be measured. They probably said, "Those were the good days back when David was in charge." And of the current king they whispered, "Why can't he be more like David?" Even Jesus himself couldn't escape being compared to David! (see Luke 1:32 and Mark 12:35-37).

If the echoes of David's reign were still being felt for centuries to come, how intimidating must it have been to be the king who immediately followed him!

David's son Solomon was his immediate successor. Solomon had to start his reign while his father was still alive, looking over his shoulder, and all of Israel was wondering how he would measure up to his dad. Is it any wonder that Solomon begged God for wisdom to rule?

When have you felt that you were in over your head and asked God for wisdom? *Many times*

If anyone ever needed to grow in wisdom, it was Solomon, the new king. In 1 Kings 3 we find Solomon still wet behind the ears and newly crowned king by his father's authority, and already he is wrongly worshiping and offering sacrifices at the high place at Gibeon.

Read Deuteronomy 12:2-4 in the margin. What does God say here about the high places? Is God vague about whether it's okay to worship at the high places?

Destroy completely all the places on the high mountains, on the hills and under every spreading tree, where the nations you are dispossessing worship their gods. Break down their altars, smash their sacred stones and burn their Asherah poles in the fire; cut down the idols of their gods and wipe out their names from those places.

You must not worship the LORD your God in their way.
Deuteronomy 12:2-4

The high places were altars at local places of worship—shrines to idols and false gods. The Books of First and Second Kings take time to deliberately spell out how each individual king dealt with the high places. A king's practice toward these places of idol worship (and thus their obedience or disobedience to God) is the biggest predictor of the success or failure of his reign.

It's possible that Solomon was sacrificing at the altars at Gibeon to worship the One True God and not the idols. However, 1 Kings 3:3 exposes Solomon's divided heart by describing his love for God and his disobedience in the same sentence. It says that Solomon loved the Lord and walked according to His commands, *except that* he sacrificed at the high places, deliberately breaking God's commands.

Most of us have an "except that" in our own lives. We love and worship God. Our lives are marked by obedience, *except that* there is one area we have not surrendered to God. It might be a habit, a wrong belief, the way we look at certain people, or the way we talk to ourselves. As a mom of young children, I sometimes compare myself with other moms who seem to be doing it way better than me. In those moments I forget that relying on God is all I need to do--that God will fully equip me for the task of motherhood. I know to do this and yet, sometimes I allow comparison to steal my joy or, even worse, to take my eyes off of God and God's good work in the life of my family. I totally trust God, "except that" I sometimes listen to that voice playing in my head instead of relying on the truth of God's sufficiency in my life.

Solomon's "except that" was his downfall, pulling him into idolatry and causing his reign and his family to fall apart.

Reread 1 Kings 3:4 (page 18). How many sacrifices do we learn Solomon has offered here at Gibeon, the most important high place?

a thousand

Remarkably, it's here in Gibeon, the site of Solomon's repeated disobedience, that God appears to him in a dream and tells Solomon to ask God for anything he wants.

In 1 Kings 3:6-9 we learn how Solomon is feeling since he has been made king. He refers to himself as "a little child" and admits that he doesn't know how to govern. Out of humility and a desire to govern rightly and follow in his father David's footsteps, he asks for wisdom, not just for his own benefit but for the benefit of God's great people that he has been appointed to rule.

God's response to Solomon's request, right at the site of Solomon's disobedience, reveals something remarkable about the character of God: He doesn't wait for us to become perfect before stepping into our lives. He doesn't hold back His love, His help, or His blessings because we are holding back parts of our lives.

I'm so grateful God doesn't wait for me to get it together in order to love me, help me, or bless me. Even when I feel less than or compare myself to others, He meets me where I am with love and grace. If you ever feel unworthy of God's love, question whether God hears your prayers and wants to help you with your struggles, or are hesitant to pray because you feel you don't deserve to have your prayers answered, then the story of Solomon's request and God's response has a message for you.

Even though Solomon was deliberately disobeying God, God loved him and wanted to help him become a better man and a better king, so He granted Solomon's request.

If God told you to ask Him for anything you wanted, as He did to Solomon, what would ask Him for? *To always show love & grace to others, to be of service to others & remember God's will for my life*

Read Philippians 4:6-7 in the margin. How do we know that God wants us to tell Him our deepest desires? *scripture tells us so many times*

What does He promise in as an outcome? *peace of God will guard your hearts & minds through Jesus*

The result of Solomon's prayer was that he received great wisdom. David may be remembered for the glory days of Israel, but Solomon is often remembered for his wisdom.

People sometimes use the word *wisdom* to mean different things: IQ, knowledge, street smarts, the insight to deal with problems that arise or relationships that are difficult. So, what kind of wisdom are we talking about here in regards to Solomon? To answer this question, let's consider several different kinds of wisdom.

Do not be anxious about anything, but in every situation, by prayer and petition, with thanksgiving, present your requests to God. And the peace of God, which transcends all understanding, will guard your hearts and your minds in Christ Jesus. Philippians 4:6-7

1. Wisdom from Acquired Knowledge or Life Experience

When the Bible speaks of true wisdom, it isn't talking about knowledge that can be gained from years of study or even life experience. This isn't knowledge from the school of the Ivy League or the school of hard knocks. The kind of wisdom Solomon was granted was a gift from God, granted because of a prayer.

Knowledge and wisdom sometimes go hand in hand, but sometimes they do not. There is more information available to us today than our ancestors just a few generations ago ever could have dreamed of. But is the world any kinder, more peaceful, or more mature? Knowledge is a wonderful thing, but wisdom is something different. It is not acquired through patience, age, experience, or study; it is something acquired from the Lord.

Read James 3:13-17. Write some of the words used to describe true wisdom:

living an honorable life, doing good works with humility, peace loving, gentle at all times, willing to yield to others, full of mercy + good deeds, shows no favoritism and is always sincere

2. Wisdom for Political Savvy

In the story that immediately precedes Solomon's dream-prayer at Gibeon, his father, David, gave him some last instructions before his death about how to run the kingdom.

Besides David's instructions to remain faithful to God, the speech sounds less like a God-fearing king and a little more like something out of the classic mob movie *The Godfather*, as David gives instructions about how to deal with enemies who have wronged their family after he passes away. "You are a man of *wisdom*," David instructs Solomon about one such situation. "You will know what to do with him. Bring his gray head down to the grave in blood" (1 Kings 2:9, emphasis added). About another situation, he advises Solomon, "Deal with him according to your *wisdom*, but do not let his gray head go down to the grave in peace" (1 Kings 2:6, emphasis added).

The wisdom to know how to deal with those who have wronged you—enemies both within and outside of your kingdom—is one kind of wisdom it takes to be king. No wonder it is immediately after this speech that Solomon begs the Lord for wisdom. But is this the kind of wisdom God grants?

God's response to Solomon's request for wisdom notes both what he asked for and what he didn't ask for.

Reread 1 Kings 3:11-14 (pages 18-19) and complete the following:

Solomon asks for *a discerning heart to govern + to distinguish right from wrong* **(v. 11) 9**

And God grants him *a wise + discerning heart* **(v. 12)**

Solomon doesn't ask for these things, but God gives them to him anyway:

1. _wealth_ _____ (v. 13)

2. _honor_ _____ (v. 13)

3. _long life_ _____ (v. 14)

God grants Solomon everything he might have asked for (but didn't) *except* the death of his enemies. In such close proximity in the text to David's reference to "wisdom" as something that enlightens one about taking revenge, God's point is not lost here. Wisdom for revenge is not what God is granting.

3. Wisdom That's Passed to the Next Generation

We might wonder if the kind of wisdom given to Solomon is the kind a father passes along to a son. Solomon is certainly famous for the many proverbs attributed to his pen, many of them addressed as wisdom from a father to a son. Is the kind of wisdom he is granted the kind that helps one raise up a child in the way he or she should go?

As Solomon's story demonstrates, wisdom isn't necessarily hereditary. Solomon's son and successor, Rehoboam, does not follow God as closely as his grandfather David did, or even as closely as his father, Solomon, did with his divided heart. Instead of following the wisdom of his elders or the example of his father, Rehoboam instead follows the advice of his peers who say: "These people have said to you, 'Your father put a heavy yoke on us, but make our yoke lighter.' Now tell them, 'My little finger is thicker than my father's waist. My father laid on you a heavy yoke; I will make it even heavier. My father scourged you with whips; I will scourge you with scorpions'" (1 Kings 12:10-11).

Not the best way to start his reign as a new king. The kingdom so artfully united by his grandfather David was divided under Rehoboam. Solomon's wisdom is not necessarily the kind that translates to the next generation.

4. Wisdom for Accumulating Wealth

Besides wisdom, Solomon is famous for the ostentatious display of wealth and luxury that he amassed, which we read about in the Old Testament. Is his wealth a result of God-given wisdom? The New Testament also mentions Solomon's great wealth and riches. But is it in a positive light?

Read Luke 12:27-28 in the margin. Is Solomon's splendor something that we are to aspire to? _probably not!_

"Consider how the wild flowers grow. They do not labor or spin. Yet I tell you, not even Solomon in all his splendor was dressed like one of these. If that is how God clothes the grass of the field, which is here today, and tomorrow is thrown into the fire, how much more will he clothe you—you of little faith!"
Luke 12:27-28

Even with all of his rich robes, Solomon's wealth is on the losing side of a comparison to a simple wildflower. God's creation is adorned more beautifully than all the wealth Solomon could produce. Wisdom to produce economic prosperity is obviously not something high on God's list of priorities.

5. Godly Wisdom— The Discernment to Rule Yourself before Ruling Others

Solomon did become a wise ruler who made wise judgments. In fact, the first story of his kingship is the legendary story of 1 Kings 3:16-28, in which Solomon makes a judgment on which of two women is the true mother of a baby. However, his true wisdom came from the discernment to rule himself before ruling others. In other words, Solomon knew that he needed to follow God before others could follow him.

Even before Solomon applied his new-found wisdom to his subjects, he applied it to himself. The first thing he did upon waking from his dream was to worship God:

> Then Solomon awoke; it had been a dream. He came to Jerusalem where he stood before the ark of the covenant of the LORD. He offered up burnt offerings and offerings of well-being, and provided a feast for all his servants.
>
> 1 Kings 3:15 NRSV

Instead of continuing to make sacrifices at the high places (something God had specifically forbidden), Solomon awoke and worshiped as God wanted—in Jerusalem before the ark of the Lord. Then he went and provided a feast for his servants.

First he worshiped. Then he served. His answered prayer led immediately to right worship and then to benevolent action. Solomon's encounter with God changed him *first* before it changed the way he governed.

The wisdom he received from God was the kind that helped him to distinguish and choose right from wrong before he ever set about making decisions for others as king. When Solomon was at his best, he remembered to control his own behavior, being obedient to God before his desires got the best of him. When he was at his worst, he forgot that before ruling others he needed to place himself under the rule of the King of kings.

Describe a time when you received wisdom from God that helped you to choose obedience before your desires got the best of you.

True wisdom is wisdom that changes us before it changes the way we minister to others. It is wisdom to let God rule us before we set out to make decisions that affect others.

Place yourself in God's hands today the way that Solomon did, coming to Him as "a little child" who needs His help and wisdom. God will honor that kind of prayer, and in your dependence on Him you will find peace.

Talk with God

Lord, grant me wisdom to place You as ruler over every area of my life. Help me to deal with the situations, relationships, and people around me with wisdom and grace. Amen.

Act on It

Think of the things in your life that require more wisdom than you possess. In the margin, list some areas or relationships in which you feel you are over your head and need wisdom from God. Below each item write the words "God, grant me wisdom." Each time one of those situations comes up this week, repeat the words "God, grant me wisdom." Listen for God's guidance throughout the week.

Day 4: A House for God

Read God's Word

David's words as he hands off the responsibility for building the Temple to Solomon:

> [2] *King David rose to his feet and said: "Listen to me, my fellow Israelites, my people. I had it in my heart to build a house as a place of rest for the ark of the covenant of the LORD, for the footstool of our God, and I made plans to build it.* [3] *But God said to me, 'You are not to build a house for my Name, because you are a warrior and have shed blood.'*
>
> [4] *"Yet the LORD, the God of Israel, chose me from my whole family to be king over Israel forever. He chose Judah as leader, and from the tribe of Judah he chose my family, and from my father's sons he was pleased to make me king over all Israel.* [5] *Of all my sons—and the LORD has given me many—he has chosen my son Solomon to sit on the throne of the kingdom of the LORD over Israel.* [6] *He said to me: 'Solomon your son is the one who will build my house and my courts,*

True wisdom is wisdom that changes us before it changes the way we minister to others.

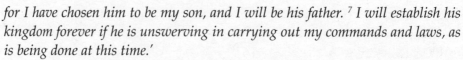

for I have chosen him to be my son, and I will be his father. ⁷ I will establish his kingdom forever if he is unswerving in carrying out my commands and laws, as is being done at this time.'

⁸ *"So now I charge you in the sight of all Israel and of the assembly of the* Lord, *and in the hearing of our God: Be careful to follow all the commands of the* Lord *your God, that you may possess this good land and pass it on as an inheritance to your descendants forever.*

⁹ *"And you, my son Solomon, acknowledge the God of your father, and serve him with wholehearted devotion and with a willing mind, for the Lord searches every heart and understands every desire and every thought. If you seek him, he will be found by you; but if you forsake him, he will reject you forever. ¹⁰ Consider now, for the* Lord *has chosen you to build a house as the sanctuary. Be strong and do the work."*

1 Chronicles 28:1-10

Solomon's words at the dedication of the finished Temple:

⁵⁴ *When Solomon had finished all these prayers and supplications to the* Lord, *he rose from before the altar of the* Lord, *where he had been kneeling with his hands spread out toward heaven. ⁵⁵ He stood and blessed the whole assembly of Israel in a loud voice, saying:*

⁵⁶ *"Praise be to the* Lord, *who has given rest to his people Israel just as he promised. Not one word has failed of all the good promises he gave through his servant Moses. ⁵⁷ May the* Lord *our God be with us as he was with our ancestors; may he never leave us nor forsake us. ⁵⁸ May he turn our hearts to him, to walk in obedience to him and keep the commands, decrees and laws he gave our ancestors. ⁵⁹ And may these words of mine, which I have prayed before the* Lord, *be near to the* Lord *our God day and night, that he may uphold the cause of his servant and the cause of his people Israel according to each day's need, ⁶⁰ so that all the peoples of the earth may know that the* Lord *is God and that there is no other. ⁶¹ And may your hearts be fully committed to the* Lord *our God, to live by his decrees and obey his commands, as at this time."*

1 Kings 8:54-61

Reflect and Respond

I grew up in church. I mean that almost literally, since one activity or another had us at the church building at least three or four times a week. On days that we had children's activities, my friends and I would run through the halls as if they were our playground, whooping and hollering and having all kinds of fun. But when we approached the sanctuary, the rowdiness stopped. When we pulled

open the heavy door leading from the education building into the sanctuary, it was as if we were entering another world, one with rich wood pews and high ceilings. On one wall was a huge stained glass depiction of the nativity, with each person dressed in a different bright color. Over the altar was a stained glass window depicting Jesus kneeling at a rock in the garden of Gethsemane. My earliest memories of God are of experiences in that room; our preschool director was standing in front of my class—a group of wiggly, wide-eyed preschoolers—as she bent down to our level and told us with a gentle, hushed voice, "This is God's house." I sensed that there. Even as a four-year-old, I could tell there was something different about that place. And when I entered there, I was different too.

What is your earliest memory of a church building or other place that seemed holy to you? *I remember Northwood Christian Church - Sunday School, VBS open windows and fans with no screens. A wasp that came in + stung my hand. Singing + stories*

With all of his politics, wisdom, and personal ups and downs, Solomon's lifelong achievement was building a house for God. His father, David, had originally set out to build the Temple, but God stopped him and gave the job to Solomon instead. Envisioning and building a Temple as a house for God was a task that spanned two generations, and it was a unique role for these two kings, father and son. It was a job that no king had done before and none would undertake after.

Unlike other buildings or monuments in the empire, the Temple was never intended to bring glory to the king. It was built entirely for the glory of God.

David delivers his instructions to Solomon with utmost urgency about the importance of his task. Solomon is to undertake the building of the Temple not only with attention to the detailed plans (and there are many details in the plans) but also with attention to his own relationship with God: "And you, my son Solomon, acknowledge the God of your father, and serve him with wholehearted devotion" (1 Chronicles 28:9). Of all the tools and plans used to build the Temple, the most important tool will be the leader himself, and the most important plan will be the plan for his own wholehearted devotion to God.

David is very direct about the fact that Solomon should follow God with his whole heart, and that if he does not it will mean his downfall: "If you seek him, he will be found by you; but if you forsake him, he will reject you forever" (1 Chronicles 28:9). Unfortunately, this statement comes true in Solomon's life in ways that we will talk about tomorrow.

Solomon shows us that our relationship with God is a gift, but it is dependent on our continual acceptance of that gift and our consecration of ourselves to Him. God offers us unconditional grace, but we must continually receive that offer and not reject God.

In what ways do we sometimes reject God, whether knowingly or unknowingly?

by doing things our way & by not not trusting him

What can we do to continually accept God's offer of grace and relationship? How can we continually consecrate ourselves to Him? *pray & talk to him continually*

While the speech in 1 Chronicles 28 is from one king to another, from one builder to another, it also is a speech from father to son.

Write the instructions David gives Solomon in 1 Chronicles 28:10 and the first sentence of 1 Chronicles 28:20.

Be strong & courageous & do the work. Don't be afraid or discouraged

Be strong & do the work

Doesn't that sound just like a father talking to a son? Be strong and courageous, and *do the work*. David wants Solomon to be sure this job gets done without the many distractions of leading a kingdom—without letting his own sins or failures get in the way.

The instructions given for building the Temple are very detailed and specific.

Read 1 Chronicles 28:11-18 and write below just a few of the items related to the building of the Temple for which David passes on instructions to Solomon. *architecture of buildings & courtyards as well as amount of gold & silver used to make items of service*

That's a lot of detailed plans! The rules and detailed plans for worship in the Old Testament show that God wants His people to take worship seriously, not lightly. It is a holy privilege to approach God in worship, and Solomon's task of building God's house is serious business. God wants hearts fully consecrated and devoted to Him, and the purpose of building a Temple is to create a place where that happens.

Consider the weight of this responsibility: being in charge of building the house of God—its formation, its care, the people who perform the roles of worship. This is the place where God's Spirit will dwell, where His people will meet with Him to receive forgiveness and enter into fellowship with Him.

Solomon certainly feels the weight of the job God has entrusted to him. When the Temple is completed, Solomon spends a day consecrating it with prayer, making the first sacrifices for which the Temple is constructed, and giving a speech to his people. This day, which must be an incredible celebration, is described in 1 Kings 8. Listen to Solomon's words as he explains to his people just why this Temple is so important, not only for their nation but also for the world:

> And may these words of mine, which I have prayed before the LORD, be near to the LORD our God day and night, that he may uphold the cause of his servant and the cause of his people Israel according to each day's need, so that all the peoples of the earth may know that the LORD is God and that there is no other.
>
> 1 Kings 8:59-60

While the Temple may be a place of worship for God's people, its true purpose is even bigger than that. The transformation of God's people that will happen there will mean that the whole world will witness how they are different from the rest of the world and will come to know that God is real.

John Oswalt puts it in a very compelling way: "It will not be the splendor of some earthly building that draws people to God. Rather it will be the glory of his own person as it is depicted in the lives of his worshipers. Solomon recognizes that unless the people of God are completely submitted to God in unreserved obedience, manifesting the life of God in their daily walk, the Temple will accomplish nothing."[4] There is nothing magical about a building that can make people know God. Instead, it is the lives of the people who are changed there that will impact the world in a very powerful way.

Is this hitting home for *you*? It should!

Read the Scriptures in the margin. What do you think it means that you are God's temple, a dwelling place of the Holy Spirit?

That God is always in us + with us

What do you think people notice about you that is different from the world around you?

The same kind of encounter with the holy that God's people had in the Temple is the kind of encounter that others are to have with you. You are a temple of the Holy Spirit.

Think again about the places you've felt God's presence. Remember the peace, the forgiveness, the stillness, the joy, the feeling that just being there makes you feel closer to Him, and different. You are a mobile temple carrying all of this around with you, offering it to others. *The beach, the mountains - places of serenity + beauty*

Also, any church or worship area

Do you not know that you are God's temple and that God's Spirit dwells in you?
1 Corinthians 3:16 NRSV

Do you not know that your bodies are temples of the Holy Spirit, who is in you, whom you have received from God? You are not your own; you were bought at a price.
1 Corinthians 6:19-20

You are a sanctuary for the people God places in your life.

You can be that place of peace for people. You are a sanctuary for the people God places in your life. You are filled with God's Spirit. You are God's house.

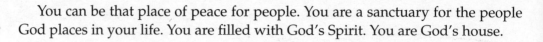

Talk with God

Holy Spirit, fill me today with love, joy, peace, patience, kindness, goodness, faithfulness, gentleness, and self-control. Help me to grow this fruit in a way that is clearly visible to other people so that when they encounter me, they will encounter a place of safety and sanctuary. Make me Your house today. Amen.

Act on It

How can you carry the peace and love of Christ with you? What spiritual practices can you engage in today that will fill you with peace so that you can be a walking sanctuary for others? If you like, make some notes in the margin.

Day 5: The Foolishness of the Wise Man

Read God's Word

23 King Solomon was greater in riches and wisdom than all the other kings of the earth. 24 The whole world sought audience with Solomon to hear the wisdom God had put in his heart. 25 Year after year, everyone who came brought a gift— articles of silver and gold, robes, weapons and spices, and horses and mules.

26 Solomon accumulated chariots and horses; he had fourteen hundred chariots and twelve thousand horses, which he kept in the chariot cities and also with him in Jerusalem. 27 The king made silver as common in Jerusalem as stones, and cedar as plentiful as sycamore-fig trees in the foothills. 28 Solomon's horses were imported from Egypt and from Kue—the royal merchants purchased them from Kue at the current price. 29 They imported a chariot from Egypt for six hundred shekels of silver, and a horse for a hundred and fifty. They also exported them to all the kings of the Hittites and of the Arameans.

11 1 King Solomon, however, loved many foreign women besides Pharaoh's daughter—Moabites, Ammonites, Edomites, Sidonians and Hittites. 2 They were from nations about which the LORD had told the Israelites, "You must not inter- marry with them, because they will surely turn your hearts after their gods."

Nevertheless, Solomon held fast to them in love. ³ *He had seven hundred wives of royal birth and three hundred concubines, and his wives led him astray.* ⁴ *As Solomon grew old, his wives turned his heart after other gods, and his heart was not fully devoted to the* LORD *his God, as the heart of David his father had been.* ⁵ *He followed Ashtoreth the goddess of the Sidonians, and Molek the detestable god of the Ammonites.* ⁶ *So Solomon did evil in the eyes of the* LORD; *he did not follow the Lord completely, as David his father had done.*

⁷ *On a hill east of Jerusalem, Solomon built a high place for Chemosh the detestable god of Moab, and for Molek the detestable god of the Ammonites.* ⁸ *He did the same for all his foreign wives, who burned incense and offered sacrifices to their gods.*

1 Kings 10:23-29; 11:1-8

Reflect and Respond

Conversation was abundant around a table at the local coffee shop. The gathered friends hooted with laughter as they talked over their lattes and caught up on the things going on in one another's lives. But when the door opened and they turned to see the new customer walking in, they became silent.

"Can you believe she'll even show her face in here?" one whispered. "I hear the affair started at work. Now people are saying she is leaving her husband for him."

"Well," said another, "I would never—I mean never in a million years—do something like that."

Perhaps the most dangerous point in our spiritual lives is when we begin to consider ourselves immune to sin. The idea that we are invulnerable to temptation or spiritually superior to those whose sin is made public can gradually lead us to neglect our connection to God and let our spiritual lives atrophy.

Among the warnings for Israel's king in Deuteronomy 17, which we will look at today, is the warning that he is not supposed to "consider himself better than his fellow Israelites and turn from the law to the right or the left" (Deuteronomy 17:20). This means the king is not above the law. The king is to be an obedient subject of the King of kings, just as everyone else. His power does not make him immune to the temptation or consequences of sin.

As a pastor, it can be easy to fill up my time doing "God's work" without really spending time with God. My schedule looks like I am doing lots of spiritual things, but unless I'm paying attention, I can do a lot of talking *about* God and working *for* God without having prayer time and conversation *with* God. Each of us, no matter how long we've walked with God or what our position of leadership or influence may be, must always keep a vigilant watch over our relationship with

> Perhaps the most dangerous point in our spiritual lives is when we begin to consider ourselves immune to sin.

God and the spiritual practices that keep us close to Him. Otherwise we will slip into doing life in our own strength and following our own temptations, and both of these things always lead to sin.

The root of Solomon's fatal flaw is the temptation to love power, privilege, and women more than he loves God. A verse in First Kings points to what would be Solomon's fatal flaw: "Solomon made an alliance with Pharaoh king of Egypt and married his daughter" (1 Kings 3:1). That one bride, that one alliance, turned into an obsession for Solomon and became the destruction of his reign.

God's people had been slaves in Egypt, and the Lord had instructed them not to go back (Deuteronomy 17:16). Solomon's alliance with Egypt—both for a bride and then for horses and chariots—directly violates God's careful instructions about the behavior of the king.

Read Deuteronomy 17:16-17 and fill in the blanks:

all of these

"The king, moreover, must not acquire great numbers of _horses_ for himself or make the people return to _Egypt_ to get more of them, for the LORD has told you, "You are not to _go to Egypt_ that way again." He must not take many _wives_, or his heart will be _turned away from God._ He must not accumulate large amounts of _silver_ and _gold_."

The decrees of this law were to be written by the king's own hand on a scroll and kept with him. He was supposed to read it all the days of his life (vv. 18-19).

Reread today's Scripture passage from 1 Kings 10-11 (pages 30-31), and then mark an X next to the commands from Deuteronomy 17:16-17 (above) that Solomon directly disobeyed.

Solomon's sinful appetite for women begins with just one wife from Egypt and escalates to the accumulation of hundreds of wives and concubines. Many of these begin as political alliances, but Scripture is clear that Solomon "clung to them in love" (1 Kings 11:2 NRSV). His love for his wives competes directly with his love for the Lord, just as his practice of burning incense on the high places does (1 Kings 3:3). In fact, Solomon's appetite for new wives reaches addictive proportions, blinding him to the spiritual idolatry that they bring into his household and his kingdom.

Remember that you can tell a good king of Israel by how he deals with the "high places" dedicated to idol worship, because this reveals how purely he is connected to God. Good kings pull down or destroy the altars at the high places, while bad kings passively leave them standing, allowing idol worship to spread and pollute God's people. Solomon's love of his many foreign wives pulls his heart so strongly away from God that he drifts away—at first slowly and then dramatically.

Solomon doesn't just leave the high places of idol worship standing. What dramatic step does he take in 1 Kings 11:7-8? *built a high place for all of his foreign wives*

As Christians we are called to give love and grace to all people, but we also must remember that those we spend the most time with *will* have an influence over us. The views of those in your closest circles are likely to impact your beliefs and actions. Offer friendship and love to everyone you meet, but be sure that you are staying grounded in the study of God's Word and have a close group of Christian friends to inspire you "as iron sharpens iron" (Proverbs 27:17).

Who are the Christian friends that inspire you "as iron sharpens iron"? *Peggy, Pam, Terry*

Solomon has another love besides women. His love for horses and chariots means that he is relying not on God to protect the kingdom but on the strength of his armies. The passage from Deuteronomy 17 is explicit that the king should not acquire too many horses, especially not from Egypt. The Egyptians are war-mongers, and God doesn't want His people to associate with them or become like them. Not only does Solomon violate this command and return to Egypt to buy horses, but he also becomes like them when he begins selling to other rulers and countries (1 Kings 10:29).

Solomon is famous for offering wisdom to other people, but he could use some of his own advice.

Read the following passages often attributed to Solomon, plus one from the psalms written by his father, David. Beside each, write a phrase containing advice that he should have taken himself.

Ecclesiastes 5:10 *Money does not bring happiness*

Proverbs 16:18 *Proud people are never aware its their problem & usually get tripped up by it*

Proverbs 12:4 *A worthy wife is a crown for her husband, but a disgraceful woman is like cancer in his bones.*

Psalm 20:7-9 *having too much of a good thing keeps you from being humble & may make one boastful*

33

As one Proverb attributed to Solomon says, "A person's own folly leads to their ruin" (Proverbs 19:3a). We may know what is best, but unless we practice it ourselves, our knowledge is nothing.

We later learn in 1 Kings 5:13 and 9:23 that Solomon oppresses his own people and uses them for forced labor. Dr. Claude Mariottini makes an interesting comparison of the workers forced to labor under Solomon to the Israelites forced to labor under the Egyptians. He writes,

> The Hebrew word for "forced labor" is *mas*, the same word that appears in Exodus 1:11. The word was used to describe the way the Egyptians oppressed the Israelites. . . . The overseers of the forced work in Egypt were ruthless and made the Israelites work hard, without mercy.[5]

Hundreds of years earlier, Egypt had enslaved and oppressed the Israelites, forcing them into harsh labor. Egypt was a cesspool of idol worship and false gods. Egypt also was an arms dealer, buying and selling horses and chariots as the machines of war upon which they relied for security and strength.

The Israelites had broken free of Egypt, but under Solomon's rule, they had become just like them. Twice the Lord appears to Solomon (1 Kings 3:5 and 9:2) to remind him of the terms of the covenant between God and David's royal family (1 Samuel 7), but Solomon fails again and again to uphold his part of the deal.

Read about God's response in 1 Kings 11:9-13.

What emotion is attributed to God? (v. 9) *very angry*

What will happen to Solomon's kingdom as a result? (v. 11) *it will be taken away + given to a servant after Solomons death but will let 1 tribe remain with his son all for the sake of David*

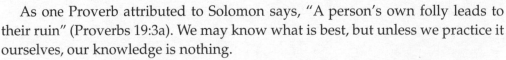

> We must let go of certain things so that we can grab hold of God with open hands.

Solomon's downward spiral is sad to watch, as he slips from a king who loves God and is filled with God's imparted wisdom to a man who is captive to his own desires.

God calls us to consecrate ourselves and act differently than our desires might dictate so that we can live truly free from slavery to those desires. We must let go of certain things so that we can grab hold of God with open hands. Holiness is both about letting go and grabbing hold, and the relationship we have with God as a result of wholehearted devotion is always worth it.

What have you needed to let go of in order to answer God's call to be holy or set apart?

What have you grabbed hold of in answer to this call?

Any failure to recognize that we are vulnerable to temptation and sin—"Well, I would never in a million years . . ."—means that we are letting our guard down and no longer relying on God for His help and guidance. Solomon relied on horses and chariots as the strength and security of his kingdom. Similarly, sometimes we forget God and rely on our own abilities or the things that we possess to be our strength and security—and these things are never adequate.

Being set apart by God means that we are different in our practices, in our faith, and in what we love and worship. It means being marked by the same holiness that characterizes God Himself.

This transformation of becoming more like Christ isn't something we do in our own strength. God alone gives us the strength and grace necessary for this process. *The Message* translation of Romans 12:2 describes in a very interesting way what happens when we are set apart:

> *Don't become so well-adjusted to your culture that you fit into it without even thinking. Instead, fix your attention on God. You'll be changed from the inside out. Readily recognize what he wants from you, and quickly respond to it. Unlike the culture around you, always dragging you down to its level of immaturity, God brings the best out of you, develops well-formed maturity in you.*

What does it look like when we become so well-adjusted to our culture that we fit in without even thinking? *you don't stretch for more, become complacent*

Where are you tempted to do this? *not learn to pray aloud with others*

In what ways have you seen God bring out the best in those who follow Him? In you? *more confident to speak of Gods goodness & grace*

As God's people, we are called to be set apart from practices that drag us down so that we don't drift away from God but, instead, grow in well-formed maturity into the best that God has created us to be. We also are called to be set apart by participating in holy habits such as worshiping God, mentoring and being mentored by other Christians, and drawing close to God through the reading of

His Word and prayer. These are practices that teach us about the character of God and help us to absorb that character as our own.

As we journey through First and Second Kings together, we will look at each of these holy habits and how it was practiced in the lives of key leaders of Israel—both kings and prophets. As we do, remember that you are loved. You are chosen. You are set apart for a relationship with God and a purpose in His kingdom. May these truths bring joy and confidence to your heart!

Talk with God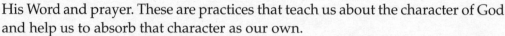

Lord, I want to be wholeheartedly Yours. Don't let me become so well-adjusted to the culture around me, like Solomon, that I fit into it without even thinking. Help me to let go of things that are not of You so that I can grab hold of You with everything I am. Amen.

Act on It

Earlier you reflected on those things that you have let go of and those things you have grabbed hold of in order to be set apart for God. Spend some moments now in prayer, asking God to reveal any areas that need renewed focus as well as any new things He might be calling you to let go or take hold of at this point in your faith journey. What specific actions do you feel led to take this week? If you like, make some notes below.

Week 1
Video Viewer Guide

"Take with you the servants of your lord, and have my son Solomon ride on my own mule, and bring him down to Gihon. There let the priest Zadok and the prophet Nathan anoint him king over Israel; then blow the trumpet, and say, 'Long live King Solomon!' You shall go up following him. Let him enter and sit on my throne; he shall be king in my place; for I have appointed him to be ruler over Israel and over Judah."

1 Kings 1:33-35 NRSV

consecrate – to set apart for _specific_ , _holy sacred_ purposes

We realize that Solomon is in trouble when we learn that he's not keeping _Gods_ _rules_.

Solomon seemed to have the misconception that he could separate his _public_ life from his _private_ life.

high places – the locations for _idol_ _worship_

God never _abandons_ us.

Through every bad ending, God makes a way for a _new_ _beginning_.

Solomon prays for wisdom. (1 Kings 3:7-9)

> Then Solomon awoke; it had been a dream. He came to Jerusalem where he stood before the ark of the covenant of the LORD. He offered up burnt _Offerings_ and offerings of well-being, and provided a feast for all his _servants_.

1 Kings 3:15 NRSV

What did Solomon do with the wisdom God gave him?

He _worshiped_.

He _served_.

Consecration is an act you have to _participate_ in.

Week 2
Elijah
Set Apart by Listening

"Lord, are You there? Do You see me? Do You hear me? Can You give me a clear answer? I don't know what to do, and I need You to guide me. I can't hear You."

Sound familiar? We beg God for a word of clarity, instruction, or encouragement, and then we wait, asking "Was that you, Lord?" But God doesn't play hide and seek. God doesn't tease us and keep quiet. God is always speaking to us if only we would learn to hear His voice.

Listening to God is a spiritual practice. It takes a training of the heart, eyes, and ears. Listening for God's voice means that we don't just assume every blaring message we hear is of God. It means slowing down and discerning the myriad of voices that compete for our attention. Which voice is God's, and how do we know it's Him? We learn from the major prophets in the Bible that it's best to take time alone in prayer and to practice listening and waiting. We have to create some margin in our schedules to listen carefully. And while God sometimes does seem to wave a banner with His word for us, most times God speaks in that quiet voice that only our hearts can hear when we are still and waiting.

Elijah's story speaks to us in so many ways this week. Mighty winds and fires sweep by him and he wonders, *Is that You, Lord?* But when the still small voice calls his name, he doesn't have to ask. He knows God's voice in the quiet moment.

This week we'll learn how we are set apart by listening for God, and we'll learn some tools that will help us discern how God speaks to us through Scripture, through his Spirit, through our common sense, and through the saints around us—those whom God uses to speak truth into our lives.

Day 1: The Unpopular Path of the Prophet

Read God's Word

²⁹ In the thirty-eighth year of Asa king of Judah, Ahab son of Omri became king of Israel, and he reigned in Samaria over Israel twenty-two years. ³⁰ Ahab son of Omri did more evil in the eyes of the Lord than any of those before him. ³¹ He not only considered it trivial to commit the sins of Jeroboam son of Nebat, but he also married Jezebel daughter of Ethbaal king of the Sidonians, and began to serve Baal and worship him. ³² He set up an altar for Baal in the temple of Baal that he built in Samaria. ³³ Ahab also made an Asherah pole and did more to arouse the anger of the Lord, the God of Israel, than did all the kings of Israel before him.

1 Kings 16:29-33

Now Elijah the Tishbite, from Tishbe in Gilead, said to Ahab, "As the Lord, the God of Israel, lives, whom I serve, there will be neither dew nor rain in the next few years except at my word."

² Then the word of the Lord came to Elijah: ³ "Leave here, turn eastward and hide in the Kerith Ravine, east of the Jordan. ⁴ You will drink from the brook, and I have directed the ravens to supply you with food there."

⁵ So he did what the Lord had told him. He went to the Kerith Ravine, east of the Jordan, and stayed there. ⁶ The ravens brought him bread and meat in the morning and bread and meat in the evening, and he drank from the brook.

1 Kings 17:1-7

Reflect and Respond

Have you ever had to tell someone the truth, even when you knew the truth would be unpopular? Imagine if this was your calling, your job. Imagine that every time you entered a room, people wondered if you'd call them out for some indiscretion or begin speaking harsh words about the misdeeds of the nation and its leaders. That was the life of an Old Testament prophet.

This week we shift our attention from kings to prophets, those unusual and often eccentric servants of God who had the courage to speak what others didn't want to hear. While kings took on battles with other nations to protect their borders, prophets often took on the battles closer to home—the ones for the hearts and minds of God's people. As dangerous as an enemy who might attack from another country might be, even more threatening was the danger that God's people would turn away from Him and begin to worship other things.

King Ahab not only tolerated the worship of false gods (as some other bad kings had), he also encouraged it and built temples and Asherah poles (places of worship) for the very idols that God had carefully warned His people about.

According to 1 Kings 16:30 and 1 Kings 16:33, how did Ahab measure up to all the other kings before him? *he did more evil & more to arouse the anger of God than any of the king before him*

During Ahab's reign, the most popular false god was the Phoenician storm god Baal, often depicted with a lightning bolt in his hand. "Since Baal was the lord of the vine and the god of fertility, Baalism taught heavy drinking and sexual license as religious duty."[1] You can see how people's choice of false gods often meant choosing what fed their appetites and desires, cherry-picking an idol to match their own wants. Worshiping the true God, on the other hand, has always meant admitting that when left to our own inclinations we make a mess of our lives, and that only through submitting to Him do we find peace.

People don't often worship idols made of clay or stone today. What are some idols that we follow that allow us to feed our own desires and appetites? *money, belongings,*

This is one of the low points of Israel's history, when the very leader of God's people is encouraging and promoting idol worship, and then in walks the prophet Elijah. He does not come bearing good news. He has the courage to stand up to King Ahab and make a declaration that is so unpopular it puts his life at risk:

> "As the LORD the God of Israel lives, before whom I stand, there shall be neither dew nor rain these years, except by my word."
>
> 1 Kings 17:1 NRSV

I love that although Elijah is standing before the throne of the king, he knows exactly who is in power here. While other people may see the throne of a king, a prophet has the sharper vision to see the throne of God, the true seat of power. And the irony of the specific consequence is rich. So you want to worship a storm god? No storms. Pray to a god who claims to rule the rains? No rain. This declaration of drought makes it clear that "Baal the storm god is no god at all."[3] God will not tolerate competition for the hearts of His people.

To put it mildly, Ahab is not pleased. This particular prophetic message would cause havoc in a land where rain meant life and drought meant death. Elijah would have to go into hiding to avoid his immediate arrest or even execution.

Extra Insight
Throughout the Old Testament, we see the Hebrews struggle with worshiping the gods of the cultures around them, most often a reference to Baal worship. The word Baal means "master" or "lord," and there were several iterations of Baal worship, depending on the region and the time period.[2]

41

Read each passage below. What are some of the strange things that other prophets did to communicate the Word of God to His people?

Ezekiel 5:1-3 *Shave his head & beard & do 3 different things with the hair to signify what would happen to Jerusalem*

Jeremiah 27:1-2 *was told to make a yoke and wear it on his neck*

Hosea 1:2-3 *was told to marry a prostitute so that some of her children would be conceived in prostitution to signify how Israel acted as a prostitute by worshiping other gods*

The actions of the prophets definitely got people's attention, and they got them listening to God. We read in the Book of Ezekiel, "Son of man, your people talk about you in their houses and whisper about you at the doors. They say to each other, 'Come on, let's go hear the prophet tell us what the Lord is saying!'" (33:30 NLT). But their actions certainly didn't make them any friends.

Being a prophet was a very solitary occupation. Elijah's words were unpopular. His occupation meant that his life was frequently at risk. He traveled alone. What was it that compelled prophets like Elijah to take on such an unpopular role that they would spend their careers as an outsider, a social pariah?

Prophets were first and foremost listeners. They kept their ears open to God and to His hopes and dreams of what the world could and should be. They were also seers. They kept their eyes open to the condition of the world around them and the ways in which it didn't match God's plans. Having open ears to God and open eyes to the world meant that prophets also had open mouths, speaking out about the difference between those two realities.

While we may never be called to confront a king, we are called to listen: to tune in so closely to God's voice that it is louder than the realities of our culture, the media, and even the standards accepted by our families and communities. The prophets' isolated path actually may have given them more time for silence and listening in God's presence. You and I are not called to live in isolation from the world, but we must take time to be alone with God, to sit in silence with Him so that even our own words aren't the center of our prayers. This kind of silence is a discipline. It takes practice. We'll talk more about this later in the week.

When we listen, sometimes God reveals to us ways that the world doesn't match His plans. And when we see those things, we are always called to pray (words of petition to God) and sometimes to speak (words of truth to those around us). Here is a helpful definition of the modern-day gift of prophecy:

> Prophecy is the gift of speaking the Word of God clearly and
> faithfully. Prophets allow God to speak through them to com-
> municate the message that people most need to hear. While
> often unpopular, prophets are able to say what needs to be said

We are called to listen: to tune in so closely to God's voice that it is louder than the realities of our culture, the media, and even the standards accepted by our families and communities.

If we want to be God's truth tellers, we first need to let the truth work in us.

because of the spiritual empowerment they receive. Prophets do not foretell the future, but proclaim God's future by revealing God's perspective on our current reality.[4]

In order to speak the Word of God, we first have to listen to the Word of God. Prophets had to be sure they were listening closely. If their connection to God was weak or if they themselves were corrupted by sin, the message they delivered to God's people would be tainted. If we want to be God's truth tellers, we first need to let the truth work in us.

Read Hebrews 4:12 in the margin. When have you experienced the Word judging the thoughts and attitudes of your heart? How did it change you?

When we are called to speak, we must do so with extreme gentleness, kindness, and an attitude of servanthood.

Read Ephesians 4:15 in the margin. *How* **are we to speak the truth? What do you think that means?**

How do we know when to speak and when to stay silent? We should beware of speaking out of anger, a judgmental attitude, or the feeling that we alone hold the truth that others need to hear. We must first let the truth work in us, knowing that we are all sinners saved by grace. We also must be willing to walk in relationship beside those we are speaking to—both before and after we speak.

Truth telling is not something we do for our own vindication or pleasure. For the ancient prophets, their call to speak the truth meant putting themselves at great personal risk. But their growing closeness to God and love for His Word meant they felt an unquenchable call to make God's voice loud enough for His people to hear so that they could turn to Him and receive His mercy.

We sometimes mistakenly think that prophets in the Old Testament were judgmental, calling down wrath on those who were not walking with God. Actually, prophets were merciful truth tellers, warning people of what would happen if they did not align themselves closely to God rather than to their own whims or the standards of the world. The consequences they spoke of were the consequences of the people's wrong beliefs and actions.

God allowed the water that the people thought they were receiving from the storm god Baal to dry up so that they would learn to cry out to Him. Instead of worshiping a false god, a figment of their imagination who had no way of bringing life-giving water, God wanted them to turn to the source of living water.

For the word of God is alive and active. Sharper than any double-edged sword, it penetrates even to dividing soul and spirit, joints and marrow; it judges the thoughts and attitudes of the heart.
Hebrews 4:12

Instead, speaking the truth in love, we will grow to become in every respect the mature body of him who is the head, that is, Christ.
Ephesians 4:15

43

See, I am doing a new thing! Now it springs up; do you not perceive it? I am making a way in the wilderness and streams in the wasteland. The wild animals honor me, the jackals and the owls, because I provide water in the wilderness and streams in the wasteland, to give drink to my people, my chosen, the people I formed for myself that they may proclaim my praise.

Isaiah 43:19-21

God is always proclaiming for His people that He is the source they are seeking, the living water that will not dry up. If you have received that kind of nourishment, sustenance, and saving grace from Him, I hope that it will make you a prophet of grace with a burning desire to proclaim to the people in your own life the love and mercy of your God.

Talk with God

Loving God, thank you for the prophets in my life—those who have spoken truth in love, pointed me to You, and reminded me of Your promises. Help me to be such a friend to others, to lovingly and boldly share Your grace and mercy and love. Amen.

Act on It

Think of a way in which in which the world around you does not match God's dream for the world. Then spend at least five minutes in silent listening prayer (letting God communicate to you without trying to form your own words or requests). Ask God to speak to your heart about ways He is calling you to speak and act in response to those areas. If you like, make some notes in the margin.

Day 2: God Provides

Read God's Word

⁷ *Some time later the brook dried up because there had been no rain in the land.* ⁸ *Then the word of the LORD came to him:* ⁹ *"Go at once to Zarephath in the region of Sidon and stay there. I have directed a widow there to supply you with food."* ¹⁰ *So he went to Zarephath. When he came to the town gate, a widow was there gathering sticks. He called to her and asked, "Would you bring me a little water in a jar so I may have a drink?"* ¹¹ *As she was going to get it, he called, "And bring me, please, a piece of bread."*

¹² *"As surely as the* Lord *your God lives," she replied, "I don't have any bread—only a handful of flour in a jar and a little olive oil in a jug. I am gathering a few sticks to take home and make a meal for myself and my son, that we may eat it—and die."*

¹³ *Elijah said to her, "Don't be afraid. Go home and do as you have said. But first make a small loaf of bread for me from what you have and bring it to me, and then make something for yourself and your son.* ¹⁴ *For this is what the* Lord, *the God of Israel, says: 'The jar of flour will not be used up and the jug of oil will not run dry until the day the* Lord *sends rain on the land.'"*

¹⁵ *She went away and did as Elijah had told her. So there was food every day for Elijah and for the woman and her family.* ¹⁶ *For the jar of flour was not used up and the jug of oil did not run dry, in keeping with the word of the* Lord *spoken by Elijah.*

¹⁷ *Some time later the son of the woman who owned the house became ill. He grew worse and worse, and finally stopped breathing.* ¹⁸ *She said to Elijah, "What do you have against me, man of God? Did you come to remind me of my sin and kill my son?"*

¹⁹ *"Give me your son," Elijah replied. He took him from her arms, carried him to the upper room where he was staying, and laid him on his bed.* ²⁰ *Then he cried out to the* Lord, *"Lord my God, have you brought tragedy even on this widow I am staying with, by causing her son to die?"* ²¹ *Then he stretched himself out on the boy three times and cried out to the* Lord, *"Lord my God, let this boy's life return to him!"*

²² *The* Lord *heard Elijah's cry, and the boy's life returned to him, and he lived.* ²³ *Elijah picked up the child and carried him down from the room into the house. He gave him to his mother and said, "Look, your son is alive!"*

²⁴ *Then the woman said to Elijah, "Now I know that you are a man of God and that the word of the Lord from your mouth is the truth."*

1 Kings 17:7-24

Reflect and Respond

Watchman Nee was a man who many have described as a prophet, living out his faith in Christ in an unlikely place and time: China, during the Communist Revolution. When he became a Christian in his teenage years, Nee began to speak boldly to his classmates about faith in Christ, and nearly all of them were converted to faith in Christ.

His mother's faith was instrumental in his own conversion. He was born Nee Shi-Tsu in November 1903, but his mother later changed his name to "Watchman" to reflect a biblical calling. He was raised in the Methodist Church in China.

During his ministry he established many churches, preached often, spoke publicly of the hope of the gospel, and published so prolifically that his collected works finally filled sixty-two volumes! Few have had such an incredible impact on the spread of Christianity in China.

Yet he knew what it was to suffer, to be in need, and to be hungry.

In the early days of his ministry in Shanghai, he described a time when he had only a little bread to eat each day. He suffered with tuberculosis for years and was later diagnosed with a chronic stomach disorder and heart disease, which were never cured. After the Communist Revolution, Nee was targeted because of his professed faith in Christ. He was falsely condemned, arrested, and sentenced to fifteen years' imprisonment in 1956. He died in prison in 1972.[6]

How can someone we would describe as a great success in ministry also suffer so much want, struggle, loneliness, and suffering? Maybe struggle and success aren't such opposites. Too often we imagine that the life of faith will be smooth sailing, that Christ's promise to provide for all our needs will mean that the life of a Christian will be lived on Easy Street. Jesus' ministry of suffering should have put those myths to an end once and for all, but in every generation we find people of faith professing that if we aren't experiencing prosperity, health, and wealth, then we're not doing the Christian faith right.

Read Philippians 4:11b-13 in the margin. What is Paul's secret for being content? *God gives him Strength*

In a moment of insight that must have been taken from his own faith and personal experience with struggle, Watchman Nee wrote these words:

> Because of our proneness to look at the bucket and forget the fountain, God has frequently to change His means of supply to keep our eyes fixed on the source.[7]

Read Philippians 4:19 in the margin. Who is the fountain? *God in his glory in Jesus*

What are some of the "buckets" God has used as the means of supplying your needs?

Elijah certainly experienced a change in supply. During the drought that he had called on God to send, affecting King Ahab and his idolatrous regime, Elijah

I have learned the secret of being content in any and every situation, whether well fed or hungry, whether living in plenty or in want. I can do all this through him who gives me strength.
Philippians 4:11b-13

And my God will meet all your needs according to the riches of his glory in Christ Jesus.
Philippians 4:19

escaped to a solitary place and hid in Kerith Ravine where he was brought food by ravens and given water to drink by a brook that ran through the ravine.

This was an unlikely "bucket" that God used to supply Elijah's needs. While he was on the run from an angry king, the bird that brought him food was considered unclean by God's people (see Leviticus 11:13-15). Yet this improbable bird became a delivery system for the food of a prophet. A bird that will normally feed its own hunger with anything it can find instead served the needs of the man who was God's mouthpiece.

When the water dried up in the brook, Elijah was driven to look for other sources to supply his needs. In another improbable move, God sent him northeast to Zarepheth. This city was a double whammy of inhospitality, because it was a Gentile city and in the area of Sidon, the home region of Elijah's enemy and King Ahab's wife, Jezebel.[8]

Just when it looked like Elijah's resources had dried up, God was simply changing the means of supply by which He provided.

Here again, Elijah was challenged to look to an unlikely source for his needs. God led him to a widow at the gates of the city who had fallen on such hard times that she was gathering a few sticks to cook her last bit of flour and bread into the final meal she and her only son would eat before they died. Astonishingly, Elijah asked her to cook this final meal and give it to him instead!

According to the following verses, how were God's people supposed to treat widows and orphans?

Exodus 22:22-24 *do not exploit — treat fairly & given a chance to restore*

James 1:27 *should be cared for*

This had to be a humbling moment for the prophet: to take food from the hungriest, to ask for provision from those he was trained to provide for. This woman was "ravenous" in the truest sense, but God's spokesperson demanded her last morsel of food; and like the ravens who provided for Elijah, she went against her own nature and complied. What a bold demand, and what bold obedience and faith she demonstrated when she did what he asked instead of keeping her meager resources for her own family.

A woman who had next to nothing provided for a prophet who had nothing. Sometimes our own experiences of scarcity inspire our generosity, because we understand what those in need are going through and have compassion on them.

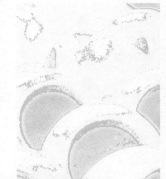

Read Luke 21:1-4 in the margin. How did this widow give what little she had? *the 2 Coins was all she had*

After the widow's kitchen miracle, she was struck by tragedy when her son died. Because she had been faithful to give to the prophet of God even in her time of need, perhaps she asked herself, *Why me?* Knowing where to turn when she needed miraculous intervention, she immediately sent for Elijah.

Read again 1 Kings 17:17-24.

What emotions do you think the widow experienced in the ups and downs of this story?

As Jesus looked up, he saw the rich putting their gifts into the temple treasury. He also saw a poor widow put in two very small copper coins. "Truly I tell you," he said, "this poor widow has put in more than all the others. All these people gave their gifts out of their wealth; but she out of her poverty put in all she had to live on."
Luke 21:1-4

Write her quote from 1 Kings 17:24 here: *what do you have against me, man of God? Did you come to remind me of my sin and kill my son?*

What did she now understand as a result of this miracle? *that Elijah was a man of God & that God words that he spoke were the truth*

God's miracles through His prophet Elijah got people's attention. They made it clear that the words from his mouth truly were from God.

Elijah started his ministry in scarcity. With no rain he turned to the ravens and the brook. When the brook dried up, he turned to the widow with the empty pantry. Yet every time his physical resources ran out, God defied all expectations by providing abundantly.

We have identified that a prophet's first job was to be a listener. It was only after listening carefully and closely to God that the prophet was able to speak God's word to God's people. No one listens as well as someone who is desperate. When we find ourselves lacking our basic needs, we lean in to God as in no other time in life, crying out for help and attending to His voice, because we realize we have nowhere else to turn.

This powerful prophet would never forget the lesson he learned in weakness and scarcity about where his power and provision came from. As followers of Jesus who are called to reach out to others in His name, this is a lesson we too must learn: nothing we have comes from our own strength. All comes from one Source, our Father in heaven.

Whether the resources in your life are flowing or drying up, remember that the amount of what you have is no indication of God's love or favor. Like the widow, you may have the opportunity to see God's abundance through what looks like your scarcity. Like Elijah, you may be called upon to humble yourself and receive blessings from the hands of someone who has very little.

In all things, rely on God as the Source. He is the ever-flowing river of living water, and His riches are never depleted. You can depend on Him!

Talk with God

God, You are the Source of my strength and all that I have. When I feel weak or depleted, help me look to You. May I give freely to others out of what You have given to me. Amen.

Act on It

Think of a charity or organization you have supported or would like to support, either personally or through your church or a nonprofit agency. Find a way to give of what you have been given this week, either financially or through your time or talents.

Day 3: Against the Odds

Read God's Word

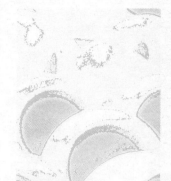

Extra Insight
Jesus' miracles included the multiplying of food beyond physical limits (see Matthew 14:13-21). He also healed children and raised a widow's son from the dead (see Luke 7:11-17). And when Jesus healed the son of a royal official in Capernaum, his explanation acknowledged the reason for the widow's declaration of belief after Elijah raised her son: "Unless you people see signs and wonders . . . you will never believe" (John 4:48).

[20] *So Ahab sent word throughout all Israel and assembled the prophets on Mount Carmel.* [21] *Elijah went before the people and said, "How long will you waver between two opinions? If the LORD is God, follow him; but if Baal is God, follow him."*

But the people said nothing.

[22] *Then Elijah said to them, "I am the only one of the LORD's prophets left, but Baal has four hundred and fifty prophets.* [23] *Get two bulls for us. Let Baal's prophets choose one for themselves, and let them cut it into pieces and put it on the wood but not set fire to it. I will prepare the other bull and put it on the wood but not set fire to it.* [24] *Then you call on the name of your god, and I will call on the name of the LORD. The god who answers by fire—he is God."*

Then all the people said, "What you say is good."

[25] *Elijah said to the prophets of Baal, "Choose one of the bulls and prepare it first, since there are so many of you. Call on the name of your god, but do not light the fire."* [26] *So they took the bull given them and prepared it.*

Then they called on the name of Baal from morning till noon. "Baal, answer us!" they shouted. But there was no response; no one answered. And they danced around the altar they had made.

²⁷ At noon Elijah began to taunt them. "Shout louder!" he said. "Surely he is a god! Perhaps he is deep in thought, or busy, or traveling. Maybe he is sleeping and must be awakened." ²⁸ So they shouted louder and slashed themselves with swords and spears, as was their custom, until their blood flowed. ²⁹ Midday passed, and they continued their frantic prophesying until the time for the evening sacrifice. But there was no response, no one answered, no one paid attention.

³⁰ Then Elijah said to all the people, "Come here to me." They came to him, and he repaired the altar of the L{\sc ord}, which had been torn down. ³¹ Elijah took twelve stones, one for each of the tribes descended from Jacob, to whom the word of the Lord had come, saying, "Your name shall be Israel." ³² With the stones he built an altar in the name of the L{\sc ord}, and he dug a trench around it large enough to hold two seahs[a] of seed. ³³ He arranged the wood, cut the bull into pieces and laid it on the wood. Then he said to them, "Fill four large jars with water and pour it on the offering and on the wood."

³⁴ "Do it again," he said, and they did it again.

"Do it a third time," he ordered, and they did it the third time. ³⁵ The water ran down around the altar and even filled the trench.

³⁶ At the time of sacrifice, the prophet Elijah stepped forward and prayed: "L{\sc ord}, the God of Abraham, Isaac and Israel, let it be known today that you are God in Israel and that I am your servant and have done all these things at your command. ³⁷ Answer me, L{\sc ord}, answer me, so these people will know that you, L{\sc ord}, are God, and that you are turning their hearts back again."

³⁸ Then the fire of the L{\sc ord} fell and burned up the sacrifice, the wood, the stones and the soil, and also licked up the water in the trench.

³⁹ When all the people saw this, they fell prostrate and cried, "The L{\sc ord}—he is God! The L{\sc ord}—he is God!"

1 Kings 18:20-39

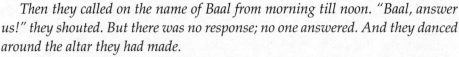

Reflect and Respond

Elijah had been in hiding for over three years as the country was rocked by the drought he had predicted.

The time he spent apart—waiting by the brook, receiving provision from God, watching miracles unfold in the widow's home—had prepared Elijah by strengthening his faith through demonstrations of God's power and by allowing him time to rest in God's presence and tune his heart to listen to God's voice. The Christian life is a rhythm of action and reflection, and perhaps no life shows this better than Eijah's. We often find him in quiet times apart from the world before and after the big public encounters of his life. Likewise, God wants us to draw apart with Him and listen to His voice as well as engage the world in community and ministry.

Describe a time when you have drawn apart from the world to be with God. What was the setting? What happened while you were there?

When Elijah finally emerged, it must have been an epic moment for him to face King Ahab after three years of drought. Ahab had been searching the kingdom for Elijah, hoping to bring him out of hiding and destroy him for the drought he believed Elijah had caused. When the two men finally met, Ahab called him "You troubler of Israel" (1 Kings 18:17).

Read 1 Kings 18:18 in the margin. How did Elijah respond to King Ahab's accusation? *Not me but you because you abandoned the Lord & followed Baal*

"I have not made trouble for Israel," Elijah replied. "But you and your father's family have. You have abandoned the LORD's commands and have followed the Baals." 1 Kings 18:18

For prophets, the phrase "Don't shoot the messenger" was more than an expression. They had hard truths to tell, and those truths produced hard reactions in their hearers. Elijah made it clear to Ahab that the trouble did not begin with him but with Ahab and his family's abandonment of God's Word. When God's truth brings conflict or resistance, it is actually a step in the right direction, because often we must hear hard truth before we can turn to God for help.

Elijah gave God's people a chance to answer, turn, and choose finally whom they would believe in and follow: "Elijah went before the people and said, 'How long will you waver between two opinions? If the LORD is God, follow him; but if Baal is God, follow him.' But the people said nothing" (1 Kings 18:21).

When God's invitation is made, no answer is actually an answer of no. If a young man makes a marriage proposal to the woman he loves and she does not answer, that in itself is a heart-breaking negative response. The people's silence spoke volumes about the loyalty of their hearts. They may have thought that they were being neutral or that they could worship Yahweh and other gods at the same time, but their disloyalty broke God's heart. The question of whom they would follow had to be resolved. An answer had to be given.

Elijah proposed a contest between Yahweh and Baal to settle once and for all the question of who was the real and true God. It would be a battle of the deities, bringing God's people together to watch so that they could decide for themselves whom to follow. The priests would prepare a sacrifice, a bull on an altar, and let the deity who was real bring down fire from heaven. Elijah made sure that the prophets of the false gods were given every advantage. He wanted there to be no question that it was Yahweh, the God of Israel, who had done a supernatural work in showing up and showing off.

Reread 1 Kings 18:26-28 (pages 49-50). How would you characterize the actions of the prophets of Baal? Circle the appropriate words below:

~~Loud~~ or quiet   ~~Violent~~ or gentle   ~~Frantic~~ or calm

Extra Insight
The priests of Baal were Jezebel's spiritual advisers. When Jezebel heard about this contest from Ahab—and the news that her prophets had been killed— she was furious and ordered for Elijah to be hunted and killed.

These prophets pulled out all of their tricks to make sure their god heard. They danced. They shouted. They cut themselves and offered their own blood. They had the advantage of going first in this contest, and they spent all day in the strange gyrations of idol worship.

Elijah taunted them to shout even louder. He mocked their impotent idol by giving him human characteristics: "Surely he is a god! Perhaps he is deep in thought, or busy, or traveling. Maybe he is sleeping and must be awakened" (1 Kings 18:27). These challenges were both amusing and humbling. The question of whether Baal was "traveling" may have been a euphemism people used for going to the bathroom.[10] What an insult! In contrast to the question about whether Baal might have been napping, God's people knew that "indeed, he who watches over Israel / will neither slumber nor sleep" (Psalm 121:4). As loud and dramatic and long as the false prophets shouted, still "there was no response, no one answered, no one paid attention" (1 Kings 18:29).

When it was Elijah's turn, the contrast was sharp. While 450 of Baal's prophets and 400 more prophets of Asherah were present (see 1 Kings 18:19), there was only one Elijah. While they had been loud, he was quiet. While they felt they needed to hurt themselves to make their false god listen, Elijah spoke with a calm and quiet voice.

As if the odds of 450 prophets to one were not steep enough, Elijah gave his opponents even more of an advantage by what he did. He engaged in heavy manual labor and repaired the altar of the Lord, gathered twelve stones, dug a trench, arranged the wood, and divided the pieces of the bull over it (vv. 30-33). Then he invited them to fill jars of water and pour it on top of the offering and wood not once, not twice, but three times until it filled the trench.

God may seem to be the underdog at times, but no one and nothing can overpower Him. In biblical stories such as Elijah facing the prophets of Baal, Esther standing up to the powers that be when she was an ethnic and religious minority, and Jesus feeding thousands with small portions of food, God shows again and again that there is never a circumstance so big that He cannot overcome it.

What obstacle seems too big for God in your life, your community, or the world? Take a moment to name it here.

With the odds stacked—the fuel and sacrifice thoroughly drenched with so much water it had run down the sides of the altar and filled the entire trench—there could be no question that if this offering was consumed by fire, it had to be the Lord. Elijah prayed a gentle prayer, asking for God's supernatural action to overwhelm the natural circumstances and to show Himself to be real and powerful for one specific reason: "Answer me, LORD, answer me, so these people will know that you, LORD, are God, and that you are turning their hearts back again" (1 Kings 18:37). And answer God did, with fire so hot that it not only burned the sacrifice and the wood but also licked up the water that had gathered in the trench. God had triumphed in power, and the people responded as Elijah had hoped, turning their hearts to worship God again.

After the scene with the sacrifice was complete, the false prophets were put to death. They had led Israel astray to the way of death for so long that death became their own sentence. Elijah declared that once again it would rain, a sign that God had shown favor to His people and a torrential downpour of grace had arrived.

Read James 5:16-17 in the margin. What insight are we given about where Elijah's victory came from?

Baal, the idol whom the people worshiped for rain, could not make it rain. Baal, the false god that people associated with fire, could not bring fire. The people could no longer deny that God alone had the power to move on earth and the interest and compassion to show up for His people.

No matter how great your circumstance, God is always bigger. No matter how great your need, you can turn to Him for help. In fact, there is no other source in this world that will bring help or hope apart from Him.

Therefore confess your sins to each other and pray for each other so that you may be healed. The prayer of a righteous person is powerful and effective. Elijah was a human being, even as we are. He prayed earnestly that it would not rain, and it did not rain on the land for three and a half years.
James 5:16-17

No matter how great your circumstance, God is always bigger.

Talk with God

Lord, I lift up to You all the impossible situations in life that I and others encounter. You alone are God, our help and hope. I pray that as You work, making Your kingdom come on earth, all people will acknowledge that You alone are God and will give You praise. Amen.

Act on It

Recall the obstacle you named above, taking it to God in prayer. Rather than rehearsing the challenges and impossible odds you are facing, rehearse the character and power of your odds-defying God. Praise God for the many ways He has helped you in times past, and thank Him in advance for the ways He will help you to overcome this current obstacle. If you like, make some notes in the margin.

Day 4: A Way Out of the Wilderness

Read God's Word

¹ Now Ahab told Jezebel everything Elijah had done and how he had killed all the prophets with the sword. ² So Jezebel sent a messenger to Elijah to say, "May the gods deal with me, be it ever so severely, if by this time tomorrow I do not make your life like that of one of them.

³ Elijah was afraid and ran for his life. When he came to Beersheba in Judah, he left his servant there, ⁴ while he himself went a day's journey into the wilderness. He came to a broom bush, sat down under it and prayed that he might die. "I have had enough, Lord," he said. "Take my life; I am no better than my ancestors." ⁵ Then he lay down under the bush and fell asleep.

All at once an angel touched him and said, "Get up and eat." ⁶ He looked around, and there by his head was some bread baked over hot coals, and a jar of water. He ate and drank and then lay down again.

⁷ The angel of the Lord came back a second time and touched him and said, "Get up and eat, for the journey is too much for you." ⁸ So he got up and ate and drank. Strengthened by that food, he traveled forty days and forty nights until he reached Horeb, the mountain of God. ⁹ There he went into a cave and spent the night.

And the word of the Lord came to him: "What are you doing here, Elijah?"

¹⁰ He replied, "I have been very zealous for the Lord God Almighty. The Israelites have rejected your covenant, torn down your altars, and put your prophets to death with the sword. I am the only one left, and now they are trying to kill me too."

¹¹ The Lord said, "Go out and stand on the mountain in the presence of the Lord, for the Lord is about to pass by."

1 Kings 19:1-11

Reflect and Respond

I should have known something was wrong when I didn't see her at church for a few weeks. Cora was always one of the first ones there on Sunday mornings, sitting on the second row with a bright smile on her face. But her seat had been empty for two or three weeks, and no one had heard from her. She also was one of the most faithful attendees of our Bible study group, so I picked up an extra copy of the new book we were going to study next before calling to see if I could drop it by her house. When she answered the door, I noticed that Cora's normally bright eyes lacked their usual sparkle; her soft voice was flat when I asked how she was doing.

"Not so well," she said. She admitted she had been feeling empty and sad, staying close to home when she didn't have to be at work. Mostly she had been on her couch watching old TV shows. Her daughter's wedding was the month before, and the energy and excitement leading up to the big day had been the highlight of the year for the family. But now Cora found herself not wanting to do the things that she usually enjoyed, avoiding calls from friends, and sleeping more than usual.

After listening intently for about thirty minutes, I gently asked Cora if she thought she might be experiencing depression. That was when she finally broke down in tears.

Depression isn't a topic that we Christians tend to discuss very often. Many feel ashamed and guilty when they experience depression, and so they choose to remain silent about it. Others tentatively share their struggles with friends in the faith only to be given pat answers such as, "Just pray about it, and it will go away." The shame Cora felt because of her feelings of depression made her wonder if it was her own fault, causing her to isolate herself from her friends and avoid church in fear that others might look down on her for being week in faith.

Though Christians may avoid the subject, the Bible is far from silent about depression. Great leaders such as Moses, Jonah, and David freely expressed feelings of doubt, misery, and despair. Even the great prophet Elijah experienced what may be the clearest depiction of depression in the Bible.

Just yesterday we witnessed a bold, victorious Elijah calling fire down from heaven to defeat the prophets of Baal. In that scene he seems almost superhuman—his prayers affecting supernatural acts of God in things such as fire and rain. But in the New Testament, James reminds us that Elijah was not superhuman.

Read James 5:17 in the margin. What does the opening statement say to us about Elijah?

Elijah was a human being, even as we are. He prayed earnestly that it would not rain, and it did not rain on the land for three and a half years.
James 5:17

We are hard pressed on every side, but not crushed; perplexed, but not in despair; persecuted, but not abandoned; struck down, but not destroyed.

. . .

Therefore we do not lose heart. Though outwardly we are wasting away, yet inwardly we are being renewed day by day. For our light and momentary troubles are achieving for us an eternal glory that far outweighs them all. So we fix our eyes not on what is seen, but on what is unseen, since what is seen is temporary, but what is unseen is eternal.
2 Corinthians 4:8-9, 16-18

The emphasis of this particular passage is on prayer, helping us keep in mind that Elijah's great acts on earth were not due to his superhuman power but his reliance on the power of God. But the fact that most stands out to me is, Elijah was completely human in every way. Today's story from First Kings emphasizes Elijah's humanity by giving us a description of his battle with depression: "He came to a broom bush, sat down under it and prayed that he might die. 'I have had enough, LORD,' he said. 'Take my life; I am no better than my ancestors.' Then he lay down under the bush and fell asleep" (1 Kings 19:4-5). Elijah inspires the Texan in me to say, "Bless his heart." What a lonely and isolating feeling this must have been for him.

Those reading Elijah's story have sometimes recognized and identified with feelings of fear, resignation, resentment, loneliness, anger, worry, anxiety, and survivor's guilt.

While biblical characters such as David, Jonah, and Job experienced depression after loss and disappointment, Elijah's most difficult time followed a great victory. As we see in Cora's situation as well, depression doesn't always follow difficult circumstances. Sometimes we can struggle after a mountaintop experience, feeling let down once the excitement has passed. At other times there is no rhyme or reason to our feelings; they simply overwhelm us at an unexpected time.

What I find notable in Elijah's story is not only the vivid description of the human struggle but also God's response of divine mercy. I love the image of an angel "touching" Elijah twice and the double commandment to "get up and eat" (1 Kings 19:5-7). This compassionate picture of touch and food seems very nurturing to me. Then comes a simple question: "What are you doing here, Elijah?" (1 Kings 19:9). God knows perfectly well why Elijah is in this location. God even commanded him to go there. The question seems to be more oriented to Elijah's state of mind; it is an invitation to pour out his heart, which he does.

Friends, this story gives us a picture of how God responds when we are at our lowest point. He doesn't blame or question; he simply enters into the difficult place with us, nurtures us, and invites us to pour out our hearts to Him.

Recall a low point in your life when you struggled with feelings of depression. How did you experience God entering into that difficult place with you? What gave you hope and encouragement during this time?

Perhaps you can identify with Elijah's experience in the wilderness. If so, my heart goes out to you. I've had wilderness experiences in my own life as well, including seasons of pain and loss that ran deep. When we're dealing with loss or stress or other difficult circumstances, sometimes depression can creep in like a thief in the night without us even realizing it. Even if you've never personally experienced a season of depression, you've probably had a friend or family member who has. So whether you're struggling yourself or wanting to help someone else, the good news is that there is hope for the hurting heart even in the darkest of times.

Though we must remember that one word of comfort or advice can never "fix" anyone's situation—and, after all, it is not our job to fix things—we can do much by simply being present with those who are hurting. Because each person's situation is different, asking gentle questions that communicate care and listening openly are the best ways to express love to someone who is struggling. Likewise, allowing others to express this same love and care for us is critical when *we* are the ones who are struggling.

Whether giving or receiving this loving care, we can learn from the example of the prophet Elijah. Let's look to his wilderness story to see four specific things that helped him to head back toward health and wholeness.

1. Take care of yourself.

All at once an angel touched him and said, "Get up and eat." . . . He ate and drank and then lay down again.

1 Kings 19:5-6

When depression strikes, the first thing we need to do is to take care of ourselves. I find encouragement in the fact that even the prophet Elijah needed to be reminded to take care of himself when he was struggling. Often when we are overwhelmed with circumstances or emotions, it's all we can do to put one foot in front of the other and just make it through the day. Yet more than ever, this is the time when we need to give careful attention to self-care. Eating, sleeping, reaching out for connection with those we love, and trying to do the things that bring us joy are all important parts of self-care.

God made us to be whole—body, mind, and spirit—and part of our spiritual growth means paying attention to how we are feeling. It's a good practice to periodically take an assessment of how we're doing, spend some time focusing on ourselves, and seek God's renewal and restoration. Elijah's story shows us that it's not selfish to take these steps so that we may recover, just as he did in the wilderness. Even the great prophet of God needed a time to lean on God and seek renewal in order to move forward in his journey.

2. Recognize the compassionate hand of God.

The angel of the Lord came back a second time and touched him and said,
"Get up and eat, for the journey is too much for you."

1 Kings 19:7

Don't miss this beautiful statement. The angel sent by God to care for Elijah is speaking empathy into Elijah's situation. God recognizes that Elijah has been on a tough journey and that it has been too much for him. So He sends an angel not once but twice.

Next time you are in a difficult place, imagine God gently touching you and saying, "I can see this has been too much for you." There is no blame or harsh tone in these words. It's simply a recognition of the difficulties we all go through.

Just as God sent an angel to convey compassion to Elijah, so God reaches out to us with tender care and compassion when we are hurting. When we are at our end, God doesn't point a finger at us and rehash every way that we went wrong. God doesn't shame us or turn His back on us. Instead, God is merciful, compassionate, and full of grace. He sends care and love.

3. Realize you are not alone.

"I am the only one left, and now they are trying to kill me too. . . ."
The Lord said to him, ". . .Yet I reserve seven thousand in Israel—all whose
knees have not bowed down to Baal and whose mouths have not kissed him."

1 Kings 19:10, 15a, 18

Elijah believed that he was the only true believer left, that he was all alone in Israel. This must have been a terribly lonely feeling, especially since there were many out to kill him for his beliefs. Queen Jezebel had issued a death threat for Elijah, which sent him fleeing into the wilderness. It truly seemed that the whole world was against him. Yet God reminded Elijah that there were still many faithful followers out there to come alongside him—seven thousand, to be exact.

We can relate to Elijah. When we are in the wilderness, we often feel isolated and alone, thinking that there is no one who really knows us or who understands—or worse, that the whole world is against us. That's why it is so important to have a confidante who can encourage us to take care of ourselves and hold us accountable when we are struggling. This person should be someone who practices active listening without judging or giving unsolicited advice. The best confidantes are those who can empathize with our pain, having been through difficult times themselves—oftentimes something similar to what we are experiencing. Of course, it is good to remember the difference between offering empathy and offering unsolicited advice.

4. Let God move you.

"Go, return on your way to the Wilderness . . . and when you arrive, anoint Hazael as king over Syria."

1 Kings 19:15

After Elijah had experienced a period of God-prescribed rest, God indicated that Elijah should get up and take action. Specifically, God told Elijah to travel and continue his work as a prophet. It's important to note that the Bible doesn't say Elijah had already recovered from his depression at this point. We do not know how long his depression lasted. What we do know is that although he had received some much needed compassion and care during this time apart, it now was time for him to continue the work that God had called him to do.

Sometimes when we are experiencing a wilderness season, it helps to return to our everyday activities before we feel like it. Resuming routine activities and especially entering back into community with others can help us begin to heal. Staying closely connected to our friends and loved ones helps to lift our spirits, offering us encouragement and hope.

Perhaps the first way you need to "get moving" is to tell a friend, pastor, or family member that you're struggling and ask for help. Or perhaps you need to offer compassion and care to someone else who may feel alone in the wilderness right now. Wherever you are on your way out of the wilderness, invite God to show you a path for moving forward. Then, just as Elijah did, be still and listen for God's voice. He will give you the direction and guidance you need.

Talk with God

Lord, the wilderness can be scary. Often we feel alone—isolated and lonely—as if we are the only ones going through our situation. Help us to lift our eyes and see that our help comes from You. I want to listen intently for Your still small voice calling me forward. Help me to take that first step now. Amen.

Act on It

Review the four "guidelines" in today's reading, asking God what you need to do to take steps toward health and wholeness or to help someone else who is struggling. Make notes in the margin, and choose one action you can take today.

Day 5: Still Small Voice

Read God's Word

⁹ *And the word of the LORD came to him: "What are you doing here, Elijah?"*
¹⁰ *He replied, "I have been very zealous for the LORD God Almighty. The Israelites have rejected your covenant, torn down your altars, and put your prophets to death with the sword. I am the only one left, and now they are trying to kill me too."*
¹¹ *The LORD said, "Go out and stand on the mountain in the presence of the LORD, for the LORD is about to pass by."*

Then a great and powerful wind tore the mountains apart and shattered the rocks before the LORD, but the LORD was not in the wind. After the wind there was an earthquake, but the LORD was not in the earthquake. ¹² *After the earthquake came a fire, but the LORD was not in the fire. And after the fire came a gentle whisper.* ¹³ *When Elijah heard it, he pulled his cloak over his face and went out and stood at the mouth of the cave.*

1 Kings 19:9-13

Reflect and Respond

Everyone loves to tell stories of prayers that were answered. I'd like to share with you a story about a prayer that wasn't.

It was one of those vacations where the memories preserved in scrapbooks—those of happy, smiling family members in front of awe-inspiring natural scenes and famous landmarks—only tell half the story. It rained on our parade, driving us inside where dispositions were anything but sunny. Someone had thought it wise to save money in the vacation budget by cramping all family members in one hotel room: a rollaway bed blocking the bathroom entrance and kids sleeping on the floor so that no one could walk without stepping on someone else. To make matters worse, the family brought along a know-it-all teenager who wasn't quite a child anymore but was still acting pretty childish. That teenager was me. I was grumpy and critical and right about everything, the way that only those who haven't lived in the grown-up world yet but already have grown-up opinions tend to be.

After several rainy evenings in the cramped hotel room, I finally discovered that the hotel had a workout area. I've never been the athletic type, but when I found it was the only area where I could escape and be alone for any period of time, I became quite the workout buff. There was a little sauna area where I could go in and close the door and no one would talk to me or make any noise. In that hot and humid little prayer closet, I poured out the struggles of the day to God and prayed, "God, change my family. God, change my circumstances. God, change my life."

After I prayed all the prayers that I could pray, I sat in silence with God. I listened, but there was no gentle whisper or still small voice—no booming one, either. Each night when the fitness center closed, I would sigh and return to the crowded hotel room to find that none of my prayers had been answered: my family, my circumstances, my life were all just as I had left them.

It wasn't until the last few days of our time together that I noticed something. While my circumstances hadn't changed, something else had. Me. I began to look forward to the silence of my time in the prayer closet sauna. When I arrived there each evening, I had less to say to God and, instead, settled into the silence quickly. I began to feel the presence of God like a heavy blanket on my chest.

The presence, stillness, and peace I experienced began to follow me out of the sauna, back to the hotel room, and into my relationships and daily interactions and activities. The silence came with me—inside of me—and I was different.

We'd like God to change our circumstances. Sometimes He does. More often He changes us. God uses times of silence to shape and form us, but often we're too busy to take time to listen.

Elijah's experience in the cave on Mount Horeb is a beautiful picture of what it is like to listen desperately for God's voice. Elijah entered this place in a state of exhaustion and depression, and he must have been relieved to know that he was about to experience "the presence of the LORD, for the LORD [was] about to pass by" (1 Kings 19:11). It is often in our most desperate times that we are willing to be silent and wait for God's voice. The rest of the time our busy lives seem to fill our ears and our souls with noise.

Elijah would have been excited to be sent to Mount Horeb to hear from God. Horeb had another name, Mount Sinai. This was the same location where Moses had heard God's voice in the burning bush. It also was the very same place where Moses returned with God's people to receive the Ten Commandments. If you wanted to hear from God, this mountain was the place to go!

Compare the experiences Elijah had when trying to listen to God's voice to other ways God has spoken in the Scriptures. Look up each verse and fill in the blanks:

**God's way is in the _____ and the _____.
(Nahum 1:3)**

The Lord spoke to Job out of a _____. (Job 38:1)

We'd like God to change our circumstances. Sometimes He does. More often He changes us.

Extra Insight
Mount Horeb, Mount Sinai, and Mount Paran are all names for the same place in Scripture references.[11]

Moses was drawn to listen to God when he witnessed a bush that was on _____. (Exodus 3:2)

When the Ten Commandments were given, the Lord descended on the mountain in _____ and the whole mountain _____ violently. (Exodus 19:18)

When God spoke to Elijah, His voice was NOT in a great and powerful _____, an _____, or a _____, but in a gentle _____. (1 Kings 19:11-12)

We can't assume that the way God has spoken to other people in the past will be the way God will speak to us. When we hear other people say "God told me…" or "God spoke to me about…," we may feel envious, wanting God to reveal Himself to us in similar ways. But God didn't speak to Moses the way He spoke to Job or Elijah.

We also need to remember that the loudest and most noticeable events are not always the voice of God. Almost every time a disaster strikes in our world, there is a spiritual leader who goes on record saying that the disaster is the voice of God's judgment. A hurricane, an earthquake, even a terrorist attack have been interpreted as God's loud judgment. Elijah's story teaches us that the loudest of noises and the most powerful of natural disasters are not always God's voice.

The voice of God can be loud and booming. It also can be as small as a whisper. The King James Version names the voice of God as "a still small voice" (1 Kings 19:12). Although I understand how a voice can be "small," I've always had trouble with the idea that a voice can be "still." A voice has volume but not movement. Yet when I read that Elijah went to the entrance of the cave and listened there intently for God's voice, I am reminded that it's we who have to be still if we want to hear from God.

What do the following verses say about being silent and listening for God?

Lamentations 3:26

John 10:27

Silence in prayer is freedom from needing to have all the right words to say to God.

The idea that I might make a mistake paralyzed my prayer life for a long time. What if my words didn't sound holy enough? What if I prayed for the wrong thing and God zapped me with some awful lesson. (How many times have you heard, "Don't pray for patience or God will give you something to be patient with"?)

Silence confirms that there are no mistakes in prayer. You don't need the right words in order to get prayer right; you simply need to bring all that you are before all that you know of God. I like that definition: prayer is bringing all that I am before all that I know of God, because it grows as we grow. My prayers grow as I learn more about who I am and who God is.

So I don't have to worry about my prayers being perfect—or being like someone else's. The question is, did I bring all of me? Bringing all of ourselves in silence means not rushing through a laundry list of requests or covering up our inner struggles by talking the whole time.

Silence in God's presence is at first an uncomfortable thing. If you ever want to know what's rattling around in your subconscious, just try to be quiet for a few minutes! Silence is a discipline that takes practice.

Dorothee Soelle says that there are three levels of silence.[12]

1. Silence of the mouth. I would expand this to include all external noises. This silence involves turning off the radio, finding a place apart from the noise of your work and family, and getting to a quiet place. For some this will be harder than others. I've known young parents who say the bathroom is the only private room in their house; others say they've even had to retreat to the garage and sit in the car to find silence!

2. Silence of the mind. Once you find a place where your ears aren't hearing any noise, your mind will begin making a noise all its own. Silence of the mind perhaps takes the most practice because silence is a discipline for an active mind. As thoughts and words come into your mind, simply let them float by as if on a stream; then center your mind again on the Lord.

3. Silence of the will. This is the stage where even our own desires are silent before the desires of God. "Not my will, but yours be done" is the proclamation of a will silent before God. Our goal in silence is not to become a blank slate but to be a vessel ready to be filled with the mind and heart of Christ.

Which of these three levels of silence is most challenging or difficult for you? Why?

Silence in prayer is freedom from needing to have all the right words to say to God.

It has been said that spending all of your prayer time talking to God without listening is like presenting all of your symptoms to the doctor without waiting in silence for the doctor to offer a diagnosis or treatment options. God has so much to offer us in prayer, but usually we do not take time to receive it.

In your time with God, be sure to take time to listen. The great physician longs not only to hear the symptoms of your heart but also to offer you the salve of peace that can only be found when you sit in silence with Him.

> God has so much to offer us in prayer, but usually we do not take time to receive it.

Talk with God

Lord, I come now to sit with You in silence. Open my spiritual ears to hear Your gentle whispers. . . .

(Spend several minutes in silence, listening for God.)

Act on It

For the remainder of this study, spend five to ten minutes each day sitting in silence with God. It will be difficult at first, but it will get easier each time you try it. If it helps, set a timer to relieve yourself of watching the clock. Try five minutes the first couple of days, and then extend that by a minute each day until you reach ten minutes. Keep a notepad handy, and write down any distracting thoughts that enter your mind, returning your focus to listening. You also may want to make some notes afterward. Discuss with your small group or with a spiritual friend what you experience during these times of silence—both frustrations and joys.

Week 2
Video Viewer Guide

Then He said, "Go out, and stand on the mountain before the LORD." And behold, the LORD passed by, and a great and strong wind tore into the mountains and broke the rocks in pieces before the LORD, but the LORD was not in the wind; and after the wind an earthquake, but the LORD was not in the earthquake; and after the earthquake a fire, but the LORD was not in the fire; and after the fire a

_____ _____ _____.

1 Kings 19:11-12 NKJV

If we take time to be _____ . . . we're much more likely to hear from Him.

Four Common Ways God Speaks to Us:

• _____

• _____

• _____

• _____

God's _____ _____ for us are all outlined in this book—the Bible.

It's also amazing how _____ God can get—how He can make something speak right to you and your circumstances.

Scripture is the recorded _____ of God.

And nothing that God will say in any other way will ever

_____ it.

God also speaks to us today through His _____ _____.

The Holy Spirit can speak _____ of us if we'll learn to get quiet

and listen.

The Spirit can also lead through _____ _____.

Since all true wisdom comes from _____, the Spirit works in us to guide

us. He uses our everyday wisdom and _____ _____.

You can always use your common sense to ask about decisions:

Is it the _____ thing to do?

Does it _____ and _____ those around me?

Do I feel God's _____ about this decision?

Does it line up with God's word in _____?

In the Bible, the word _____ is not reserved for the most holy of people.

If you want to hear from God, make sure that you are living in close

_____ with other Christians.

Week 3
Elijah and Elisha
Set Apart by Mentoring

If I asked you to name two or three of the most influential people from your childhood, would you be able to name them quickly? What would you say about their influence on you? Did they teach you about God? Did they pass on a love for a particular sport? Did they teach you to appreciate music? Did they give you a second chance or show you grace after a trust was broken? You may not realize it, but your past is made up of a chain of mentors who, at various points in your life, poured into you something that makes you who you are today.

parents! grandmother-Mimi Aunt Genetta

I remember my piano teacher. She was patient, affirming, and kind, but she also called me to a standard in music that wouldn't allow me to just get by or simply go through the motions. She wanted me to love music, to be swept up in music—to do more than sit down and play notes on a page. My love for music today comes largely from her influence in my young life.

Whether we know it or not, people around us have influence on our lives, and we have influence on the lives of others. In the spiritual life, we need mentors to point us back to Jesus when we get confused about who we are or where we are going. We need people who will encourage us and call us to a higher standard when we get stuck going through the motions. And whether we know it or not, others are looking to us to point them to Jesus, encourage them, and lift them up as well.

This week we will discover the ways in which our mentors have shaped our spiritual lives. We'll also explore the ways in which we might be mentors to others. You see, we weren't meant to live the life of faith on our own. God has placed in our lives spiritual mentors to teach and encourage us, and God has made us mentors to teach and encourage others. Together we create a beautiful chain—a spiritual legacy—that continues throughout the generations.

Day 1: The Call of Elisha

Read God's Word

¹³ . . . *Then there came a voice to him that said, "What are you doing here, Elijah?"* ¹⁴ *He answered, "I have been very zealous for the* LORD, *the God of hosts; for the Israelites have forsaken your covenant, thrown down your altars, and killed your prophets with the sword. I alone am left, and they are seeking my life, to take it away."* ¹⁵ *Then the* LORD *said to him, "Go, return on your way to the wilderness of Damascus; when you arrive, you shall anoint Hazael as king over Aram.* ¹⁶ *Also you shall anoint Jehu son of Nimshi as king over Israel; and you shall anoint Elisha son of Shaphat of Abel-meholah as prophet in your place.* ¹⁷ *Whoever escapes from the sword of Hazael, Jehu shall kill; and whoever escapes from the sword of Jehu, Elisha shall kill.* ¹⁸ *Yet I will leave seven thousand in Israel, all the knees that have not bowed to Baal, and every mouth that has not kissed him."*

¹⁹ *So he set out from there, and found Elisha son of Shaphat, who was plowing. There were twelve yoke of oxen ahead of him, and he was with the twelfth. Elijah passed by him and threw his mantle over him.* ²⁰ *He left the oxen, ran after Elijah, and said, "Let me kiss my father and my mother, and then I will follow you." Then Elijah said to him, "Go back again; for what have I done to you?"* ²¹ *He returned from following him, took the yoke of oxen, and slaughtered them; using the equipment from the oxen, he boiled their flesh, and gave it to the people, and they ate. Then he set out and followed Elijah, and became his servant.*

1 Kings 19:13b-21 NRSV

Reflect and Respond

We learn best in relationship with others. In families it's called parenting; in trade-work, apprenticeship; in sports, coaching; in business, mentoring; in faith, discipleship or Christian mentoring. Whatever we call it, we grow by being with those who are more experienced than we are and who will teach by their words and actions how we can grow up into a life of fullness and maturity.

Hebrews 13:7 is a pivotal verse in Scripture about discipleship, or what we might call Christian or spiritual mentoring.

Remember your leaders, who spoke the word of God to you. Consider the outcome of their way of life and imitate their faith.

Hebrews 13:7

Refer to the preceding verse to answer the following questions:

Who are we to remember?

Leaders are those who did what?

What are we to consider?

What are we to imitate?

Compared with the kind of mentoring that happens in an office, on a sports field, or at a job site, the specific terms of this verse mean that Christian or spiritual mentoring takes place on a whole new level. When God places those in our lives who will help us to grow, it is specifically their faith we are called to imitate.

Does this verse bring someone to mind whose faith you would like to imitate? If so, write his or her name below. *Melody, Judy, Kathy, Mary Lee*

Last week we looked into the strange and wonderful ministry of the prophet Elijah. The beautiful story of how he heard from God on Mount Horeb is one that has inspired many people who long to hear the "still small voice" of God. But we often forget to ask: *What did that voice tell him?*

Elijah cried out to God in a state of loneliness: "The Israelites have forsaken your covenant, thrown down your altars, and killed your prophets with the sword. I alone am left, and they are seeking my life, to take it away" (1 Kings 19:14 NRSV). It seems God's response to Elijah's state of depression included not only God's presence, care, and comfort but also a call to action.

Reread 1 Kings 19:15-16a (page 68). What does God's still small voice command Elijah to get moving and do? *anoint a kings & a prophet to replace himself*

Being a signpost for God's choice of a new king and anointing the king in an act of divine appointment were normal duties for a prophet. But then God calls Elijah to make another appointment. He wants him to select his own replacement: "And you shall anoint Elisha son of Shaphat of Abel-meholah as prophet in your place" (1 Kings 19:16b).

In verses 16-18, God seems to be saying, "Don't feel so alone. There are actually seven thousand more of my followers left. And out of them I have chosen an apprentice, a disciple, a companion for you. You don't have to do this alone."

God's spiritual comfort often comes in the physical company of another person. When we ask for His presence to surround us, sometimes that presence comes in the form of friends who are present with us. This was certainly true of the relationship of Elijah and Elisha. While Elisha benefitted from the wisdom and training of the man who was prophet before him, Elijah was no longer alone in facing the crowds of Baal followers.

> **God's spiritual comfort often comes in the physical company of another person.**

Has there been a time in your life when God sent a person to communicate His comfort? If so, describe it below.

Although we might expect the disciple, not the teacher, to be the one who benefits most from a mentoring relationship, God intends all of our relationships to be two-way streets. Mentoring relationships bring richness to the life of both the leader and the one being led. We should enter every relationship expecting not only to give but also to receive; God always intends for us to do both.

When have you expected to be on the giving end of a relationship but ended up receiving as well?

Elijah must have been quite eager to pass the buck to the next leader, who would be God's unpopular mouthpiece known as a prophet, because when he found Elisha, he didn't slow down enough for an introduction or explanation. Elisha was a farmer, out plowing his father's fields. Elijah caught up with him, threw his mantle across the young man's shoulders, and then kept going.

Elijah is a strange sort of man. (Actually, all of the prophets were!) But this kind of kamikaze appointing of a new prophet is quite odd even for one in such a peculiar occupation.

Reread 1 Kings 19:19 and describe what Elijah did to indicate that Elisha would succeed him as prophet.

Even without the benefit of a verbal explanation, Elisha knew exactly what was happening. It was as if Elijah was saying to him: "Tag! You're it!" Elijah's mantle, a simple dark cape worn over his clothes to ward off cold, was a symbol here of his authority and role as a prophet. To pass it onto Elisha's shoulders held great significance. This story became the origin of a phrase we still use today: "the passing of the mantle."[1]

In a way this scene makes me a little envious of Elisha. After I felt called to serve God in ministry, it took me most of my twenties to reach ordination as a pastor in my tradition, since the requirements included four years of college, four years of seminary (postgraduate) training, psychological testing, interviews with multiple boards, multiple papers, and finally a two-year probationary period of serving under another pastor's authority. At the end of this process—during a ceremony with friends, family, and many others gathered to watch—a bishop laid hands on my head and solemnly spoke these words: "Jessica, take thou authority to preach the Word of God and to administer the Holy Sacraments." It was an honor. And a relief. After all of that, Elisha's one-second ordination to become a prophet looks a little appealing in its simplicity!

Elisha's life had changed in a moment. He jumped down off of his plow and ran after his new teacher, the prophet who couldn't slow down even to give an explanation of what had just happened. To Elisha's credit, he didn't ask for an explanation, a job description, or an itinerary. He simply wanted to go home and say a handful of goodbyes.

Elijah responds, "What have I done to you?" (v. 20)—basically saying "What's it to me?"—and allows Elisha to return to bid his former life farewell.

We know very little about Elisha's background, but we do know that his parents were people of God. They made that clear when they named their son, for Elisha means "My God is salvation." The name of his mentor, Elijah, sounds so similar to our ears because it has a similar meaning: "My God is The Lord."

For many of us, the clearest lasting record of our faith that will remain after we are long gone is how we were able to pass down our faith to our children and others in whom we've invested, in the next generation. Elisha's life began with parents who started him off with a dedication to the Lord, and then later he was given a mentor who had that same devotion.

Elisha's background and upbringing instilled in him enough faith to make him ready to receive and respond to an instantaneous call from God that would change his life. Yet He was close enough to his family that he wanted to be sure to tell them goodbye. We're not given a glimpse of this family, but we know they were a people of some means. Any farming family that owned twelve yoke of oxen was doing pretty well for themselves.

Reread 1 Kings 19:21 (page 68) and answer the following questions:

What does Elisha do with the plow and yoke of oxen he has been working with?

Extra Insight
There were three types of mantles worn in biblical times. The mantle of Elijah was the *ádderet*, a cloak that could be made of animal hair and was a garment of distinction worn by kings and especially by prophets. The mantle was the official garment of a prophet, marking him as a spokesman of God.[2]

71

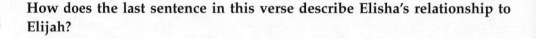

How does the last sentence in this verse describe Elisha's relationship to Elijah?

The title *servant* that Elisha took on meant that he would follow Elijah not only as a learner but also as one who would serve the older man's needs. The word for servant here is the same word that was used when Joseph served Pharaoh in Genesis 39:4. Elisha would become known as the man who "used to pour water on the hands of Elijah" (2 Kings 3:11). In addition to growing into a great prophet himself, it was an honor for Elisha to serve one of the greatest prophets Israel had ever known.

When you want to grow to become like someone in faith and maturity, one of the best ways is to assist this person in his or her calling. If you believe in the vision this person is proclaiming, sometimes the best thing you can do is volunteer to help make the individual's vision become a reality.

Do you know someone leading a movement, community, church, or family in a way that expands the kingdom of God? How can you serve this person and the vision God has given him or her? How might you learn from this person in the process?

When the son of a wealthy landowner "up and left" to become the servant of a poor prophet, it had to cause quite a stir. As if the decision to leave home and seek a brand new life by becoming a prophet of God wasn't controversial enough, Elisha decided to slaughter the very oxen he had been driving, build a bonfire with his plow, cook them up, and serve them to the people.

The choice to carry out this spectacle as his last hurrah in his hometown made Elisha fit in with the people called prophets from this first act. Prophets often did things physically to signal a spiritual truth, and they did it in a way that made people take notice and talk about it for a long time to come.

One thing that Elisha's act communicated was that there was no turning back for him. The symbols of his past life were consumed and gone. If anyone ever literally burned his bridges, it was Elisha! He didn't follow God's call while still keeping the option open of returning to his past life. He also fed the cooked oxen to the people, signifying that this role of prophet would be one that was not selfish but that would feed God's people. Both Elijah and Elisha would participate in miracles that would provide for God's people physically during times of scarcity and drought, and certainly their acts of faith provided for God's people spiritually in a world that was starved for God's grace.

In the end, Elijah never anointed the two kings that the "still small voice" of God had commanded him to anoint—Hazael and Jehu. We don't know why he never got around to fulfilling this command that God had given him on Mount Horeb. What we do know is that it was his mentee, Elisha, who basically carried out the ministry that his mentor had been charged with, albeit in very unorthodox ways.

Read 2 Kings 8:7-15. Instead of anointing Hazael, Elisha makes a prediction about him. Describe the prediction and how it comes to pass.

The king Ben-hadad will live & Hazael will be king - Hazael murders the king & he becomes new king

Now read 2 Kings 9:1-3 and describe what is strange about the anointing of King Jehu. *after being anointed as king of Israel told to run for his life*

You could say that Elijah never completed the task God gave him, or you could say that it was completed *through* him—through the ministry that he passed down to his protégée and follower. Elisha's only formal training as prophet came from his time with his mentor, Elijah. Where did his confidence come from when he was called to face down kings? He learned it from the one who had done it before him.

We can build great buildings and grow great ministries, but it's the act of investing in others so that they can grow to imitate our faith that produces new and strong disciples of Jesus (see Hebrews 13:7).

If we look back at the origin of our life of faith, we see that it was a gift from God through others. We received it like a mantle handed down. In small, forgettable conversations. In epic moments. In times of observing someone else's interactions. In relationships. Whether we were aware or not, we were receiving a priceless gift.

Thank God that He uses people to help grow other people. Who are you serving and observing? Who are you passing the mantle down to? Let's keep this chain of faith going!

> If we look back at the origin of our life of faith, we see that it was a gift from God through others.

Talk with God

Lord God, thank You for those who have gone before me who loved You and served You. Thank You for the ways they invested in me. Open my eyes to see the people You've placed in my path today so that I can give that love away in a way that lasts for generations to come. Amen.

Act on It

Recall the person you named who is leading a movement, church, or family in a way that honors the kingdom of God. Now review the way you identified that you can help or serve this person. What step—small or big—can you take *today* to act on this idea? Remember that by serving a person of God, you are serving God, and you can learn and grow in the process too.

Day 2: Marked

Read God's Word

¹⁵ When the servant of [Elisha] the man of God got up and went out early the next morning, an army with horses and chariots had surrounded the city. "Oh no, my lord! What shall we do?" the servant asked.

¹⁶ "Don't be afraid," the prophet answered. "Those who are with us are more than those who are with them."

¹⁷ And Elisha prayed, "Open his eyes, Lord, so that he may see." Then the Lord opened the servant's eyes, and he looked and saw the hills full of horses and chariots of fire all around Elisha.

2 Kings 6:15-17

¹ Now Jethro, the priest of Midian and father-in-law of Moses, heard of everything God had done for Moses and for his people Israel, and how the LORD had brought Israel out of Egypt. . . .

⁵ Jethro, Moses' father-in-law, together with Moses' sons and wife, came to him in the wilderness, where he was camped near the mountain of God. ⁶ Jethro had sent word to him, "I, your father-in-law Jethro, am coming to you with your wife and her two sons."

⁷ So Moses went out to meet his father-in-law and bowed down and kissed him. They greeted each other and then went into the tent. ⁸ Moses told his father-in-law about everything the LORD had done to Pharaoh and the Egyptians for Israel's sake and about all the hardships they had met along the way and how the LORD had saved them.

⁹ Jethro was delighted to hear about all the good things the LORD had done for Israel in rescuing them from the hand of the Egyptians. ¹⁰ He said, "Praise be to the LORD, who rescued you from the hand of the Egyptians and of Pharaoh, and who rescued the people from the hand of the Egyptians. ¹¹ Now I know that the LORD is greater than all other gods, for he did this to those who had treated Israel arrogantly." ¹² Then Jethro, Moses' father-in-law, brought a burnt offering and

other sacrifices to God, and Aaron came with all the elders of Israel to eat a meal with Moses' father-in-law in the presence of God.

[13] The next day Moses took his seat to serve as judge for the people, and they stood around him from morning till evening. [14] When his father-in-law saw all that Moses was doing for the people, he said, "What is this you are doing for the people? Why do you alone sit as judge, while all these people stand around you from morning till evening?"

[15] Moses answered him, "Because the people come to me to seek God's will. [16] Whenever they have a dispute, it is brought to me, and I decide between the parties and inform them of God's decrees and instructions."

[17] Moses' father-in-law replied, "What you are doing is not good. [18] You and these people who come to you will only wear yourselves out. The work is too heavy for you; you cannot handle it alone. [19] Listen now to me and I will give you some advice, and may God be with you.

Exodus 18:1, 5-19

Reflect and Respond

In the first week of school, a seminary professor looked out at us, a brand new class of young students who would someday be the leaders of the church. "You are so green you don't even know what you don't know yet," he said, "and what you don't know is a lot." He had piercing eyes and a very direct style that made us believe every word he said. We were nodding our heads in agreement and almost begging for a solution to our own stupidity.

"You need to get more than an education. You need to get a life. And because of that, you need more than a class. You need a mentor." He went on to challenge each of us to make it a practice of always placing ourselves in a "Mentor Sandwich"—to find someone who knew more than we did and enter into a relationship with that person as our mentor; and also to find someone we could help to guide along life's path. We would be mentored by one person and provide mentoring to another, which put us right in the middle of the sandwich. He went on to challenge each of us to do this within six months of moving to a new place, since after six months our lives and schedules would be so established we would be hesitant to add new roles and responsibilities.

That was sound advice, and it suddenly reminded me of words I had heard somewhere before. My professor's challenge sounded remarkably like words of wisdom my mother used to send me off with when I went on a school trip or to a week of camp as a teenager: "Be on the lookout: someone is there for you, because you need something from them, and you will be there for someone else, because you have something to offer or teach them. God is giving you a chance to find both of those people, so keep your eyes open." I was learning the same thing in class that she had told me years ago. That made me wonder if I might have been able to save some of the money I spent for post-graduate education if I had just listened to my mother!

The word *mentor* isn't found in the Bible. It's actually derived from Homer's classic, *The Odyssey*. In the story, Odysseus asks his friend Mentor to watch over his young son while he goes away to war. The word has come to mean a trusted advisor or guide who invests time and wisdom in another.

Some of the greatest leaders in the Bible began their ministries serving or following a mentor. In preparation for their own roles of leadership, they needed to learn and grow with the help of a trusted advisor. In the Apostle Paul's second letter to his protégé Timothy, we even find a description of something similar to a Mentor Sandwich.

> *You then, my son, be strong in the grace that is in Christ Jesus. And the things you have heard me say in the presence of many witnesses entrust to reliable people who will also be qualified to teach others.*
> *2 Timothy 2:1-2*

Read 2 Timothy 2:1-2 in the margin. Who is he naming as Timothy's mentor? Who is Timothy to invest in? *himself (Paul)*
others

How will they then carry on the mentoring practice

The Bible includes many great mentoring relationships. Let's take a look at a few of them:

Jethro and Moses (Exodus 18)
Jethro was Moses' father-in-law, who admired God's work through Moses. When Moses was overwhelmed with the day-to-day work of leadership, it was Jethro who suggested a way to find and empower leaders whom Moses could mentor.

Eli and Samuel (1 Samuel 1)
Eli raised Samuel from a young age when Samuel's mother, Hannah, dedicated him to service in the Temple. Eli helped Samuel hear and discern the voice of God. Though Eli's own sons were disobedient to God, Samuel was his true successor.

Elijah and Elisha (1 Kings 17–2 Kings 13)
Elijah was the chief prophet of Israel, and Elisha was his apprentice. Elisha took over for Elijah as the chief prophet when God took Elijah to heaven in a windstorm accompanied by a chariot of fire.

Mordecai and Esther (Esther 4)

Mordecai was Esther's uncle who raised her when she lost her parents. When she was chosen to be the Queen of Persia, Mordecai coached Esther to see her role as a leader and rescuer of her people.

Paul, Priscilla and Aquila, and Apollos (Acts 18, Romans 16:3-4, 1 Corinthians 16:19)

Priscilla and Aquila were a first-century missionary couple who worked and traveled with the Apostle Paul. They also helped mentor Apollos in the ways of God.

Paul and Timothy (1 and 2 Timothy)

Timothy traveled with Paul and became his disciple and coworker in the Gospel. In Philippians 2:19-23 Paul says of Timothy, "I have no one like him."

Jesus and his disciples (The Gospels)

These are some of the best examples of mentoring and discipling in Scripture. (More on this in Day 5.)

Before we look further at Elijah and Elisha's relationship, I'd like to shine the spotlight on Moses and Jethro. The story told of them in Exodus 18 illustrates how we can benefit from being in the middle of a Mentor Sandwich by suggesting four mentoring principles we can follow.

Mentoring Principle #1: A good mentor listens without judgment.

It's clear that Jethro and Moses had a trusted relationship. Moses was married to Jethro's daughter Zipporah before he had his burning bush experience in Exodus 3. In fact, he was Jethro's employee, tending flocks that belonged to his father-in-law, when he heard a voice from God calling him to go and rescue his people (Exodus 3:1-2).

After Moses led the Israelites out of Egypt, he ended up with a much larger "flock" than the sheep he had originally been entrusted with! Now he was in charge of the entire nation of Israel. Moses was glad to see his father-in-law (and his wife as well, we hope!) once again after the long journey. Beginning in Exodus 18:8, we read how Moses recounted to Jethro the story of what had transpired. He probably shared the struggles with a hard-hearted Pharaoh, his own self-doubt about leadership, the miracles and plagues, and the heartbreaking final plague of death of the firstborn in Egypt while God's people were saved through the Passover. The story of the crossing of the Red Sea must have been both thrilling and suspenseful. Then Moses must have told about the difficult journey they had begun through the desert toward the Promised Land.

Extra Insight

Jethro, Moses' father-in-law, was a worshiper of God (Exodus 18:10-11), and some infer that he was a descendant of Abraham through Midian (Genesis 25:1-2).[3]

This is a picture of a healthy mentoring relationship. I love that Moses was able to share his own journey—both the ups and downs—with his father-in-law. Often if a mentor is someone in an "official" capacity in our lives—such as a boss or superior in our work, for example—we are hesitant to tell the bad with the good for fear that it will affect our job. For that reason and others, we often need someone with outside perspective to listen to our experiences.

Who is someone you feel comfortable sharing honestly with, including both the ups and downs of your own story?

Mentoring Principle #2: A good mentor affirms the work of God in your life and praises God for all He has done in and through you.

After listening carefully to all that Moses told him, Jethro then responded.

Read Jethro's response in Exodus 18:9-12. *affirmation + Praised God - moses*

What was Jethro's first response? To whom was it directed?

What was Jethro's second response? To whom was it directed?
offering + sacrifices - to God

I love that Jethro first affirmed to Moses that God had done miraculous things through him. A good mentor will help you look back at your journey and identify where God has been actively changing, preparing, and calling you. And then Jethro turned his attention to God, thanking Him for all He had done by burning an offering.

Who has affirmed God's work in your own life?

Mentoring Principle #3: A good mentor speaks the truth even when it is difficult to hear and continues to walk with us as this truth helps us change our behavior for the better.

The following day Jethro had a front-row seat to see Moses' new responsibility in action, and he noticed that Moses was overwhelmed with all of the things he was doing for God's people. In Exodus 18:13-16 we see that Moses was worn out from serving the people from morning to nightfall. Because of the relationship that existed between the two men and the trust they had already established, Jethro spoke up and confronted Moses about the situation: "What is this you are doing for the people? Why do you alone sit as judge, while all these people stand around you from morning till evening?" (Exodus 18:14).

Moses' answer is convicting to us as we seek to serve others. He said, "Because the people come to me to seek God's will" (Exodus 18:15).

Because the people. That's why he was worn out. The people were demanding his time and energy. The people had needs. The people wouldn't let up because their needs knew no end.

Do you ever feel that way? Pulled this direction and that because of the needs of other people? Worn out because you are at the mercy of everyone else's demands? It's not a sign of true servanthood or effective leadership. It's a sign of lack of boundaries.

Jethro had the wisdom and life experience to know this wasn't going to be good for either Moses or the people in the long run. He said to Moses, "What you are doing is not good. You and these people who come to you will only wear yourselves out (Exodus 18:17-18).

Those are the words of a trusted mentor: "What you are doing is not good." Only someone we truly trust can speak those words in a way that calls us out for our weaknesses and mistakes—in this case, Moses' lack of boundaries and trying to do too much instead of asking others for help.

If you have someone who is able to observe your life and often listens to you talk about your struggles, why not ask this person: "Do you have any wisdom for me? What would you do in my situation? Is there anything I'm doing that is not good, and how can I change it for the better?"

When has a mentor or friend spoken words that called out a difficult truth for you? What was the outcome?

Mentoring Principle #4: A good mentor helps us develop a plan of action that will be best both for us and for those we serve.

Jethro followed his difficult words of truth with great words of wisdom and advice. He helped Moses to create a whole new system of leadership for the Israelites. What was it? Basically it was a Mentor Sandwich.

Read Exodus 18:18-23. What was Jethro's plan?

Select worthy help & capable

Jethro's instructions to Moses helped him to see that he was not doing a favor for the people he led or for himself by heading at a breakneck speed toward burnout. Often we think we are helping people by doing things for them, but in reality if we assist them in developing their own gifts and sense of responsibility, we give them confidence and empower them to be future leaders.

Moses would choose the next generation of leaders that he would mentor in positions of authority and ways of God's wisdom. This would both save Moses from burnout and develop leadership skills among God's people.

Keep in mind that Moses didn't dodge responsibility. He continued in a place of authority. Exodus 18:26 tells us, "The difficult cases they brought to Moses, but the simple ones they decided themselves."

This is how wisdom is passed down—from generation to generation in faith. We stand between the people who have done great things before us and the people who need us to lead and guide them. This is true in families, churches, schools, and communities. If one generation neglects to teach the next generation the truth they have learned, then we all miss out on something very important.

> We stand between the people who have done great things before us and the people who need us to lead and guide them.

Elijah and Elisha's Mentor Sandwich

When we look at the story of Elijah and Elisha in First and Second Kings, we have a clear picture of how Elisha looked up to Elijah, his mentor, for wisdom and guidance. He even called Elijah "Master" and took on the role of his servant as he followed him. But the story of how Elisha passed down the faith isn't quite as clear. We do know that after Elijah was gone, Elisha himself had a servant. This may not have been the same kind of mentoring relationship that Elijah entered into with Elisha in order to raise up a replacement for himself as prophet, but we know that Elisha taught his servant wisdom and helped guide him to understand the miracles of God. We learn this from today's passage from Second Kings.

Reread 2 Kings 6:15-17 (page 74). What did Elisha teach his servant on this occasion? *prayed to God for him to see the bigger picture*

When has someone spoken encouragement and faith into a particular situation in your life? Is this person someone who has served or who could serve as a mentor in your life?

My prayer is that you will have a leader, mentor, or guide who helps to open your eyes to God's power and presence in your life. Remember: Someone is there for you; you are there for someone. You are the heart of the sandwich, the center that keeps this chain of faith going. Keep your eyes open, and you will find them both.

Talk with God

Lord, show me someone You have placed in my life to teach and guide me. Give me the courage to ask this person to speak truth and the courage to listen and change with her or his help. Amen.

Act on It

Spend some time in prayer this week, inviting God to show you who might be included in your mentor sandwich. By whom would you like to be mentored? Who is someone you might offer to mentor? Maybe you already have these relationships established. If so, write a letter to your mentor, thanking this person for pouring so much into your life. If you are already mentoring someone, write your mentee a letter of encouragement.

Day 3: The Ministry of Multiplication

Read God's Word

¹ When the LORD was about to take Elijah up to heaven in a whirlwind, Elijah and Elisha were on their way from Gilgal. ² Elijah said to Elisha, "Stay here; the Lord has sent me to Bethel."

But Elisha said, "As surely as the LORD lives and as you live, I will not leave you." So they went down to Bethel.

³ The company of the prophets at Bethel came out to Elisha and asked, "Do you know that the LORD is going to take your master from you today?"

"Yes, I know," Elisha replied, "so be quiet."

⁴ Then Elijah said to him, "Stay here, Elisha; the LORD has sent me to Jericho."

And he replied, "As surely as the LORD lives and as you live, I will not leave you." So they went to Jericho.

⁵ The company of the prophets at Jericho went up to Elisha and asked him, "Do you know that the LORD is going to take your master from you today?"

"Yes, I know," he replied, "so be quiet."

⁶ Then Elijah said to him, "Stay here; the LORD has sent me to the Jordan."

And he replied, "As surely as the LORD lives and as you live, I will not leave you." So the two of them walked on.

⁷ Fifty men from the company of the prophets went and stood at a distance, facing the place where Elijah and Elisha had stopped at the Jordan. ⁸ Elijah took his cloak, rolled it up and struck the water with it. The water divided to the right and to the left, and the two of them crossed over on dry ground.

⁹ *When they had crossed, Elijah said to Elisha, "Tell me, what can I do for you before I am taken from you?"*

"Let me inherit a double portion of your spirit," Elisha replied.

¹⁰ *"You have asked a difficult thing," Elijah said, "yet if you see me when I am taken from you, it will be yours—otherwise, it will not."*

¹¹ *As they were walking along and talking together, suddenly a chariot of fire and horses of fire appeared and separated the two of them, and Elijah went up to heaven in a whirlwind.* ¹² *Elisha saw this and cried out, "My father! My father! The chariots and horsemen of Israel!" And Elisha saw him no more. Then he took hold of his garment and tore it in two.*

2 Kings 2:1-12

Reflect and Respond

My heart beat fast as I held the receiver to my ear, listening to the phone ring. I felt as if I was calling to ask someone out on a date: *What would I say if the person answered? What would the answer be to my invitation?*

But I wasn't calling to ask for a date. I was calling to ask for a mentor. A week earlier I sat in a crowded auditorium listening to an amazing woman in her late sixties teach on prayer. She talked about Jesus as if she'd just had coffee with Him that morning. And to tell the truth, she probably had. Although there was almost half a century's difference in our ages, I was determined to get to know her. There was something about the way she prayed—and talked—that I knew I needed in my own life. I was looking for guidance and help with the everyday ins and outs of following Christ day by day.

Somehow once she answered the phone and I explained who I was, I managed to ask: "Would you disciple me? Could we spend some time together once in a while and talk about how to do this thing called the Christian life?"

"Well of course, honey!" she said with a warm laugh.

And that was how Margaret Therkelson became my mentor. That was how I had the privilege of sitting on her couch every few weeks with a cup of tea, talking about living life with Jesus and praying together. Mrs. Therkelson had written wonderful books and had given great messages on prayer, but they were nothing compared to sitting with her while she talked with Jesus in person. She prayed with certainty that God was real, present, and listening intently. I had never heard anyone pray quite like her. The time I spent in her living room taught me far more than any book, lecture, or sermon.

What does the Bible say about the things that can happen in our lives because of mentoring? Read each verse, and then write a word or phrase for each:

become wise from the wise

Proverbs 13:20 *get in trouble with fools*

Proverbs 27:17 *as iron sharpens iron, so a friend sharpens a friend*

Ecclesiastes 4:10 *If one person falls, the other can reach out and help. But someone who falls alone is in real trouble*

Once during a visit to Margaret Therkelson's living room, after we had prayed and I was getting my coat to leave, I gave her what I believed was a compliment.

"Mrs. Therkelson," I said, "I hope one day I can be half the woman of prayer that you are."

Her response was quick, her voice sharper and more direct than I had ever heard it before.

"Don't do that, honey," she said. "Don't you ever wish to be half of me. Don't you know the story of Elijah and Elisha?"

I did. But that night I went back and read it again just to see what she was talking about. It was early in the book of Second Kings but late in the great prophet Elijah's life and ministry. He had performed incredible miracles, faced down evil, changed the future of nations. But his greatest investment, the thing he would leave behind that would make the most difference, was a single relationship— the one with his student and follower, Elisha.

Elisha had followed Elijah everywhere, and he was determined to follow him to the end. As they went on one last journey together to Bethel, then Jericho, then to the Jordan River, Elisha had two different interchanges with groups of local prophets who warned him that Elijah soon would be leaving (see 2 Kings 2:3, 5). As a result, Elisha stuck as closely as possible to Elijah, twice disobeying direct orders to stay put and let Elijah leave him behind.

When they reached the Jordan, seemingly at a dead end, Elijah suddenly took his mantle and struck the river, causing it to part and allowing the two men to walk to the other side on dry ground. Then Elijah turned to Elisha and spoke: "Tell me, what can I do for you before I am taken from you?" (2 Kings 2:9). His words seem abrupt to me, reminding me of his first words to Elisha: "Go back again; for what have I done to you" (1 Kings 19:20).

I wonder if Elisha looked back at the Jordan in that moment, his mouth still hanging open from the miracle he had just witnessed. No doubt he was thinking of his master's great life of ministry and miracles when he uttered his reply.

Look back at 2 Kings 2:9-10. What did Elisha request?

let me inherit a double portion of your spirit

How would Elisha know if he received his request?

This request for a "double portion" of his master's spirit seems pretty bold and gutsy. Who would dare ask such a thing of the great prophet Elijah?

Elisha did. And it's exactly what Mrs. Therkelson was encouraging me to do. Instead of saying, "I want to be half the woman you are someday," she wanted me to make this kind of bold request: "I want to be *twice* the woman you are someday." She was right in encouraging me to pray that bold kind of prayer.

If you could have a double portion of someone's faith, whose would it be?

Clearly Elisha didn't have to look for his mentor. He was simply plowing a field when Elijah came to him. Sometimes a mentor just shows up in our lives, but other times we have to look for them. Where do we begin?

First, let me acknowledge that there are different kinds of mentors and multiple avenues for finding one. Here are some possibilities for finding a good fit:

Spiritual mentor or spiritual director

A spiritual mentor or spiritual director is not a counselor or therapist but someone mature in faith who voluntarily helps you to grow closer to Christ and discern and respond to God's work in your life. A spiritual director can be a pastor or lay person who is trained to listen to your spiritual journey and offer guidance.

Vocational mentor

A vocational mentor is someone who mentors you in what you are called to do. It may be a boss or someone you know who has accomplished something great in your field. Remember that a vocation is a calling but not necessarily a paid job. So your vocational mentor also might be a mom of older children whose family you look up to, or someone whose volunteer work or philanthropy has something to teach you. Keep in mind that someone doesn't need to have walked the exact same path the same way to help you on yours.

Educational mentor

An educational mentor is someone who has knowledge in an area you'd like to learn more about. Seek out people who know the things you'd like to know about and ask them to share their knowledge and experience with you.

Peer mentor

A mentor doesn't have to be older or further in her or his journey than you. It may be that one of your friends or peers offers wisdom and support on your journey.

Family mentors

Mentoring doesn't always happen one-on-one. Spending time with a family whose relationships you admire may have a lot to teach you about the kind of family you'd like to have. The same is true for married couples spending time with other couples whose relationships they admire.

Unofficial mentors

You may find the people you learn from have never officially been named your "mentor." Make sure to pay attention to the people God puts along your path.

Wherever we find our mentors and whatever we call them (teacher, boss, mom, pastor, friend), the goal is for them to help us grow in some way—personally, professionally, and/or spiritually. You may need or want more than one kind of mentor, but as a follower of Christ, it is especially important to seek out a spiritual mentor who can encourage and guide you in the faith.

Elijah was a spiritual mentor to Elisha. The two men had grown so close that even though the younger man started out calling the older "Master" and acting as his servant, in their final moment together he called Elijah something much more intimate.

Reread 2 Kings 2:11-12 (page 82). What name does Elisha call Elijah in the end?

my father

These men had developed such a close relationship that Elisha thought of Elijah as a father. It's interesting to note that the oldest son in a family inherited a double portion of his father's estate.[4] But here, instead of land or assets, it's a double portion of his *spirit* that Elisha is looking for.

According to verses 11-12, how do we know that Elisha received his request?

tore his garment in two

Depending on how you count miracles (a hard task with the stories of these prophets since so much of what they did was outside of normal human ability), the Bible records that Elisha performed roughly double the number of miracles of his mentor, Elijah. Sometimes the story even goes to great lengths to compare the miracles of the two men, making sure we realize that Elisha did the same kinds of things his mentor did, sometimes even double.

Extra Insight
Elisha was a prophet of Israel during the reigns of Jehoram, Jehu, Jehoahaz, and Joash (903-838 B.C.).[5]

Below is a chart of some miracles performed by Elijah and Elisha. Look up the Scripture passages for Elisha's miracles 1 and 7 in the chart. After reading about each miracle, write a title for these two miracles in the chart.

Miracles of Elijah		Miracles of Elisha	
1. Causing the rain to cease for several years	1 Kings 17:1	1. *Parted the waters of the Jordan*	2 Kings 2:13-14
2. Miracle of the jar of flour and jug of oil	1 Kings 17:13-16	2. Healing of the waters	2 Kings 2:19-22
3. Resurrection of the widow's son	1 Kings 17:19-23	3. Curse of the she bears (this is a strange one!)	2 Kings 2:23-24
4. Calling of fire from heaven on the altar	1 Kings 18:36-38	4. Filling of the valley with water	2 Kings 3:16-20
5. Causing it to rain	1 Kings 18:41-45	5. Deception of the Moabites with the valley of blood	2 Kings 3:14-22
6. Calling down fire from heaven on 102 soldiers	2 Kings 1:10-12	6. Miracle of the vessels of oil	2 Kings 4:3-6
7. Parting the Jordan River	2 Kings 2:8	7. *Resurrection of a young boy*	2 Kings 4:32-37
8. Caught up to heaven in a whirlwind	2 Kings 2:11	8. Healing of the gourds	2 Kings 4:38-41
		9. Miracle of the bread	2 Kings 4:42-44
		10. Healing of Naaman	2 Kings 5:14
		11. Cursing Gehazi with leprosy	2 Kings 5:27
		12. Floating of the axe head	2 Kings 6:6
		13. Vision of the chariots	2 Kings 6:17
		14. Taking away/restoring sight to the Syrian army	2 Kings 6:18-20
		15. Deception of the Syrians with the sound of chariots	2 Kings 7:6
		16. Resurrection of the man touched by Elisha's bones	2 Kings 13:21

How does each of these miracles reflect a similar miracle of Elijah?

Elisha's miracle #1 reflects Elijah's miracle # _____1_____ **because . . .**

Elisha's miracle #7 reflects Elijah's miracle # _____3_____ **because . . .**

Scholars count the miracles of Elijah and Elisha with slight differences, but the overall effect is an almost exact doubling in the next generation. The stories go to such length to make a point of Elisha's request being answered that even the number of people raised from the dead is doubled from Elijah to Elisha.

Recall the person you named earlier whose faith you would like to receive a double portion of. What if you were to grow in your faith to twice the person of God that he or she is? What if instead of saying, "I wish I was half the person that he or she is," you prayed, "I would like to have twice the love for others, twice the impact on my community, twice the grace and patience and forgiveness"?

Turn your double portion dream into a bold request, writing your prayer to God below:

Just imagine if in every generation the strength of God's people on earth doubled because we learned the secret of Elisha and Elijah—the secret of absorbing all we can from the generation before and investing all we can in the generation that will come after us. Imagine what the world would look like in two generations, and ten, and twenty. Just imagine. And dare to pray boldly!

Talk with God

Jesus, I am so grateful that You place people in my life who have wisdom and experience beyond my own. Open my eyes to notice the potential mentors around me, and give each of us the courage to ask for even more of You in our generation than the last. Amen.

Act on It

Review the list of types of mentors. Can you think of someone in one of these areas who could mentor you? Can you identify someone who might be a spiritual mentor? Reach out today to this person—or persons—with a phone call or e-mail, asking to spend time together.

Day 4: Stepping Up

Read God's Word

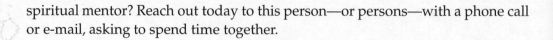

⁸ *Elijah took his cloak, rolled it up and struck the water with it. The water divided to the right and to the left, and the two of them crossed over on dry ground.*

⁹ *When they had crossed, Elijah said to Elisha, "Tell me, what can I do for you before I am taken from you?"*

"Let me inherit a double portion of your spirit," Elisha replied.

¹⁰ *"You have asked a difficult thing," Elijah said, "yet if you see me when I am taken from you, it will be yours—otherwise, it will not."*

¹¹ *As they were walking along and talking together, suddenly a chariot of fire and horses of fire appeared and separated the two of them, and Elijah went up to heaven in a whirlwind.* ¹² *Elisha saw this and cried out, "My father! My father! The chariots and horsemen of Israel!" And Elisha saw him no more. Then he took hold of his garment and tore it in two.*

¹³ *Elisha then picked up Elijah's cloak that had fallen from him and went back and stood on the bank of the Jordan.* ¹⁴ *He took the cloak that had fallen from Elijah and struck the water with it. "Where now is the LORD, the God of Elijah?" he asked. When he struck the water, it divided to the right and to the left, and he crossed over.*

¹⁵ *The company of the prophets from Jericho, who were watching, said, "The spirit of Elijah is resting on Elisha."*

2 Kings 2:8-15

Reflect and Respond

I stood on a platform filled with great leaders, professors, and mentors looking out at a chapel full of students starting a new year of classes. The president of the seminary from which I had graduated a dozen years before stood up to lead us in a litany of commitment for the new academic year. First, he invited the students to say their part, committing themselves to Christ in their studies and relationships. I found myself, out of habit, reading the part aloud with the students, but then suddenly I stopped myself. I wasn't a student this time. It was my first service of this kind to experience from the other side. Now I was standing as a leader on a platform full of leaders, having recently been invited to serve as pastor of this community, a role called Dean of the Chapel. This time I was committing myself to Christ as a mentor, not a pupil. It was more than a little hard to believe. I was standing on the same platform from which I had first heard my mentor Margaret Therkelson (and many other great leaders) speak over fifteen years before. Now it was my turn to step up and lead.

We need mentoring as a spiritual practice because it helps us grow into the faith-filled followers God has called us to be. While this is true, there is also another side to the relationship that we need to examine. Each of us also needs to mentor others. We need to learn to recognize and reach out to the next generation of followers of Christ in order to help them grow in faith. As difficult as it might be to swallow your fear of rejection and ask someone to be your mentor, it may be even more difficult to recognize that it's now your turn to be the mentor, that the mantle of leadership has passed to you.

Recall one of the first times you were named or recognized as a leader. What was your first reaction?

Most of us react with feelings of disbelief and unworthiness when we are told that we are being looked to for wisdom, strength, and leadership.

If Elisha's mouth had dropped open when he saw his mentor Elijah use his mantle to part the waters of the Jordan, imagine his reaction when he stood witness as Elijah was taken up to heaven in a whirlwind on a chariot of fire.

What did Elisha do when his mentor was taken from him and it was his turn to lead? Let's look briefly at four actions he took.

1. Elisha mourned. We read in 2 Kings 2:12, "And Elisha saw him no more. Then he took hold of his garment and tore it in two" (2 Kings 2:12).

Many of us have had difficult experiences when we have lost a mentor, either to death or relocation or changes in life situations. Because mentoring relationships can mean so much to us, when they are gone or changed drastically we are left feeling a deep loss. It can be an experience of grief.

We also have had to mourn a gap in leadership when no other leaders emerged. It's appropriate to mourn a lack of leadership. Sometimes a leader dies or moves on, and those left behind look around at one another and wonder who will take the place of leadership. Mourning a lack of great leaders is often the thing that makes us realize we need to step up and step into leadership ourselves.

2. Elisha picked up the mantle. In the next verse we read, "Elisha then picked up Elijah's cloak that had fallen from him" (2 Kings 2:13). We've seen this cloak or mantle belonging to Elijah before.

What did Elijah do with his mantle in 1 Kings 19:19?

Extra Insight
The tearing of garments, or clothes, in the Scriptures is an expression of deep grief, mourning, distress, or sometimes repentance.[6]

Notice that in the scene in 1 Kings 19:19 where Elijah selects Elisha as his successor, the mantle is handled by Elijah. He is the active agent choosing Elisha. But in the scene in 2 Kings 2:13 where Elijah departs, Elisha has to choose for himself to follow in Elijah's steps.

Each of us must recognize and choose for ourselves that it is time to transition from only being mentored to mentoring others as well.

3. Elisha did what he had seen his mentor do. No sooner had Elijah departed than Elisha imitates his teacher. Only six verses separate their identical actions.

Read and compare verses 8 and 14 in 2 Kings 2. What did both Elijah and Elisha do?

Our relationships with our mentors often show us in a very visible way what is good and right to do in certain situations. When you come to a tricky situation or decision, you might try picturing a mentor you've admired and asking what she or he would do. What an incredible confirmation of Elisha's new ministry that he was able to perform the same miracle that his mentor had just performed!

4. Elisha called out to God. As Elisha struck the water with Elijah's cloak, he called out to God, "Where now is the LORD, the God of Elijah?" (2 Kings 2:14). His mentor was no longer with him, and he had to stop relying on Elijah as a conduit for God's voice. Elisha knew that he must call out to God himself. And God responded. God doesn't want us to seek Him secondhand through someone else. He wants us to seek Him with all of our hearts.

Can you think of a situation when someone you depended on for spiritual support was no longer able to be there for you? Did you find yourself calling out to God in that moment? Briefly describe what happened:

As a result of the actions Elisha took, he was able to step up into leadership and assume the role that his mentor Elijah had been preparing him for all those years. And we see from the text that Elisha's leadership was quickly recognized by others.

Reread 2 Kings 2:15 (page 88). What did the prophets who were watching say about Elisha?

God calls us to lead, but other faithful people in our lives can confirm that call. If you are being asked to lead in your church, family, or community, or if people are coming to you for advice or a listening ear, it may be a confirmation that God is nudging you to step up and lead.

Who have you shared your life with? Name at least one person who has looked to you for help and guidance.

Now that you've been encouraged to find someone you can mentor, how do you actually mentor someone? There are many ways to mentor others, but let's consider five foundational practices of mentoring.

1. *Spend time together.* Pray for God to show you someone you can invest in. It may be a younger person you want to invest in. It may be someone who is struggling that you long to help. God will open your eyes to someone, and you can begin by praying for this person. Then invite the individual to coffee or to go with you on an errand or to an event. Be clear that you want to help the person to grow. Let her or him know your intention, and ask how you can help.

2. *Share your life.* Mentoring is not always about what you say. It also is about what you see. You are mentoring when someone is watching you make decisions, interact with people, prioritize your time and attention, and other normal things you do as you go about your day. Have someone spend time with you in your everyday activities. If the person is paying attention, she or he will learn more than you can teach with words.

Read 1 Thessalonians 2:8 in the margin. What two things was Paul determined to share with the Thessalonians? *The gospel & their lives*

3. *Share stories.* Stories teach great lessons. Jesus used them often. Tell stories of times when you made mistakes, were successful, and were challenged by disappointment and heartache. Often it's stories that we remember most.

4. *Encourage.* People are hungry to hear that they are noticed, appreciated, and loved. Think of a list of positive things about the person you want to mentor. Each time you talk, be sure to mention at least one thing. Take time to send notes of appreciation by e-mail, text, and snail mail. Think of yourself as God's instrument to give this person good news about God's plan for her or his life.

Read Philippians 4:8 in the margin. Think of a person you would like to encourage, and make a list of things you can praise about this person.

Because we loved you so much, we were delighted to share with you not only the gospel of God but our lives as well.
1 Thessalonians 2:8

Finally, brothers and sisters, whatever is true, whatever is noble, whatever is right, whatever is pure, whatever is lovely, whatever is admirable— if anything is excellent or praiseworthy— think about such things.
Philippians 4:8

5. *Tell the truth.* If you see some behavior or habit in your friend's life that is hurtful—whether to himself or herself, or to others—pray about bringing it up in conversation. Speak gently but truthfully. Be sure your words of confrontation are few and surrounded by encouragement and a continual commitment to be there as she or he grows.

Read Ephesians 4:15 in the margin. When has someone spoken the truth in love to you?

Instead, speaking the truth in love, we will grow to become in every respect the mature body of him who is the head, that is, Christ. Ephesians 4:15

The message is the person. Hear again the Apostle Paul's words to the Thessalonians: "We were delighted to share with you not only the Gospel of God but our lives as well" (1 Thessalonians 2:8). If you want the world to be a better place, the best thing you have to invest is yourself. And the best way to invest yourself is in relationship with another person.

As he watched his mentor go from him, Elisha realized that the time had come for him to step up and lead. In future years he would be the one to take on roles of leadership for God's people. If Elisha had assumed he could never be as great a mentor or leader as Elijah, we wouldn't have record of the amazing witness of his ministry.

Each of us is called to learn from others and to find ways to invest our lives in others. You are gifted with wisdom and strength from God that you may never know you have until you choose to give it away to someone else.

Perhaps the time has come for you to step up and pick up the mantle. God will give you the wisdom and words you need.

Talk with God

Lord God, thank You for the amazing men and women who have shown me Your light. Show me one person this week I can help to grow in faith in You. Amen.

If you want the world to be a better place, the best thing you have to invest is yourself. And the best way to invest yourself is in relationship with another person.

Act on It

Begin to pray about people God has placed in your life for you to invest in. Make a list of people in your family, job, church, and other areas of influence you might have. Choose one person to contact this week with words of encouragement, and see if God leads you to invest more deeply in this person's life.

Day 5: The Footsteps of Jesus

Read God's Word

¹ After six days Jesus took with him Peter, James and John the brother of James, and led them up a high mountain by themselves. ² There he was transfigured before them. His face shone like the sun, and his clothes became as white as the light. ³ Just then there appeared before them Moses and Elijah, talking with Jesus.

⁴ Peter said to Jesus, "Lord, it is good for us to be here. If you wish, I will put up three shelters—one for you, one for Moses and one for Elijah."

⁵ While he was still speaking, a bright cloud covered them, and a voice from the cloud said, "This is my Son, whom I love; with him I am well pleased. Listen to him!"

⁶ When the disciples heard this, they fell facedown to the ground, terrified. ⁷ But Jesus came and touched them. "Get up," he said. "Don't be afraid." ⁸ When they looked up, they saw no one except Jesus.

⁹ As they were coming down the mountain, Jesus instructed them, "Don't tell anyone what you have seen, until the Son of Man has been raised from the dead."

¹⁰ The disciples asked him, "Why then do the teachers of the law say that Elijah must come first?"

¹¹ Jesus replied, "To be sure, Elijah comes and will restore all things. ¹² But I tell you, Elijah has already come, and they did not recognize him, but have done to him everything they wished. In the same way the Son of Man is going to suffer at their hands." ¹³ Then the disciples understood that he was talking to them about John the Baptist.

Matthew 17:1-13

Reflect and Respond

Yesterday we witnessed the amazing end of Elijah's story with the account of his being taken up in a whirlwind on a chariot of fire. His disciple, Elisha, stood amazed and stared into the clouds, watching Elijah depart. The door closed on Elijah's earthly ministry, and he was never to be heard from again. Except . . .

Except that the Bible has a lot more to say about Elijah! The very last sentences of the Old Testament talk about Elijah:

"See, I will send the prophet Elijah to you before that great and dreadful day of the LORD comes. He will turn the hearts of the parents to their children, and the hearts of the children to their parents; or else I will come and strike the land with total destruction."

Malachi 4:5-6

These were the last sentences written by the prophet Malachi, which God's people had to hold onto for hundreds of years while God remained silent. During this period, they hoped that Elijah would return to them to prepare the way of the Messiah, the promised one whom God would send to rescue them.

In the New Testament, Elijah is mentioned nearly thirty times.[7] Of all the Old Testament figures that are talked about in the New Testament, only Moses, David, and Abraham are referenced more than Elijah. When Jesus began performing miracles, people speculated that perhaps He was the Elijah they had been waiting for.

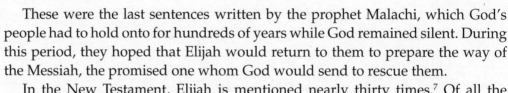

Read Luke 9:18-20.

Who do the disciples say that Jesus is rumored to be? *John the Baptist, Elijah or another ancient prophet*

Who does Peter say that Jesus is? *the Messiah*

It's not surprising that people were guessing Jesus might be Elijah returned to earth:

- Elijah spent time in the desert early in his ministry (1 Kings 19:1-9).
- Jesus went to the desert to be tempted early in his ministry (Matthew 4:1-11).
- Elijah helped a widow by performing a miracle and turning a small amount of oil into an abundance (2 Kings 4:1-7).
- Jesus helped his mother by performing a miracle when she asked him to replenish a supply of wine that had run out (John 2:1-10).
- Elijah raised a widow's son from the dead (2 Kings 4:33-35).
- Jesus raised the daughter of a ruler from the dead (Matthew 9:24-25) and also the son of a widow (Luke 7:11-17).

To the people of God, who were longing for the days when prophets walked among them performing great miracles, Jesus' actions looked a lot like those of Elijah. They hoped this would usher in the days of the Messiah coming to earth. What they didn't realize is that Jesus wasn't there to prepare the way for the Messiah; He *was* the Messiah. Instead of sending another messenger or prophet, God had come in person to set things right.

Jesus finally set things straight on an amazing mountain climbing experience with the disciples Peter, James, and John. As they reached the top of a steep mountain, an amazing transformation happened.

Extra Insight

Jesus said that John the Baptist went forth as Elijah in spirit, making him the symbolic fulfillment of the prophet's mission (Matthew 11:14, Mark 8:28, and Luke 1:17).[8]

Matthew

Read John 17:2-3.

How does Jesus' appearance change? *face shone like sun + clothes became white as the light*

Who is there with him, and what are they doing? *Peter, James, John climbing up a mountain*

At the end of this experience in which the disciples were awestruck, witnessing a place where heaven and earth seemed to intersect, they remembered what had been said about Elijah coming to prepare the way for the Messiah. They asked Jesus: "Why then do the teachers of the law say that Elijah must come first?" (Matthew 17:10). After witnessing this incredible miracle, that probably would not have been the only question on my list!

Jesus cleared things up by explaining that the prophecy about a "new Elijah" who would come to prepare the way for the Messiah was actually about John the Baptist (Matthew 17:11-13).

Read the words in Luke 1:16-17 (in the margin) that the angel told John's father before he was ever born. How is this a fulfillment of the prophecy in Malachi 4:5-6?

"He will bring back many of the people of Israel to the Lord their God. And he will go on before the Lord, in the spirit and power of Elijah, to turn the hearts of the parents to their children and the disobedient to the wisdom of the righteous— to make ready a people prepared for the Lord." Luke 1:16-17

With all of the similarities that caused people to speculate about connections between Elijah and Jesus, one of the most important has to do with mentoring. Both Elijah and Jesus practiced mentoring in a specific way. They didn't just teach their followers with words; they invited them to follow, observe, and learn from the way they lived on a daily basis. This style of passing down knowledge—not in a classroom or on a page but through life in the real moments of every day— follows the principle that "one living sermon is worth a hundred explanations."[9]

Has someone been a *living* sermon for you? If so, briefly describe something you have learned from this person.

Both Jesus and Elijah found their disciples practicing a profession (the disciples were fishermen; Elisha was a farmer) and expected them to leave behind their possessions and their families. Leaving home, family, friends, a profession—these were high expectations. The things that Elisha and the disciples had to leave behind were costly, but the rewards of their new lives with their new mentors were amazing.

In John's account of the calling of the disciples, Andrew hears and believes in Jesus first and then enthusiastically goes to get his brother so that he, too, can follow Jesus.

> *Andrew, Simon Peter's brother, was one of the two who heard what John had said and who had followed Jesus. The first thing Andrew did was to find his brother Simon and tell him, "We have found the Messiah" (that is, the Christ). And he brought him to Jesus.*
>
> *Jesus looked at him and said, "You are Simon son of John. You will be called Cephas" (which, when translated, is Peter.)*

John 1:40-42

Andrew basically said to his brother: follow me, and I will show you someone you can follow. When we follow someone who follows Jesus, walking in his or her footsteps helps us to walk in the footsteps of Christ Himself.

Teaching us to follow Christ is something the best mentors have as their goal, because the end result of our time with them is not just to soak up their wisdom, emulate their actions, or imitate their character. These are helpful outcomes of mentoring, but the best outcome is a closer walk with Christ. Time spent with people who are following Jesus makes us want to be followers of Jesus ourselves.

Is there someone you've "followed" and spent time with who makes you want to follow Christ more closely? If so, write her or his name below:

How has observing and imitating this person impacted your walk with Christ?

Listen to the words of a woman named Dorothy as she describes how her grandmother, with whom she lived with for a while when she was a child, mentored her in faith:

> My grandmother was a staunch Methodist, so we were in church every time the door was open. She'd never gone to school, but she had gotten her brothers to teach her to read well enough so that she could read her Bible. So she made sure I was at Sunday school, even though I was just three years old. They'd give us a little snack there, but you had to say a blessing before you got it. And the only blessing I knew at the time was "Jesus wept." The teacher said to me, "That's a very short blessing. Don't you know something a bit longer than that?"

So I went home and told my grandmother that I was embar-rassed because all I knew was "Jesus wept."

When my grandmother heard this, she decided to teach me the twenty-third Psalm. Three years old, I learned the entire thing, because I felt I could do it. We went over it every night. She wanted me to be proud of myself in that classroom.

And so the next Sunday I not only recited the twenty-third Psalm in Sunday school, but the teacher was so impressed, she told the minister. Before they dismissed church, she said, "You know, little Dorothy has something to say," and I stood there before the whole congregation and recited the twenty-third Psalm. I felt really good about myself for being able to do that. It made me feel wonderful. The whole church was just so pleased that little Dorothy could do this, and I think that was the message my grandmother was giving me—that you never have to feel ashamed of your capabilities. My grandmother taught me that I have a lot to be proud of. She taught me that I was somebody important, that I was somebody smart.[10]

Dorothy's grandmother was able to instill faith in herself while teaching her faith in Christ. Christian mentors have as their goal not only our own self-confidence and self-worth, which is a deep need each of us has, but also confidence in the worth of Scripture and faith in Christ.

The disciples had the amazing opportunity to follow literally in Jesus' footsteps, watching his actions and listening to his words firsthand. But after Jesus ascended—being taken up from them before their eyes, another similarity to Elijah's life and ministry—the disciples themselves must have had disciples of their own. And those followers must have passed the faith down to the next generation of believers. You and I are able to follow Jesus today because this same pattern has been repeated in every generation since.

God wants you to function as a human link in this ongoing chain of believers. He wants to give you mentors who will let you walk beside them, see their own faith and actions, and ultimately follow them in the footsteps of Christ. He also wants to use you to reach out to those who need strength and wisdom, offering them a human link that will connect them to Christ. The Apostle Paul said, "Follow my example, as I follow the example of Christ" (1 Corinthians 11:1). May these words become the living message you communicate as you invite others to be part of the great chain of faith.

Talk with God

Lord, help us look to Jesus as the ultimate mentor, as the perfect example of what it means to love You and be loved by You. Help us to follow in His footsteps and lead others on His path. Use Your Holy Spirit to work within us, guiding us to be more like You. Amen.

Act on It

Sometime this week, go on a prayer walk. With every step you take along the path, consider the Apostle Paul's words in 1 Corinthians 11:1: "Follow my example, as I follow the example of Christ." Meditate on his words and on who might be following you as you follow Christ.

Week 3
Video Viewer Guide

So Elijah went from there and found Elisha son of Shaphat. He was plowing with twelve yoke of oxen, and he himself was driving the twelfth pair. Elijah went up to him and threw his cloak around him. Elisha then left his oxen and ran after Elijah. "Let me kiss my father and mother goodbye," he said, "and then I will come with you."

"Go back," Elijah replied. "What have I done to you?"

So Elisha left him and went back. He took his yoke of oxen and slaughtered them. He burned the plowing equipment to cook the meat and gave it to the people, and they ate. Then he set out to follow *Elijah and became his* servant.

1 Kings 19:19-21 NIV

When God calls you to bigger and better things, you need to believe that there is no turning back.

A chain represents the place that you have as a link in the Christian faith.

On the chain shown here or on a paper chain provided for you in your group:

Write your name on the middle link.

On the top link, write the name of someone who has invested in you.

On the bottom link, write the name of someone God has entrusted to you—someone who is learning from the way you live your life.

Remember your ___leaders___, who spoke the word of God to you. Consider the outcome of their way of life and ___imitate___ their faith.

Hebrews 13:7 NIV

Your masterpiece is probably going to be a ___person___.

And that's the kind of masterpiece that has ___lasting___ value.

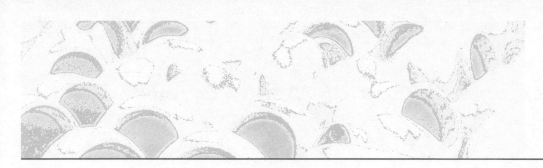

Week 4
Elisha and Naaman
Set Apart by Practicing Humility

Let's face it. Humility does not come naturally to most of us. Instead, we tend to want to be the favorite, the one who is picked, the one who is recognized and admired. We want people to know our skills, talents, degrees, certifications, pedigrees, and expertise. We prefer to be known by our successes, wearing our victories so that we will be acknowledged and accepted. Anything less might mean being looked down upon or considered ordinary.

But as followers of Jesus, we are called to practice humility. Note the word *practice*—after all, none of us is going to get it exactly right in our time here on earth! Still, we are called to imitate Christ, who we are told "did not consider [even] equality with God something to be used to his own advantage; rather he made himself nothing" (Philippians 2:6-7). If anyone could walk this earth with bragging rights, it was Jesus. After all, He was the perfect Son of God. But instead he took a different route, choosing humility all the way to a cross. Jesus humbled himself in order to fulfill God's rescue plan, giving His very life to save us.

This week we will explore the story of the prophet Elisha and a man named Naaman, a man who had enough credentials to be full of himself—and he was. Yet he would have to humble himself—to come down from his high horse and wade in the waters of the people—in order to be healed of his disease. As we consider his story, we will see that we all need experiences along our faith journeys to check ourselves for humility. In addition to learning about humility, we also will have opportunities this week to practice it. Let's invite God to remove our pride and replace it with humility, making us fully dependent on Him alone.

Day 1: Defining Details

Read God's Word

¹ Now Naaman was commander of the army of the king of Aram. He was a great man in the sight of his master and highly regarded, because through him the LORD had given victory to Aram. He was a valiant soldier, but he had leprosy.
² Now bands of raiders from Aram had gone out and had taken captive a young girl from Israel, and she served Naaman's wife. ³ She said to her mistress, "If only my master would see the prophet who is in Samaria! He would cure him of his leprosy."
⁴ Naaman went to his master and told him what the girl from Israel had said.

2 Kings 5:1-4

Reflect and Respond

A friend of mine worked in Washington, DC, for several years for a ministry located right in the heart of Capitol Hill. One year he was present during the pomp and circumstance of a presidential inauguration. For several weeks the capitol city was scrubbed and scoured as attention was given to making it look its best for the big day.

The day before the inauguration, the head of the ministry my friend worked for gave him an unusual order: "I want you to meet me downtown at 3:00 a.m. tomorrow at the beginning of the route that the inaugural procession will take." Not knowing what to expect, he got up while it was still dark and met his boss on the cold streets where they walked the route together while it was still quiet. That's when he saw what his mentor wanted him to see: police vans were driving along the route, and periodically officers were getting out, rounding up the homeless people from the streets, and packing them into the vans to take them to jail for the day. There they would be out of view of the tourists and TV cameras that would crowd the streets that day. Later that day all eyes would focus on a single figure in a black limousine winding its way down that street; but the least, the last, and the lonely would be hidden from the public eye.

It can be uncomfortable for us to come face to face with the least, the last, and the lonely—the most humble of society; yet encountering true humility can be one of the most transformative experiences in our lives. This week we will focus on the practice of humility by looking to a story in Second Kings that involves a familiar friend, the prophet Elisha. Before we get to Elisha's part in the story, we need to meet the two other characters whose personal stories spin the events into action.

Naaman is listed first, and he would have it no other way. He is the commander of the Aramean army, a five-star general. Everywhere he goes, people bow and scrape, flattering him with their words and preparing for him the nicest rooms and most lavish banquets. The words given to describe him include accolades and adjectives that build him up as a man of power.

Reread 2 Kings 5:1 (page 102) and circle the titles and adjectives describing Naaman that indicate his power and prestige. Then write them below:
Commander of army, great man, highly regarded, valiant soldier

After Naaman's grand entrance, the Scripture jumps quickly to introduce the secondary character, a servant girl. It's as if the story makes the two of them stand side by side so that we may look back and forth from one to the other and see their differences clearly—although chances are they never would have stood next to each other because of the great gap in their status.

Reread 2 Kings 5:2 (page 102) and circle any clues that describe the servant girl. Then write them below: *young, served*

Look at the two groups of words you've written above, and note the stark differences between them. Write your thoughts below:
highly vs lowly, regarded

There is perhaps no deeper contrast between two characters portrayed in the same story in the Bible. This girl is little and young; she is a foreigner and a slave. She is a victim of human trafficking, having been taken from her country against her will. She has no status; we aren't even given her name. Her home country of Israel serves as a clue to how despised she is.

You see, Israel is not well-thought-of in Aram. Aram has raided Israel and taken prisoners to become slaves. The servant girl's country of origin is considered weak and inferior. If being from Israel isn't enough, we are told she comes from the region of Samaria, a territory despised in Israel. Many years later this despised region would be named in a story about a Samaritan woman who conversed with Jesus (John 4:4-42)—shocking because of her gender and place of origin—and a story Jesus would tell of a good Samaritan (Luke 10:25-37)—shocking because the people who heard the story would have considered the Samaritan hero to be far beneath them.

In essence, Naaman has every privilege and advantage in Aram, while the servant girl has every imaginable disadvantage in this foreign culture in which she lives and serves against her will. Their cultural status is obvious, yet there is one little detail about each of them that keeps them from being totally defined by their status. You might call it a redefining detail.

Naaman's redefining detail is the last word of the last sentence used to describe him in 2 Kings 5:1. Write the word below. *leprosy*

Naaman's redefining detail is a dreaded skin disease called leprosy. Actually, there is some debate among scholars as to what kind of skin disease it is since he remains in social contact with others throughout the story, unlike the lepers of the New Testament who are shunned to protect others from catching a very contagious disease. Even so, his desire to be cured and the inclusion of the story in Scripture imply that he is distressed by the implications of his diagnosis.

A skin disease such as leprosy has changed the way people respond to Namaan. It's likely that the worse the disease gets, the more people want to stay away. As we can imagine, Naaman may be nervous about losing his place of power. Perhaps some are even waiting in the wings to take his place. Instead of being the great and esteemed Naaman, he is now redefined as a leper.

The servant girl's redefining detail is her faith. Though no one in Naaman's kingdom knows how to cure him, she remembers a prophet back home in Israel named Elisha. She has faith in Elisha's God—her God—to heal anyone, even her braggadocio boss, Naaman. So she says to Naaman's wife, her mistress, "If only my master would see the prophet who is in Samaria! He would cure him of his leprosy" (1 Kings 5:3).

This young girl who thus far has been defined by her lowly status is now redefined: she is faithful and brave. Though she may have been humble in her approach to reaching Naaman with her idea, she is not timid or weak in her confidence that her God can heal this disease. Regardless of her cultural status, she is an example of how God uses unexpected characters to bring about His plans.

What are the details of your cultural status? What would "the world" list when it comes to your accomplishments, your assets, and your worth?
free country, comfortable home, plenty to eat, riches

What would you say is your redefining detail—the thing that keeps you from being totally defined by your cultural status? It might be something that lifts you up or something that brings you down a notch.
share with others

What strikes me in this story is not only the young servant girl's faith but also her compassion. She could have been the kind to snicker under her breath when humiliating marks began appearing on her master's face and body. She might have thought he deserved it. But she had compassion. She wanted to see him get better. Her faith is shown not only in her confidence that healing is found through God but also in her compassion and desire to connect all those around her to God's healing power—even the ones who have destroyed her life.

True confessions time. If you were to hear that someone who has said or done something awful—whether to you or to someone you care about—is now suffering, what would you think and feel? Would you be glad that bad things are happening to this person, or would you pray for him or her? Write your thoughts below. (You will not be asked to share these with your group!)

I have thought before someone got what they deserved, but later regretted feeling that way

Perhaps we all should pray to have a heart like the servant girl, showing compassion even toward those who have meant us evil. I know there's room for more compassion in my own heart.

In this story we have two residents of the same household: one is at the head of the table; the other is scrubbing floors in the kitchen. But each of them has a redefining detail, a thing God uses that has nothing to do with his or her cultural status. God uses the frailty of the human body to reroute Naaman's destiny, and He uses faith to redefine the story of a slave girl. God sees their hearts, not their status. Status means nothing to God.

In the Book of Acts we read, "Then Peter opened up his mouth, and said, Of a truth I perceive that God is no respecter of persons (10:34 KJV). What does this mean? God certainly respects and loves human beings. He made us and cherishes us. To be "no respecter of persons" means that God has no need for human titles, achievements, or accomplishments. We cannot impress God with *what* we are. He simply loves us for *who* we are. We see this clearly in the life and ministry of Jesus.

In the fourth chapter of the Gospel of Luke, Jesus returns to his hometown of Nazareth and has the opportunity to preach his first sermon in his home synagogue. Having stood in the pulpit of my own childhood church after becoming a pastor and looking out at the people who had known me since I was a preschooler, I can tell you that it is an intimidating prospect. Yet the message Jesus gives on this day is one of his most powerful and memorable statements recorded in Scripture. Using the words of the prophet Isaiah, Jesus defines his mission on earth:

> *"The Spirit of the Lord is on me,*
> *because he has anointed me*
> *to proclaim good news to the poor.*
> *He has sent me to proclaim freedom for the prisoners*
> *and recovery of sight for the blind,*
> *to set the oppressed free,*
> *to proclaim the year of the Lord's favor."*
>
> Luke 4:18-19

> We cannot impress God with *what* we are. He simply loves us for *who* we are.

105

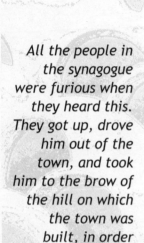

At first the people are amazed. They are impressed by Jesus' gracious words and delivery. They remember him as a little tyke. "Isn't this Joseph's son?" they ask (v. 22).

But Jesus doesn't want them to miss his true message. He knows that the poor, the prisoners, the blind, and the oppressed are not necessarily the ones other people think he should help. He is speaking to a room full of Jews—insiders in the faith, those with religious status. But He wants them to know that He has a heart for the outsiders, something he knows they won't be too happy about.

Jesus gives them two examples of the kinds of people God has helped in the past, drawing from two of the stories we are studying in First and Second Kings.

First, in verses 25 and 26, he reminds them of the widow who was the recipient of the miracle of multiplication of oil through the hand of the prophet Elijah. She wasn't an insider at all. She was from Zarephath, a city in the region of Sidon. This was outside the bounds of where God's people resided. According to those in the synagogue, she wasn't deserving of God's help.

Then in verse 27 comes an interesting turn. Jesus reminds them of the very story we are studying this week, the story of Naaman, the great general of Aram. (Since we are not yet to the climax of Naaman's story, I feel the need to give a spoiler alert here. But I'm counting on the fact that you either already know what happens to Naaman or will agree that the relevancy of the point I'm making is worth the early reveal!) Jesus reminds them that when Naaman was healed by the prophet Elisha, there must have been many suffering with leprosy in the nation of Israel. But God chose to use Elisha to heal a foreigner, a man of great power who had attacked and raided the nation of Israel—even kidnapped some of its young people and forced them to become slaves.

Suddenly, in Jesus' telling of the story, Naaman is not a man of status. He's an enemy of the people of Israel—and yet God healed him.

We can tell how seriously offensive Jesus' words are by the reaction of the people. These are the people of his hometown, the friends of his parents and grandparents.

Read Luke 4:28-29 in the margin and describe the people's reaction.

In Second Kings, Naaman is a person of earthly power and position. In the Gospel of Luke, he is an outsider and enemy of God's people. Human opinion is fickle. Social hierarchies can change, and those who are revered one day may be destitute and despised the next. We see this lived out from Hollywood to Washington, DC. We know it to be true from the playground to the boardroom. One minute someone is revered and loved by all only to become yesterday's news tomorrow.

When and how have you experienced the fickle nature of human opinion?

Here's the good news for us: God can look at both a great ruler and a small child and see His beloved, one who needs His help and hope and healing. What matters is not what the world sees when it looks at you but what God sees.

What does God see when He looks at you? How does God define you?

What do you see when you look at others? Do you have eyes like God's eyes? A heart like God's heart? Making the shift from a human perspective to God's perspective is hard for us. But with His help, we can see "children of God" all around us—from the one riding in the black limo to those living on the streets it may pass.

What could help you to have God's eyes and God's heart—to have God's perspective of others?

Jesus once told a story about a great banquet where the host commanded his servants to "Go out quickly into the streets and alleys of the town and bring in the poor, the crippled, the blind and the lame" (Luke 14:21). The master rounded them up, not to throw them in jail where they would be out of sight of the important guests, but to bring them to the table—to welcome them, to sit with them, and to offer them a feast.

That's the kind of God we serve—One who invites us all to the table to sit side by side at a feast for all of His children. You see, we don't get to choose who is important. All our degrees, certificates, and experience—none of that matters at God's banquet table. The servant girl is invited to sit next to the high-ranking official. All are welcome. All are children of the most-high King!

Talk with God

Lord, forgive us for being fickle. Create in us humility to love and accept those who are different from us. Help us to look at all people as Your beloved and to see ourselves as Your beloved. Thank You for the invitation to sit at Your table where all are welcome. Amen.

> *What matters is not what the world sees when it looks at you but what God sees.*

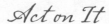

Act on It

On the left side below, list the first three people who come to your mind when you think of power, status, and prestige. Try to have at least two of them be people you have met personally. Now, on the right side below, list the first three people (or categories of people) you think of when you think of humiliation, weakness, and contempt. Reflect on these questions: How does God feel about each group of people? Is one group more important to God or more loved by Him? Now pray for each person in both lists.

Day 2: Preoccupied with Pride

Read God's Word

⁴ *Naaman went to his master and told him what the girl from Israel had said.* ⁵ *"By all means, go," the king of Aram replied. "I will send a letter to the king of Israel." So Naaman left, taking with him ten talents of silver, six thousand shekels of gold and ten sets of clothing.* ⁶ *The letter that he took to the king of Israel read: "With this letter I am sending my servant Naaman to you so that you may cure him of his leprosy."*

⁷ *As soon as the king of Israel read the letter, he tore his robes and said, "Am I God? Can I kill and bring back to life? Why does this fellow send someone to me to be cured of his leprosy? See how he is trying to pick a quarrel with me!"*

⁸ *When Elisha the man of God heard that the king of Israel had torn his robes, he sent him this message: "Why have you torn your robes? Have the man come to me and he will know that there is a prophet in Israel."* ⁹ *So Naaman went with his horses and chariots and stopped at the door of Elisha's house.* ¹⁰ *Elisha sent a messenger to say to him, "Go, wash yourself seven times in the Jordan, and your flesh will be restored and you will be cleansed."*

¹¹ *But Naaman went away angry and said, "I thought that he would surely come out to me and stand and call on the name of the LORD his God, wave his hand over the spot and cure me of my leprosy.* ¹² *Are not Abana and Pharpar, the rivers of Damascus, better than all the waters of Israel? Couldn't I wash in them and be cleansed?" So he turned and went off in a rage.*

2 Kings 5:4-12

Reflect and Respond

"You're so vain. You probably think this song is about you." Carly Simon's catchy tune was the emblem of vanity and pride for a generation. There has been wide speculation about whom the song is about, with a number of famous friends from Simon's past rumored to be the one. In an interview to the *Washington Post* in 1983, Simon commented that Warren Beatty actually called her once to thank her for the song.[1]

Vanity and pride are vices that are often easier to recognize in others than in ourselves. "I'm not proud," we may think. "I'm actually pretty critical of myself." Not many of us sit and stare into our mirrors like Snow White's stepmother, believing ourselves "the fairest one of all." If we get close enough to our mirrors, we're more likely to be examining our pores, blemishes, or wrinkles—sorry, "character lines"—pointing out our imperfections, not our superior qualities.

Although we certainly have proud moments, not many of us strut around believing ourselves to be superior in appearance or talent or wisdom to those around us. Still, if we define pride only as seeing ourselves as the best or better than our peers, we may escape the tough lesson Naaman's story has to teach us.

So far our discussion of pride and humility—the major themes of Naaman and Elisha's story—has been focused on others: how we view others based on their status in the world, and how we should see all people through the status of being God's child. But now it is time to turn our gaze inward.

First, let's dismiss the false notion that pride is simply believing ourselves to be the best at something. If that is our understanding, we may have mixed feelings when we encourage our children or loved ones to take pride in their accomplishments or tell them we're proud of them.

Rebecca Konyndyk DeYoung has written a book on pride called *Vainglory: The Forgotten Vice*. In it she writes, "Pride is the vice of putting yourself at the center of all things, in God's place, choosing your own way to happiness and believing that any goodness or happiness you have is due to your own power and merit....A prideful disposition says, in effect, 'I will decide on what happiness is for me, and I will provide it for myself.'"[2] Instead of considering ourselves the best, pride is simply considering ourselves before others. It can mean that we consider ourselves superior to someone else, but it also can mean we spend our time and energy trying to elevate our appearance in other people's eyes— that we wish to attract what DeYoung calls the three A's: Attention, Affirmation, and Applause.[3]

What are some common ways we consider ourselves before others?

> Instead of considering ourselves the best, pride is simply considering ourselves before others.

humility
modest
compassionate
humble
true humility is
invisible to
themselves

109

Humility, the opposite of pride, is also frequently misunderstood. Humility is "often mischaracterized as an unduly low estimation of oneself, a self-deprecating, self-undermining sense of one's own debased status."[4] If being down on yourself were true humility, one might mistake a lack of self-esteem as a positive trait. Just as taking pride in your accomplishments is not the true sin of pride, neither is practicing self-deprecation a virtue of humility.

Don't we struggle with this? I may get a compliment about one of my sermons or even about something I'm wearing, and sometimes instead of giving a genuine "thank you" what comes out is, "I wish I could have put more time into my message this week" or "Oh, I got this at the thrift shop." These are silly examples, but they represent a common struggle for many of us. We mistake humility for self-deprecation. We trade a chance to receive a spoken kindness from someone with humble gratitude in order to put ourselves down or make sure others know we aren't that great.

Rather than having a low opinion of yourself, humility simply means that you do not put yourself first in your thoughts and actions. It has been said that "humility is not thinking less of yourself but thinking of yourself less."[5]

Name some people you believe to be truly humble. What about these individuals causes you to see them as humble?

Mary Lee

Let's check in on Naaman. Picking up where we left him only three verses into 2 Kings 5, there really is nothing in the text to indicate that he is either a prideful or a humble man. He is described as a commander, a great man, and a highly regarded and valiant soldier. Those are, we might say, "just the facts, ma'am."

We might even start off considering him a man of wisdom, since he listens to those of low status rather than ignore them. He does take the advice of his young servant girl and decides to find the prophet whom she says can heal him. When he asks the king of Aram for permission to make the trip, the king sends a letter with him to the king of Israel.

Reread 2 Kings 5:6-7 (page 108). What does the letter say? What is the king of Israel's response?

Here's quite a picture of someone caught up in pride and self-importance! The king of Aram believes that he can command someone's healing the way he commands a military attack. The king of Israel, on the other hand, knows that he has no power to heal. He panics, wondering what will happen to his country when he can't deliver.

> Rather than having a low opinion of yourself, humility simply means that you do not put yourself first in your thoughts and actions.

Reread 2 Kings 5:8 (page 108). What is Elisha's response when he hears that his king has torn his robes?

Though Elisha's words may sound like pride, drawing attention to himself, we must remember that Elisha is God's messenger—God's anointed representative among His people. His words acknowledge that he knows healing is from God alone, not something to be commanded by any human king. So Elisha sends a message to the king, telling him to send Naaman to him.

I love what happens next. Naaman pulls up at Elisha's house—his horses and chariots kicking up a magnificent cloud of dust as they come to a halt. Naaman—with a flourish, I'm sure—jumps down from his chariot and knocks boldly on the door, only to be greeted not by the prophet himself but a messenger with an unwelcome prescription: "Go, wash yourself seven times in the Jordan, and your flesh will be restored and you will be cleansed" (2 Kings 5:10). And just like that, the door is shut in Naaman's face. He isn't invited in to see the famous prophet, and he certainly doesn't get the show of bowing and scraping he might have expected upon his arrival.

This is when Naaman's true character is revealed. (It's often when things don't go the way we expect that the dregs of our hearts show themselves, isn't it?) He pouts and complains that things aren't going his way. He criticizes the prophet and his prescription, turns his nose up at the thought of entering the Jordan River, and scoffs that he has better rivers back home, wondering why he even made the trip. Then he stomps away in a tantrum like a toddler.

This is the problem with pride. Naaman believes that the way he is treated and the healing he is offered are beneath him, so he flexes his muscles—and his temper—to show those around him the image he wants to project: a strong and prestigious man who never should have been stood up by a lowly prophet. It takes all kinds of energy and bluster for Naaman to protect the image that he wants the world to see. And we are just like him.

So much time and energy go into thinking about how people see us. As DeYoung points out, we long for acknowledgement, approval, and adulation.[6]

If you are honest with yourself, what are some ways you spend time and energy seeking acknowledgment, approval, or adulation from others?

In the Gospel of Luke, we read about an occasion when Jesus acknowledges our human tendency to focus our energy on crafting the image we want others to see. He responds by telling a parable:

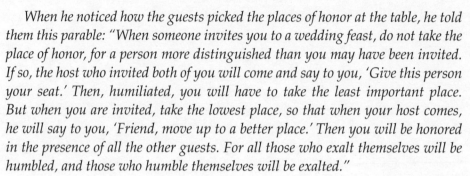

When he noticed how the guests picked the places of honor at the table, he told them this parable: "When someone invites you to a wedding feast, do not take the place of honor, for a person more distinguished than you may have been invited. If so, the host who invited both of you will come and say to you, 'Give this person your seat.' Then, humiliated, you will have to take the least important place. But when you are invited, take the lowest place, so that when your host comes, he will say to you, 'Friend, move up to a better place.' Then you will be honored in the presence of all the other guests. For all those who exalt themselves will be humbled, and those who humble themselves will be exalted."

Luke 14:7-11

Write the last sentence in your own words below. Replace the words "exalt themselves" and "humble themselves" with your own language or examples.

Seeking the "best place at the table" can take on many forms. As in Jesus' story, it might be an obvious desire to sit where those of high status and acclaim would sit at a party, attracting attention to our importance. Or it might be saying yes to too many obligations, hoping that those who extended the invitations would see us as a saint or a servant. It even could be a hypersensitivity to the opinions of others, constantly worrying what everyone from a close friend to a complete stranger thinks of us.

When my mother and grandmother came for a visit my first semester in seminary, I wanted to show them how I was thriving in my new environment and how much I had learned and changed. Over dinner on their first night there, my grandmother asked me to tell her about the classes I was taking. I didn't get past the first one, which was philosophy of religion, because I began to pontificate on all of the deep lessons I was learning in the class: existential arguments for the proof of God's existence, discussions of the root of consciousness, explanations about how bad things happen even though God is good. When I finished— probably close to thirty minutes later—my eighty-year-old grandmother, who was a woman of deep faith, smiled and patted my hand as she said, "All I know is that you have to have the faith of a little child. The faith of a little child."

I realized suddenly that I had been trying to impress her, this woman whose love for me began far before I learned to crawl. I had been working hard to create some image that she would notice, praise, and admire. I had seated myself at the table in a place to exalt myself, and I found myself humbled.

In what areas of your life do you think about your "place at the table"?

How do you try to influence the way others see you or think of you?

When it comes down to it, all the energy we expend projecting for ourselves an image that we want the world to see is useless, because it is God's opinion of us that matters. I love how the Apostle Paul explains his motivation in life to the Galatians.

Read Galatians 1:10 in the margin. What does Paul say about trying to please people?

> *Am I now trying to win the approval of human beings, or of God? Or am I trying to please people? If I were still trying to please people, I would not be a servant of Christ. Galatians 1:10*

Pride is simply thinking too much about the wrong person's opinion of us—whether that person be you or someone (real or perceived) you long to impress. God's opinion alone is the one that matters, which He made clear long before you could impress anyone, long before you were even born. And God's opinion of you is this: you are a beloved child. His thoughts toward you are love. Simply love. When you grasp that, all the striving and posturing stop. Your identity is formed. Your soul relaxes. And you realize that the humblest seat at His table is actually preferred seating.

> All the energy we expend projecting for ourselves an image that we want the world to see is useless because it is God's opinion of us that matters.

Talk with God

Lord, thank You for the reminder that Your opinion is the only one that matters. I'm so thankful that You love me just as I am. Help me to relax in my identity in You and take my place at Your table. Amen.

> Pride is simply thinking too much about the wrong person's opinion of us.

Act on It

Write this definition on an index card and place it somewhere you will see it often: *Humility – putting others above yourself in your thoughts and actions.* Each day this week, look for a specific way that you can practice humility by putting others above yourself both in thought and action. Then be sure to follow through with the action. At the end of the week, reflect on what happened and be prepared to share with your group.

Day 3: Our Weakness, His Strength

Read God's Word

¹⁰ *Elisha sent a messenger to say to him, "Go, wash yourself seven times in the Jordan, and your flesh will be restored and you will be cleansed."*

¹¹ *But Naaman went away angry and said, "I thought that he would surely come out to me and stand and call on the name of the LORD his God, wave his hand over the spot and cure me of my leprosy.* ¹² *Are not Abana and Pharpar, the rivers of Damascus, better than all the waters of Israel? Couldn't I wash in them and be cleansed?" So he turned and went off in a rage.*

¹³ *Naaman's servants went to him and said, "My father, if the prophet had told you to do some great thing, would you not have done it? How much more, then, when he tells you, 'Wash and be cleansed'!"* ¹⁴ *So he went down and dipped himself in the Jordan seven times, as the man of God had told him, and his flesh was restored and became clean like that of a young boy.*

¹⁵ *Then Naaman and all his attendants went back to the man of God. He stood before him and said, "Now I know that there is no God in all the world except in Israel. So please accept a gift from your servant."*

¹⁶ *The prophet answered, "As surely as the LORD lives, whom I serve, I will not accept a thing." And even though Naaman urged him, he refused.*

¹⁷ *"If you will not," said Naaman, "please let me, your servant, be given as much earth as a pair of mules can carry, for your servant will never again make burnt offerings and sacrifices to any other god but the LORD.* ¹⁸ *But may the LORD forgive your servant for this one thing: When my master enters the temple of Rimmon to bow down and he is leaning on my arm and I have to bow there also—when I bow down in the temple of Rimmon, may the LORD forgive your servant for this."*

¹⁹ *"Go in peace," Elisha said.*

2 Kings 5:10-19

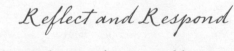

Reflect and Respond

I walked into the hospital room of a sweet, older man from my congregation who had suffered a stroke the month before. Bobby's wife, Maureen, was standing at his bedside, talking with a doctor who had come by to check on him. When I mentioned that I could wait outside, they both motioned for me to stay, so I perched on the narrow couch by the bed.

This is what she told the doctor:

> The therapy seems to be working well. We can see his body getting stronger every day, but he's struggling with something else. Bobby used to be the one to take care of the rest of us. He would fix our adult kids' cars when they had trouble, climb on the roof to clean out the gutters, even bring his toolbox when we visited the grandkids at college, insisting on fixing things in their dorm rooms. He's not used to us taking care of him, and it has really become an even greater struggle than what's going on with his body. He tells me he lies here and thinks about that one tree branch at home hanging over the garage, worrying, *What if it falls before I can get better and climb up there to cut it?* What do you think we can do to help his anxiety and worry?

As soon as the doctor left, I apologized for having been present to overhear such a personal conversation, but she placed her hand gently on my arm and said, "I'm so glad you were here to hear that. We want you to pray with us for Bobby's healing—not just for his body, but for his mind and heart as well. This stroke has showed him how much he needs to learn to need other people."

Humility does not come naturally to us. From the time we learn to speak as toddlers, we begin to demand: "I can do it myself!" Early childhood brings one developmental lesson after another, and we gain independence with every step, breaking free of our dependence on our parents and caregivers. We learn those lessons so well that life seems to be a series of victories, growing stronger with each step of independence and learning to care for ourselves in a world where individuality reigns supreme. But God's plans for us are the opposite. God declared over the first human being, "It is not good for man to be alone" (Genesis 2:18). He created us to live in community and in full reliance on God.

One of the greatest teachers of the lesson that we are not supreme beings capable of fully autonomous living is the human body. Nothing makes us more aware of our own limitations than the constraints our bodies place on us. Our bodies remind us that we are human by growing tired and requiring rest, by getting sick and requiring healing, and by aging and making us aware of our mortality. If we did not experience any of these things, we might think ourselves godlike in our capabilities and believe we have no need to rely on God.

When have you been the most aware of the limitations of your body?

Think of a group you've participated in where you've listened to one another's prayer requests. What has been the most common type of request offered by the group? In my experience, members of small groups are most willing to share requests related to struggles with health and money. Please pray for my husband's surgery, my friend's cancer, or my neighbor's job search. These seem to be the two areas that we know we are helpless and need God's intervention. Often it's the limitations of our bodies that often drive us to our knees and remind us of our dependence on God.

What do these verses tell us about the limitations of the human body?

Genesis 2:7

Psalm 103:13-18

Isaiah 40:30-31

Here in 2 Kings 5, we see that Naaman certainly is a man who does not accept human limitations. He is a leader, a conqueror, someone who overcomes every obstacle placed in his path. When he finally faces an obstacle that he has no power to conquer, he is at a loss. Only the limitation of his human body can teach Naaman that there is One more powerful than he.

We can see how desperate Naaman is for healing, because he follows the advice of a lowly, foreign slave girl. I imagine him trying every other cure possible in his own country before admitting that he needs healing so badly he is willing to seek it from an unknown prophet in a land his country has raided.

Even as he seeks healing, Naaman maintains his facade of control and authority. He has his king send a letter ahead to establish his clout. Then he arrives on Elisha's doorstep with a flourish and knocks on the door as if he can command healing. Despite the arrogance of his method of asking for healing, God hears his request and gives him a path to healing, even though it isn't the solution Naaman wants to hear. One of the lessons Naaman's story teaches us is that God not only cares for our souls but our bodies as well.

What do we learn from these verses about God's relationship to our physical bodies?

Psalm 139:13-16

Isaiah 43:1

1 Corinthians 6:19-20

Like Naaman, most of us live with the illusion that we are in control until something in our world reminds us that this simply is not so. The humbling method by which God offers His healing to Naaman is exactly what he needs, but it isn't what he expects or wants.

What kind of healing does Naaman imagine he will receive? What is the prescription he is offered instead?

Whether it's because of an illness or something else that humbles us, we all have been in Naaman's shoes at one time or another, realizing we are not in control and being offered help that is different from what we expected or wanted.

Recall a time when you realized you were not in control and needed help. Describe it briefly below:

Were you offered any kind of help that was different from what you expected or wanted? What happened?

When Naaman tries to storm off in indignant rage, it is his servant who gently encourages him to try the prophet's advice. After all, they have traveled so far. Once again we find that the sensible ones offering wisdom in this story are the servants. Those of low stature have no illusion that their own strength can save them, so they know to look for one higher in authority and power. Naaman's physical weakness and resulting desperation are the only things that can make him seek God. And so, finally, he chooses to obey the prophet's instructions.

Naaman's portion of the story ends in a beautiful way.

Reread 2 Kings 5:15-19 (page 114). What does Naaman say he has learned, and what does he want to do in response?

Naaman returns to Elisha's house (and this time gets to meet the prophet) and declares his faith in Elisha's God, the God who has made him well. For the first time in his life, Naaman's weakness has put him in touch with God's strength, and his natural response is gratitude.

The Apostle Paul writes about weakness leading to God's strength in his second letter to the Corinthians.

> "Naaman was commander-in-chief of the army of Syria, and was nearest to the person of the king, Ben-hadad II, whom he accompanied officially and supported when he went to worship in the temple of Rimmon, (2 Kings 5:18)."[7]

117

Read 2 Corinthians 12:7-10 in the margin. What does Paul learn about God through his weakness, and what is his response?

Therefore, in order to keep me from becoming conceited, I was given a thorn in my flesh, a messenger of Satan, to torment me. Three times I pleaded with the Lord to take it away from me. But he said to me, "My grace is sufficient for you, for my power is made perfect in weakness." Therefore I will boast all the more gladly about my weaknesses, so that Christ's power may rest on me. That is why, for Christ's sake, I delight in weaknesses, in insults, in hardships, in persecutions, in difficulties. For when I am weak, then I am strong."

2 Corinthians 12:7-10

Paul writes that he has an undefined physical problem—something he calls a thorn in his flesh—that makes him weak. But it is this very weakness that makes Paul rely on the strength of Christ.

Whether it is experiencing physical or other kinds of limitations, our weakness is a powerful reminder of our dependence on God.

How have you discovered God's strength in your own weakness?

Like Naaman, it's good for us to remember that help doesn't always arrive in the way we request. Not only are we not in complete control of our bodies, we also do not get to determine the method or timing of God's response to our prayers for healing. This is true not only for physical healing but for all manner of healing. Whether it is obvious to us or not, God hears every cry of our hearts and responds with the grace we need in that moment.

Donald E. Demaray describes five types of miraculous healing in his book *Experiencing Healing and Wholeness: A Journey in Faith*:[8]

- The miracle of supernatural touch—God can and does heal miraculously.
- The miracle of the doctor and modern medicine—The gifts of modern medicine are gifts God has given us through human ingenuity.
- The miracle of nature—Our bodies are created to heal themselves in many amazing ways.
- The miracle of the victorious crossing—Ultimate healing comes when we pass from this world with its inevitable pain and suffering into the full presence of God for eternity.
- The miracle of grace sufficient—God can meet us in our suffering and give us the grace to not only endure but witness to others how He helps us in our need.

Dr. Demaray describes this last kind of healing, the healing of grace sufficient, in the story of a woman named Mavis who was miraculously healed. Mavis' husband, George, tells the story of how his wife struggled for twelve years with an undiagnosed illness that manifested itself in weakness of her muscles.

She was often unable to lift her limbs and sometimes lacked strength to lift her drooping eyelids, and then one day she felt God's touch and her body began to gain strength, slowly and miraculously, until her body was totally restored. As George tells about Mavis' miraculous healing, she interrupts him, wanting readers to know that God was present in a very powerful way throughout the twelve years of her illness, not only in the miracle at the end. She says,

> Though I am *so* grateful for the miracle of God's "healing touch," as great a miracle to me was His "keeping touch" for those twelve long years that kept me from ruining what He was planning to do. When my mind or my emotions, or people, created times of confusion for me, such as feeling sorry for myself or questioning my own ability to interpret what God's will really was, the Holy Spirit would whisper, "Just leave it alone, Mavis, and trust Me." And always, along with the whisper, He gave the *power* to leave it alone, until my physical responses were overcome by His abiding presence. I became aware that my spiritual muscles were growing stronger, while my physical muscles were growing weaker. God and His plans for me became much more important than my plans.[9]

Mavis discovered the miracle of grace sufficient during those twelve years. Though her body failed her every day, she discovered that her God never failed her.

A few years after my conversation with Maureen and Bobby in the hospital room following his stroke, I walked with Maureen into the sanctuary to sit with his open casket before the funeral. At one point she smiled through her tears and said this:

> You know, Bobby and I have been in love since we were teenagers. But we never had a love so deep as we did after the stroke. It was the stroke that taught us that we could really depend fully on each other. If I had to go back and choose life with the stroke or life after the stroke, I would choose the stroke.

God is with us through every moment of need. Whatever drives us to our knees can be a grace-filled reminder of our dependence on Him. Though often it is hard to praise God in the midst of struggles, it is in the times of our greatest weakness that we discover His greatest strength. Like the prophet Naaman and my friend Maureen, may our response to God's sufficient grace always be one of gratitude and praise.

Extra Insight
Many interpretations have been given to Paul's "thorn in the flesh." Some have said that it was impiety or unbelief or a bad temper. Others have speculated it was a pain in the ear or head, epileptic fits, poor eyesight, or some other physical ailment.[10]

Though often it is hard to praise God in the midst of struggles, it is in the times of our greatest weakness that we discover His greatest strength.

119

Lord, help us learn what it means to be humble—to think of others before ourselves and to remember that all we have, all that we are, and all that we need is found in You alone. Amen.

Act on It

Today or another day this week, reach out to someone who is in a moment of need. Make a meal for someone, send a card or a note of encouragement, or invite someone to get coffee. Offer strength, faith, or hope for someone who is "running low."

Day 4: Intentional Humility

Read God's Word

[19] *After Naaman had traveled some distance,* [20] *Gehazi, the servant of Elisha the man of God, said to himself, "My master was too easy on Naaman, this Aramean, by not accepting from him what he brought. As surely as the* LORD *lives, I will run after him and get something from him."*

[21] *So Gehazi hurried after Naaman. When Naaman saw him running toward him, he got down from the chariot to meet him. "Is everything all right?" he asked.*

[22] *"Everything is all right," Gehazi answered. "My master sent me to say, 'Two young men from the company of the prophets have just come to me from the hill country of Ephraim. Please give them a talent of silver and two sets of clothing.'"*

[23] *"By all means, take two talents," said Naaman. He urged Gehazi to accept them, and then tied up the two talents of silver in two bags, with two sets of clothing. He gave them to two of his servants, and they carried them ahead of Gehazi.* [24] *When Gehazi came to the hill, he took the things from the servants and put them away in the house. He sent the men away and they left.*

[25] *When he went in and stood before his master, Elisha asked him, "Where have you been, Gehazi?"*

"Your servant didn't go anywhere," Gehazi answered.

[26] *But Elisha said to him, "Was not my spirit with you when the man got down from his chariot to meet you? Is this the time to take money or to accept clothes—or olive groves and vineyards, or flocks and herds, or male and female slaves?* [27] *Naaman's leprosy will cling to you and to your descendants forever."*

Then Gehazi went from Elisha's presence and his skin was leprous—it had become as white as snow.

2 Kings 5:19-27

Reflect and Respond

"Pride goes before a fall."

There are some statements so common that most people don't even know they're quoting Scripture when they say it. This one is actually a reference to Proverbs 16:18: "Pride goes before destruction, / a haughty spirit before a fall." I personally have proved this verse over and over again! I've walked into a meeting feeling pretty sure of myself, thinking people were staring at me for some complimentary reason, when I suddenly realized I had baby spit-up down my sleeve. I've launched self-assuredly into a conversation with a couple of parents about a situation involving their teenage son, trying to project with warm, pastoral confidence that I was keeping up with their needs and praying for them, only to be gently corrected five minutes into the conversation that it was their daughter they had requested prayer for. I would give you more embarrassing examples of how I've started into a situation with pride only to be reminded quickly that humiliation is one of the quickest paths to humility, but I'm too embarrassed to name any more of those moments here.

Recall an embarrassing moment that got you in touch with humility:

Humility often is seen as the root of all virtues, the one bright spot of goodness from which all other goodness may grow. Missionary Andrew Murray once said that "humility is not so much a grace or virtue along with others; it is the root of all, because it alone takes the right attitude before God, and allows Him as God to do all."[11] Conversely, the sin of pride keeps us from opening our hearts to God's transforming grace, and the hardness of heart it produces may lead to a snowball effect of sin. Murray wrote, "Pride must die in you, or nothing of heaven can live in you."[12]

It's clear, then, that we should do everything possible to nurture humility in our souls and to root out pride. But how? One of the toughest things about the ultimate virtue of humility is that often we receive it through means we have no control over. As we've seen this week with Naaman, an illness or injury of the body can remind us that we need other people to care for us. Or a mistake or blunder can take us down a notch when we might have been puffed up with pride otherwise. Perhaps it is fitting that the path to humility itself is usually out of our control.

But if we truly are *seekers* of humility, there are spiritual practices that can help us arrive at its door in ways other than by accident. Before exploring these practices, let's take a trip back into Naaman and Elisha's story to find out what *not* to do. Recall how Naaman reacted to the miracle of healing he received when he humbled himself and obeyed Elisha's instructions and was healed:

> *Then Naaman and all his attendants went back to the man of God. He stood before him and said, "Now I know that there is no God in all the world except in Israel. So please accept a gift from your servant."*
>
> *The prophet answered, "As surely as the LORD lives, whom I serve, I will not accept a thing." And even though Naaman urged him, he refused.*
>
> 2 Kings 5:15-16

Naaman praised God, which was an appropriate response. But he was so grateful that he also wanted to give a gift to the prophet Elisha, the mouthpiece of God's healing instructions. Prophets were not affluent people. There's not much money in a vocation that involves confronting leaders with difficult truths about themselves and their kingdoms. Elisha, whose family owned land and had enough money for at least twelve pairs of oxen, had left a life of comfort to follow Elijah and God's calling into the modest life of ministry. Why not receive some reward now? Surely Naaman had enough to spare.

Perhaps Elisha knew that if Naaman gave him money after being healed, Naaman might leave with the feeling that he had paid for his miracle and was in the position of control once again. So Elisha turned down the offer of a gift "even though Naaman urged him" (2 Kings 5:16). Elisha was not looking out for his own gain but for God's glory, and nothing would tempt him away from that.

Elisha's servant, Gehazi, on the other hand, saw an opportunity for personal gain, and the results were tragic. Let's trace Gehazi's missteps and discover what we can learn about what *not* to do if we want to be seekers of humility.

1. Gehazi believes he knows better than his master.
Reread 2 Kings 5:19-20 (Page 120). What does Gehazi say to himself?

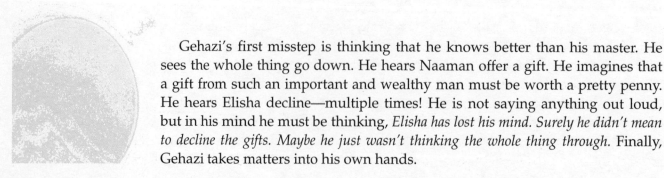

Gehazi's first misstep is thinking that he knows better than his master. He sees the whole thing go down. He hears Naaman offer a gift. He imagines that a gift from such an important and wealthy man must be worth a pretty penny. He hears Elisha decline—multiple times! He is not saying anything out loud, but in his mind he must be thinking, *Elisha has lost his mind. Surely he didn't mean to decline the gifts. Maybe he just wasn't thinking the whole thing through.* Finally, Gehazi takes matters into his own hands.

A sure sign of a lack of humility is thinking that we know better than those around us. Gehazi wasn't thinking about Elisha's point of view. He wasn't thinking about the big picture. Instead, he was only thinking about his personal gain, so much so that he became convinced that his ideas were superior to Elisha's.

2. Gehazi lies to Naaman.

Reread 2 Kings 5:21-22. What is the lie that Gehazi tells Naaman?

Now we see Gehazi make his move. He's going after Naaman to get that gift. He's got a great idea—he'll tell Naaman that he needs some extra resources to show hospitality to some surprise guests. That way, he's saying, "we didn't need a gift before, but now we do because some members of a group of prophets just showed up." Never mind that, by telling Naaman that his master sent him, Gehazi is misrepresenting the authority of his boss. He is committed to his plan at this point; there's no going back.

If we find ourselves needing to "tweak" the truth, we should ask ourselves why and how we are trying to benefit. Often it is to protect our image or interests. Sometimes we can become so committed to the lie that we get caught up in it and, like Gehazi, become somewhat obsessed with our own gain.

3. Gehazi acts deceptively.

Reread 2 Kings 5:23-24. What are Gehazi's deceptive actions?

When Gehazi approaches the camp where Elisha might see him, he takes the goods from Naaman's servants and carries them back himself. Then he hides what he has taken. Originally he said to himself that his master had "been too easy on Naaman," but it is clear by his deceptive actions that he is keeping the material goods for his own gain. He puts them away in the house; he doesn't run to Elisha and show him what a wonderful thing he has done.

If there's some material thing you long for, be watchful that you don't want it more than the clear conscience of following God. No matter how this story ends, Gehazi will have to live with the consequence of having been deceptive and greedy. It's the same for us. When we sneak around to get ahead or deceive others for our own prosperity, we forfeit the freedom that a life with God offers. Instead of freedom, we are enslaved to the lie.

4. Gehazi covers a lie with a lie.

Reread 2 Kings 5:25 (page 120). What does Elisha ask Gehazi, and how does he respond?

Extra Insight
The Bible portrays Gehazi as a man of questionable character. In addition to his deception and lies surrounding a reward for Naaman's healing, he once tried to force a grieving woman away from the prophet (2 Kings 4:27) and was unable to restore a child to life despite Elisha's commission (2 Kings 4:31).

He did testify to the king of Elisha's good deeds and helped a widow to get her lands restored (2 Kings 8:1-6).[13]

Gehazi covers up a lie with a lie. When Elisha asks where he went, Gehazi tells him that he didn't go anywhere. That was a bold-faced lie. It might seem like a small lie. After all, it's not as if anyone got hurt or lost anything—except Gehazi himself, as we'll read in the next verses. But small lies often lead to bigger ones. Bigger lies are needed to cover up those small ones until the story has spun out of control. That's why we need to be on guard against even the smallest of lies so that deception doesn't creep into our relationships.

When was the last time you found yourself "tweaking" the truth about something? What was the reason?

Were there negative consequences of the lie you told? Did it lead to more deception in word or action?

One of the ironic lessons of Gehazi's story is never to lie to your boss, especially when your boss is a prophet! Elisha knows exactly where Gehazi has been and what he has done.

Reread 2 Kings 5:26-27 (pages 120-121). What does Elisha say will be the consequence of Gehazi's actions?

Elisha recognizes that the curse Gehazi has brought on himself will be to receive the very disease of which Naaman has been cured. It is a reversal of fortunes. Naaman, who was leprous and proud, has become humble and healed. Gehazi, though he started out as a servant of God, has become filled with self-interest to the point of deceiving others. When his prideful nature takes over, disease takes over his body.

While Elisha refuses a gift from the man he has helped to heal, knowing the credit belongs to God alone, Gehazi approaches the situation thinking only of himself, wondering, *How can this benefit me?* This question is at the root of the pride we wish to avoid.

Turn to Philippians 2 and read the instructions found in verses 3-4. What are we told not to do? What are we encouraged to do?

Now read verses 5-11. Describe the example of ultimate humility given here.

Thanks to Gehazi, we now know what *not to do.* He shows us that selfish ambition and vain conceit are not the most fruitful path in life. Thank goodness we have a perfect example of what *to do* in our practice of humility—to value others above ourselves and look to the interests of others. We have in Jesus Christ a beautiful picture of this. He demonstrates true humility, setting aside his own will for God's will, laying down his life for ours. Now let's consider some "keys" to practicing his kind of humility.

Service

If we want to become humble like Christ, we must follow the example of his servanthood. When Jesus took on "the very nature of a servant" (Philippians 2:7), he didn't do so in name only. He performed jobs that others considered beneath them. He put others' needs before his own image or comfort. He washed the feet of his friends, he sat at tables with sinners, he stopped to listen to children, he touched people who had been isolated and avoided at all costs. He did not throw around his royal status but set it aside to show love to the least among us.

Jesus practiced humility as a way of life. It was his nature, his character. He humbly gave of himself to heal, minister, encourage, teach, and ultimately to save. We don't have to wait for mission trips or service projects to serve. We can serve the interests of others every day.

What can you do today that would make someone's life easier, whether it is someone in your own family, workplace, church, or neighborhood?

Self-Denial Through Solitude, Silence, and Fasting

The spiritual discipline of self-denial is helpful to us when we want to steep our hearts in humility. Sometimes we need to hit a reset button in our souls and make some blank space to hear from God. In order to do that, we can practice

125

acts of self-denial—giving something up in order to take in more of God. Solitude, silence, and fasting are ways in which we can remove ourselves from the trappings that surround us on a daily basis and get real with God.

Solitude or intentional silence can be intimidating for some. It's not easy to be alone for a time and give up the noise of the television, social media, and our phones. Silence creates room to be confronted with our own thoughts and feelings, and that can be scary. But God is ready and willing to meet us and help us to process who we are and what we think about when the noises of life stop.

In order to practice the solitude of silence, you have to plan it. Put it on the calendar and tell your loved ones that you are either going away or that you are intentionally remaining silent for a time—not because you don't want to talk to them anymore, but because you need to hear from God. Invite God to speak into your life as you shut out the noise of the world.

Fasting is another spiritual practice of self-denial that helps us to experience the frailty and hunger of the human body. Our hunger and need can drive us to rely on Christ and to remember that we are not superhuman. It's difficult to give up food when it's so easy to grab something from the pantry whenever we feel the need. But denying ourselves and depending on God to fill up the empty space pushes us to a deeper place with God and helps us to humble ourselves before Him.

Recall a time you denied yourself something—through solitude, silence, fasting, or something else. How did this help to remind you of your human limitations and needs?

🔑 Community

Now that we've considered solitude as a practice that leads to humility, it may seem strange to talk about community as another means to humility. Yet both are necessary and helpful in cultivating a humble attitude. Community helps us not only to discover our gifts but also to uncover our flaws. Togetherness with other people often reveals our need to change. A friend once told me, "When I'm alone, I can believe I'm perfect. It's when I get around other people that I realize that is far from the truth."

The highest kind of community is made up of friends who call us to the best version of ourselves—when honesty, humility, and growth are a way of life. Our closest relationships are often the safe places that expose our faults and failings. The desire to be the best parent, friend, daughter, sister, or spouse that we can be is sometimes the thing that drives us to see the truth about ourselves. When we are confronted with our imperfections of the heart and give ourselves to others in intentional community, the only solution is transformation.

What is one fault or failing you've discovered about yourself by being in community with other people? How has this realization led to greater humility?

Humility doesn't have to be an accidental virtue, learned only when we are surprised by a random mishap that leads to embarrassment. It's something the Bible encourages us to *pursue*. With God's help, we can face our own flaws and find the transformation that only He can bring.

John Newton, the former slave trader who came to know and experience God's amazing grace, was asked at age eighty-two what he recalled about his life. He replied, "Although my memory is fading, I remember two things very clearly: I am a great sinner, and Christ is a great Savior."[14] The result of that realization in his life was beautiful music—literally. Newton's life dramatically changed from slave ship captain to minister of the Gospel. The humility he found in knowing what he was capable of doing without God drove Him into Jesus' arms forever, and the good he did there is still sung in churches and elsewhere around the world.

Humility is a gift, but it is a gift we can grab hold of, pursue, and praise God for. We must practice humility just as we must practice the piano or the guitar or tennis. We practice putting others first, regarding others higher than us, laying down our lives. We do this in small ways such as giving up the best seat in the room or the best parking spot in the lot. We do this by walking away from the computer to fully engage with our families. We do this through spiritual practices such as fasting, silence, and solitude. When it comes to a life of humility, practice makes perfect.

> With God's help, we can face our own flaws and find the transformation that only He can bring.

Talk with God

Lord, thank You for laying down Your life for my sake and being the ultimate example of humility. Transform me to be more like You. Amen.

Act on It

Look at your calendar this week and mark one block of time to practice fasting, silence, or solitude. Tell your family about your commitment so that they will know you are not ignoring them during this time. Spend the time clearing your mind and heart of clutter and depending solely on God. Invite Him to set you apart for a life of humility.

Day 5: Playing Favorites

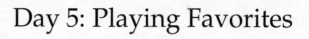

Read God's Word

⁴⁶ And Mary said:

> *"My soul glorifies the Lord*
> *⁴⁷ and my spirit rejoices in God my Savior,*
> *⁴⁸ for he has been mindful*
> *of the humble state of his servant.*
> *From now on all generations will call me blessed,*
> *⁴⁹ for the Mighty One has done great things for me—*
> *holy is his name.*
> *⁵⁰ His mercy extends to those who fear him,*
> *from generation to generation.*
> *⁵¹ He has performed mighty deeds with his arm;*
> *he has scattered those who are proud in their inmost thoughts.*
> *⁵² He has brought down rulers from their thrones*
> *but has lifted up the humble.*
> *⁵³ He has filled the hungry with good things*
> *but has sent the rich away empty.*
> *⁵⁴ He has helped his servant Israel,*
> *remembering to be merciful*
> *⁵⁵ to Abraham and his descendants forever,*
> *just as he promised our ancestors."*

Luke 1:46-55

Reflect and Respond

This week the story of Naaman and the prophet Elisha has given us some insight into the relationship between humility and healing. Let's review the events.

A proud man was made desperate by the weakness of his body and resorted to the advice of a servant girl about where to seek help. When Naaman arrived to ask the prophet Elisha for help, he was not received with the respect and honor he felt he deserved, and he almost missed his chance to receive the healing he was offered. Yet another servant urged him to humble himself and lower himself into a river seven times as the prophet instructed. Once Naaman was healed, he returned to Elisha, praising God and declaring his faith. He wanted to offer Elisha a gift in return for his healing, but the prophet refused, knowing that it might make him feel he had earned his healing and thus was in control of

God. Finally, Elisha's servant lied and received goods in exchange for Naaman's healing, and immediately the servant was stricken with the same disease that Naaman had had.

There are several reversals of fortune in this story. The proud are humbled, the sick are healed, and the servants become leaders. We see that those who humble themselves are elevated and used by God, but those who are proud suffer the opposite fate. Naaman may have tried many cures before he resorted to following the advice of a young servant girl, but ultimately he humbled himself and did what he had been instructed to do. The best general description of what happened to Naaman may be found in a verse in the New Testament.

Read James 4:10 in the margin. According to this verse, what happens when we humble ourselves?

This kind of reversal of the proud and the humble is not an isolated occurrence in Scripture. In fact, some have suggested that this theme recurs so often throughout the Bible that it seems God plays favorites, rescuing those who are down and out and snubbing those who are self-reliant. They say that Scripture portrays a God who goes out of His way to seek and save those who are vulnerable and desperate while railing against those who consider themselves privileged insiders.

Read Isaiah 66:2 in the margin. Who is identified as having God's favor?

Do you think this verse gives support to the idea that God plays favorites? Why or why not?

Mary's Magnificat, which is our Scripture reading for today, is another example in the Bible where we see the theme of God rescuing and blessing the lowly. In this beautiful song that Mary sings when her cousin Elizabeth acknowledges that the baby Mary is carrying is the Lord, she begins by expressing her praise to God for the great things He has done in her life. Then quickly she turns her attention to God's acts throughout the world.

Turn back to today's Scripture reading from Luke 1 (page 128) and follow these instructions:

   1.   **Circle the word humble, which is mentioned twice.**

Humble yourselves before the Lord, and he will lift you up.
James 4:10

"Has not my hand made all these things, and so they came into being?" declares the LORD.

"These are the ones I look on with favor: those who are humble and contrite in spirit, and who tremble at my word."
Isaiah 66:2

129

2. Now circle any other mentions of people who are characterized as being in a humble state (e.g., the hungry, poor, lowly).

3. Underline words that name or describe those who are in a proud state (e.g., rulers, the rich).

4. Next to statements that talk about bringing someone low or lifting someone up, draw an arrow indicating the direction they are taking.

What do you observe about God in this passage?

Mary's song certainly seems to paint a picture of a God who prefers the lowly and needy, who longs to help those in distress. It also portrays a God who brings down those who take credit for their own power and authority, going out of His way to make sure they are toppled from their pedestals.

Read James 4:6 and 1 Peter 5:5 in the margin. What does God do to the proud? What does He offer the humble?

If we go back to the beginning of God's relationship with His people, we see that He gives them instructions again and again to care for the orphans, the widows, and the aliens—those foreigners among them who would have been in a vulnerable and destitute state away from home and family. It seems God wanted His people to have favorites as well when it came to prioritizing whom to help.

Even Jesus' litany of blessings commonly known as the Beatitudes (Matthew 5:3-12) depicts an intentional preference for those who are in humble positions—the poor, grieving, and meek.

Underline words and phrases that describe those in humble positions:

"Blessed are the poor in spirit,
*   for theirs is the kingdom of heaven.*
Blessed are those who mourn,
*   for they will be comforted.*
Blessed are the meek,
*   for they will inherit the earth.*
Blessed are those who hunger and thirst for righteousness,
*   for they will be filled.*

Blessed are the merciful,
for they will be shown mercy.
Blessed are the pure in heart,
for they will see God.
Blessed are the peacemakers,
for they will be called children of God.
Blessed are those who are persecuted because of righteousness,
for theirs is the kingdom of heaven.

"Blessed are you when people insult you, persecute you and falsely say all kinds of evil against you because of me. Rejoice and be glad, because great is your reward in heaven, for in the same way they persecuted the prophets who were before you."

Matthew 5:3-12

Now think of people you know who fit the descriptions you've underlined above, and write their initials next to the lines that describe them.

Extra Insight
The word "Beatitude" comes from a Latin word meaning "happy" or "blessed."[15]

What are we to make of this preferential God who seems to play favorites with the poor and vulnerable? It would be disappointing to think that although God is for us, He may be for some of us more than others, wouldn't it?

But let's consider another possibility. What if these "preferential" acts are actually a sign that God loves all of us, not just a few? Think about it: neither pride nor humility is a permanent state. There are not two distinct types of people on earth—"the proud" and "the humble." It's more accurate to say that each of us fits these descriptions on different days and at different times in our life. So, in effect, the Scriptures are telling us that God prefers one attitude rather than another. That sheds a different light on things, doesn't it?

When we are humble, we are much more aware of our need for God. Humility, at its core, is a state of knowing our helplessness and our need for God. God knows that when we recognize our need for Him and have no illusion of "being in control" or "having it all together," we are most likely to cry out for His saving grace. Pride, on the other hand, assures that we will continue in the blind assumption that we can make it through life on our own merit, strength, and competence. So, saying that God prefers the humble is saying that God prefers us to recognize our need for Him so that we may receive His mercy and grace.

If we are honest with ourselves about our own daily battle between pride and humility, it's much easier to see the two in a more fluid light. Suddenly "the proud" are no longer the people we point our fingers at, shaking our heads at their privileged position. Instead, we recognize that we are both: we are the proud, those in need of a reminder of our base human stature, and we are the humble, those in need of God's help. When we feel proud, we tend to think we can manage on our own. But when we feel humble, we tend to seek help.

When we feel proud, we tend to think we can manage on our own. But when we feel humble, we tend to seek help.

131

Recall a time when you felt proud and thought you could manage on your own. What happened?

Now recall a time when you felt humble and recognized your need for help. What happened?

"For those who exalt themselves will be humbled, and those who humble themselves will be exalted."
Matthew 23:12

You might say that humility is the only way to God's heart because it is the only way we allow our hearts to be open to Him. Naturally, God prefers us to remain in the state that drives us to open ourselves to Him. So, God's preference for "the humble" is simply a preference for each of us, whom He dearly loves, to be humble in heart and ready to seek His help. Likewise, His opposition to "the proud" simply means that when we forget our great need, we can expect to be humbled so that once again we will open ourselves to His love and grace.

Read Matthew 23:12 in the margin. What does Jesus promise in this verse?

I love that Jesus didn't merely talk about humility but lived it out in a way unlike anyone else before or after Him. Jesus declared, "Truly I tell you, unless you change and become like little children, you will never enter the kingdom of heaven. Therefore, whoever takes the lowly position of this child is the greatest in the kingdom of heaven" (Matthew 18:3-4). Who would know this truth better than the One who left His exalted place in heaven to be born a little child, humbling himself to take the most vulnerable human form?

Jesus explained to His disciples, "Whoever wants to become great among you must be your servant, and whoever wants to be first must be your slave—just as the Son of Man did not come to be served, but to serve, and to give his life as a ransom for many" (Matthew 20:26-27). Later Jesus modeled what he was saying by washing His disciples feet, taking the form of a servant.

Read John 13:12-17. What explanation did Jesus give to his disciples for what He had done?

Jesus' actions in washing the feet of his disciples seemed at the time to be the ultimate sign of humility. No doubt they thought that this selfless and status-less act definitively showed that He did not put Himself above even the lowliest of tasks for their sake. But if washing their feet seemed to be a great sacrifice, it was nothing compared with the humiliation of the cross.

Read Philippians 2:8 in the margin. How was the cross the ultimate demonstration of Jesus' humility?

Humility not only reminds us of our great need for God; it also helps us to identify more closely with our Savior, who was willing to die the most humiliating of deaths because of His great love for us.

How has an experience of humility in your own life helped you to identify more closely with Jesus?

If you come face to face with your own limitations today, your own human nature, consider yourself blessed. If you are convicted of sin or reminded of your own predisposition to stray or to doubt, ask God to give you the grace to seek Him in that moment. Remember that when you discover your humility, you are most like Jesus—the One who demonstrated humility in the ultimate way, the One who calls us to imitate Him and to be transformed into His likeness. When we become like Jesus, we live out the set apart life, pointing others to God.

When you know how much you cannot do on your own and seek God for help, He always answers. God loves a humble heart that seeks Him. If you come to Him in humility, you can be sure that He will lift you up.

Talk with God

Lord, humility is difficult. We like to be first, to be celebrated, and to get the best spot—the best of everything. Help us to imitate Christ, seeking a spirit of humility as we follow after You. Amen.

Act on It

Write Philippians 2:5-11 (or some portion of this passage) on an index card and carry the card around with you all week. Recite the verse five to ten times a day until it is written on your heart. As you internalize the words, meditate on Christ's humility and what it means for you as you practice humility.

And being found in appearance as a man, he humbled himself by becoming obedient to death— even death on a cross! Philippians 2:8

When you discover your humility, you are most like Jesus.

133

Week 4
Video Viewer Guide

Now Naaman was commander of the army of the king of Aram. He was a great man in the sight of his master and highly regarded, because through him the LORD *had given victory to Aram. He was a* __valiant__ *soldier…*

2 Kings 5:1 NIV

He was a valiant soldier, but he had __leprosy__.

2 Kings 5:1 NIV

Now bands of raiders from Aram had gone out and had taken captive a young girl from Israel, and she __served__ *Naaman's wife.*

2 Kings 5:2 NIV

"I thought that he would surely come out to me and stand and call on the name of the LORD *his God,* __wave__ *his* __hand__ *over the spot and cure me of my leprosy."*

2 Kings 5:11 NIV

So he went down and dipped himself in the Jordan seven times, as the man of God had told him, and his flesh was restored and became clean like that of a __young__ __boy__.

2 Kings 5:14 NIV

Instead of, "Do you know who I am?" Naaman finally recognizes who God is. Suddenly he is identifying himself more with the __servants__ in the story than with those in __power__.

It was the spiritual practice of __humbling__ himself, of obeying God and what He asked of him…that finally brought __healing__ to Naaman.

It's a __gift__ when we realize that we are not the ones in __control__.

Week 5
Hezekiah
Set Apart by Worshiping God

When we consider the practice of worship in our lives, many of us think first of going to church on Sundays. If we are regular church attendees, we may be tempted to check that box on our list of to-dos and pat ourselves on the back. Participating in worship with the gathered church is important. But as we'll see this week, worship as a spiritual practice is more than showing up at church on Sunday. Our location on Sunday mornings doesn't tell the whole story about our loyalty to God.

Worship as a spiritual practice is about identity, priority, focus, and trust. It's not a place but a lifestyle. We, God's people, worship by putting God first, seeking God first, and trusting God's plan for our lives. With so many things in this world competing for our attention and allegiance, true worshipers look to God as the sole keeper of our hearts. Practicing a life of worship means identifying and turning from the things we have given our hearts to in the past and continually searching for and clearing out the idols we have set up in our lives along the way.

This week we'll see God's people struggle with a lack of trust in their God, and we'll watch their misguided efforts when they began to worship a gift over the Giver. Have you ever struggled with that—holding more tightly to the gift than the One who gave the gift? That's where God's people found themselves when Hezekiah became king. Through his leadership, we'll see idols destroyed and God's people return to faithfulness and true worship.

Day 1: Catching Up with the Kings

Read God's Word

²⁶ *Jeroboam son of Nebat rebelled against the king. He was one of Solomon's officials, an Ephraimite from Zeredah, and his mother was a widow named Zeruah.*

²⁷ *Here is the account of how he rebelled against the king: Solomon had built the terraces and had filled in the gap in the wall of the city of David his father.* ²⁸ *Now Jeroboam was a man of standing, and when Solomon saw how well the young man did his work, he put him in charge of the whole labor force of the tribes of Joseph.*

²⁹ *About that time Jeroboam was going out of Jerusalem, and Ahijah the prophet of Shiloh met him on the way, wearing a new cloak. The two of them were alone out in the country,* ³⁰ *and Ahijah took hold of the new cloak he was wearing and tore it into twelve pieces.* ³¹ *Then he said to Jeroboam, "Take ten pieces for yourself, for this is what the LORD, the God of Israel, says: 'See, I am going to tear the kingdom out of Solomon's hand and give you ten tribes.* ³² *But for the sake of my servant David and the city of Jerusalem, which I have chosen out of all the tribes of Israel, he will have one tribe.* ³³ *I will do this because they have forsaken me and worshiped Ashtoreth the goddess of the Sidonians, Chemosh the god of the Moabites, and Molek the god of the Ammonites, and have not walked in obedience to me, nor done what is right in my eyes, nor kept my decrees and laws as David, Solomon's father, did.*

³⁴ *"'But I will not take the whole kingdom out of Solomon's hand; I have made him ruler all the days of his life for the sake of David my servant, whom I chose and who obeyed my commands and decrees.* ³⁵ *I will take the kingdom from his son's hands and give you ten tribes.* ³⁶ *I will give one tribe to his son so that David my servant may always have a lamp before me in Jerusalem, the city where I chose to put my Name.* ³⁷ *However, as for you, I will take you, and you will rule over all that your heart desires; you will be king over Israel.* ³⁸ *If you do whatever I command you and walk in obedience to me and do what is right in my eyes by obeying my decrees and commands, as David my servant did, I will be with you. I will build you a dynasty as enduring as the one I built for David and will give Israel to you.* ³⁹ *I will humble David's descendants because of this, but not forever.'"*

⁴⁰ *Solomon tried to kill Jeroboam, but Jeroboam fled to Egypt, to Shishak the king, and stayed there until Solomon's death.*

1 Kings 11:26-40

Reflect and Respond

We've been talking for several weeks mostly about the prophets of Israel, but in the meantime strange things have been happening with the kings and the kingdom itself. The last two weeks of our study will deal with the lives of two pivotal kings in Israel's history, but first we need to catch up on some important happenings that have left God's people not with one king but two kings at once.

When King Solomon, David's son, died in 796 B.C., Israel was still one kingdom under one king. Israel was a people organized into twelve tribes named for the sons of Jacob (whose name was changed to Israel by God), each living on their own tribal land. All of the kings of the people had come from the tribe of Judah.

When Solomon died, his son Rehoboam became king. Jeroboam, who had been one of Solomon's chief officials, led the people to Rehoboam and asked if he could go easier on them than his father Solomon had. They said: "Your father put a heavy yoke on us, but now lighten the harsh labor and the heavy yoke he put on us, and we will serve you" (1 Kings 12:4).

Rehoboam asked for three days to think about it, and he consulted his father's officials for wisdom and advice. What an important thing for a young king to do! The officials advised him, "If today you will be a servant to these people and serve them and give them a favorable answer, they will always be your servants" (1 Kings 12:7). What wise advice they gave him: be kind to your people today and they will follow you forever.

But the young king rejected their advice and consulted the young men serving with him, who advised him to be even harsher than his father had been. Not wanting to seem weak, Rehoboam stumbled into pride and ignored the lesson of humility. The text tells us that he answered the people harshly, saying, "My father made your yoke heavy; I will make it even heavier. My father scourged you with whips; I will scourge you with scorpions" (1 Kings 12:13-14).

I can remember a few times early in my ministry when I tested the waters regarding the kind of leader I would be. I didn't want to be the weakest one at the table, but I didn't want to seem overbearing. I wanted everyone to know that I knew what I was talking about, but I didn't want to seem like a know-it-all.

When you're young, leading with strength seems like the right choice—you want to prove you're up to the task. But as we get a little older, we get a little wiser, don't we? We realize that leading with kindness and the heart of a servant actually yields more cooperation and trust.

Have you ever been tempted by pride to "prove yourself" as Rehoboam was—whether by asserting your power and authority or demonstrating your abilities and qualifications? If so, describe briefly what happened:

Threatening his people was Rehoboam's key mistake. He assumed that no matter how badly he treated them, they would always follow him. One little detail that may have gone unnoticed by Rehoboam was a prophecy that had been delivered to Jeroboam while Solomon was still alive.

Look back at our Scripture reading for today, 1 Kings 11:26-40. In an encounter with God's prophet Ahijah, the future division of the kingdom of Israel had already been foretold to the official Jeroboam. He knew ahead of time that someday he would be declared king over the majority of the people of Israel. Solomon knew it too, and so he tried to have Jeroboam killed; but Jeroboam hid until Solomon's death.

Reread 1 Kings 11:30-31 (page 136). What was the physical object used to depict how the kingdom would be torn? *new cloak*

According to 1 Kings 11:33, what was the reason that God would split the kingdom apart? *because the people worshipped other Gods, were not obedient to God nor done what was right*

The division of the nation of Israel was caused by the people's rebellion. They had begun to worship false gods. God specifically lists three gods they had worshiped, because they wanted to be like the nations surrounding them. Worship matters to God. It matters that His people give their hearts only to Him. Despite their calling to be set apart from the idol worshipers in neighboring nations and recognized as a people who worshiped the One True God alone, God's people were flirting with idolatry.

So when Solomon's son Rehoboam declared that his reign would be about tyranny and oppression of God's people, the kingdom was finally torn in two. The ten tribes from the northern region retreated back to their homes and no longer recognized Rehoboam as their king. They were now called the nation of Israel. And they wanted their own king.

THE KINGDOMS OF ISRAEL AND JUDAH

SCALE OF MILES

When all the Israelites heard that Jeroboam had returned, they called him to the assembly and made him king over all Israel. The two tribes in the southern region became known as the nation of Judah and continued to follow Rehoboam, Solomon's son, as their king. "Only the tribe of Judah remained loyal to the house of David" (1 Kings 12:20)

Now we have two separate kingdoms with two separate kings. And the kings' names may be as easy for us to confuse as those of the prophets Elijah and Elisha! Jeroboam was king of the nation of Israel in the North. Rehoboam (Solomon's son) was king of the nation of Judah in the South.

Jeroboam was a first generation king. His ancestors had been common people, and now suddenly he was thrust into a position of royalty and leadership. God had prepared him for his new position by giving him warning through a prophet to prepare himself for this moment. God even promised to take care of him during his reign: "I will take you, and you will rule over all that your heart desires; you will be king over Israel" (1 Kings 11:37). But his leadership would be conditional on one piece of advice.

Look back at 1 Kings 11:37-38 (page 136). What did God require of Jeroboam in order to stay with him and give him a long dynasty? *if he did what God commanded, was obedient to God, did what was right*

With the knowledge that his position in the kingdom rested entirely on his commitment to worship God alone, you would think that Jeroboam would take every opportunity to remind his people that they were called to worship the One True God. The nations around them not only flirted with idolatry but sold their souls to false gods. Yet Israel was God's people. Surely Jeroboam, who had been warned, would lead them accordingly.

Jeroboam, however, had a concern. He was afraid that if he allowed people to travel to Jerusalem in the southern kingdom of Judah to worship at the Temple there, they would go back to following King Rehoboam.

Read 1 Kings 12:28-29 in the margin. What did King Jeroboam decide to do? *created 2 idols for his people to worship in 2 cities other than Jerusalem*

Can you think of a time when fear or insecurity caused you to compromise your dedication to God? If so, describe it briefly below:

After seeking advice, the king made two golden calves. He said to the people, "It is too much for you to go up to Jerusalem. Here are your gods, Israel, who brought you up out of Egypt." One he set up in Bethel, and the other in Dan. 1 Kings 12:28-29

I find it interesting that both young Rehoboam and the newly named King Jeroboam sought advice early in their kingship. Rehoboam ignored the wise advice to be a servant leader of his people and instead declared that he would be a harsh and powerful leader. Jeroboam sought advice and decided that protecting his own power was more important than heeding God's voice. While Moses' brother Aaron had created one golden calf for God's people to worship as an idol, Jeroboam made two!

Both of these kings chose to put their own self-interest first, and the results were tragic for their people. Saul, David, and Solomon—Israel's first three kings—each had Jeroboam's flaws, but the roller coaster of leadership that followed in the divided kingdom was unquestionably worse than anything the people of Israel and Judah ever had experienced. The Books of First and Second Kings introduce us to the many kings who reigned in each kingdom, providing details such as the length of the king's reign and the quality or character of his leadership.

We find that each king is defined as being bad or good by whether he worshiped God alone and whether his reign was a good one for his people. Not surprisingly, there is a direct correlation between these two factors. Those kings who gave their hearts to God and listened for His voice were known as good rulers of the people. Those who worshiped idols had reigns filled with disastrous decisions that caused their people to suffer.

Extra Insight
"The only notable act of [Jeroboam's] reign marked him with infamy, as the man 'who made Israel to sin.' It was the idolatrous establishment of golden calves at Bethel and Dan that the people might worship there and not at Jerusalem."[1]

Take a look at the charts below and answer the following questions:

How many kings ruled each kingdom? *20*

What was the total number of kings? *40*

How many good kings were there in all? *8*

Over which kingdom did the good kings reign? *Judah*

Kings of Israel (10 Tribes in North)	Bad or Good	Years of Reign	Scripture
1. Jeroboam I	B	22	1 K 11:26–14:20
2. Nadab	B	2	1 K 15:25-28
3. Baasha	B	24	1 K 15:27–16:7
4. Elah	B	2	1 K 16:6-14
5. Zimri	B	7 days	1 K 16:9-20
6. Tibni	B	7	1 K 16:21-22

7. Omri	B	12	1 K 16:23-28
8. Ahab	B	22	1 K 16:28–22:40
9. Ahaziah	B	2	1 K 22:40, 52-54; 2 K 1:1-18
10. Jehoram	B	12	2 K 3:1–9:25
11. Jehu	B	28	2 K 9:1–10:36
12. Jehoahaz	B	17	2 K13:1-9
13. Jehoash	B	16	2 K 13:10–14:16
14. Jeroboam II	B	41	2 K 14:23-29
15. Zechariah	B	6 months	2 K 14:29–15:12
16. Shallum	B	1 month	2 K 15:10-14
17. Menahem	B	10	2 K 15:14-22
18. Pekahiah	B	2	2 K 15:23-26
19. Pekah	B	20	2 K 15:27-31
20. Hoshea	B	9	2 K 15:30; 17:1-6

Kings of Judah (2 tribes in South)	Bad or Good	Years of Reign	Scripture
1. Rehoboam	B	17	1 K 11:42–14:31
2. Abijah	B	3	1 K 14:31–15:8
3. Asa	G	41	1 K 15:8-24
4. Jehoshaphat	G	25	1 K 22:41-55
5. Jehoram	B	8	2 K 8:16-24
6. Ahaziah	B	1	2 K 8:24–9:29
7. Athaliah	B	7	2 K 11:1-20
8. Jehoash	G	40	2 K 11:1–12:21
9. Amaziah	G	29	2 K 14:1-22
10. Uzziah (or Azariah)	G	52	2 K 15:1-7
11. Jotham	G	16	2 K 15:32-38
12. Ahaz	B	16	2 K 15:38–16:20
13. Hezekiah	G ✓	29	2 K 16:20; 18:1- 20:21
14. Manasseh	B	55	2 K 21:1-18
15. Amon	B	2	2 K 21:19-26
16. Josiah	G ✓	31	2 K 22:1–23:30
17. Johoahaz	B	3 months	2 K 23:30-34
18. Jehoiakim	B	11	2 K 23:34–24:6
19. Johoiachin	B	3 months	2 K 24:6-16
20. Zedekiah	B	11	2 K 24:17–25:30

We'll spend the next two weeks learning about the last two good kings of Judah, Hezekiah and Josiah. By the time these two kings came along, they had to spend time and energy reforming the kingdom from the negative choices that

141

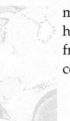

many bad rulers before them had made. Hezekiah and Josiah are known for having a heart for God and being good leaders of their people. And as we learn from the example of the kings of Israel and Judah, these two factors have a direct correlation.

Have you found in your own experience that those who have a heart for God make strong leaders? Explain your answer.

Your heart is precious to God. He counts it as one of the greatest treasures of His kingdom!

Today we've done some important "background prep" for our week of study, but there is an important takeaway I don't want you to miss. Worship matters to God. What we give our hearts to matters immensely. This is why the Bible tells us, "Above all else, guard your heart, for everything you do flows from it" (Proverbs 4:23). The way that we guard our hearts and keep from flirting with idolatry is by worshiping God alone. Remember, your heart is precious to God. He counts it as one of the greatest treasures of His kingdom!

Talk with God

God of Grace, our quest for power on this earth can make us do terrible things. It can be so easy to take our eyes off of You when it seems to us that our way is better. Forgive me, God, for forging my own way without You. Help me to look to You for guidance and leadership. Amen.

Act on It

In the margin, make a list of the things you give your heart to other than God—perhaps your family, ~~your job~~, or a particular passion or project. Invite God to examine your heart and be sure that none of these has become an idol in your life. Ask God to be the Lord of all of your life, receiving your worship and praise for all the good gifts He has given you.

Day 2: Firing Our Idols

Read God's Word

¹ In the third year of Hoshea son of Elah king of Israel, Hezekiah son of Ahaz king of Judah began to reign. ² He was twenty-five years old when he became king,

and he reigned in Jerusalem twenty-nine years. His mother's name was Abijah daughter of Zechariah. ³ He did what was right in the eyes of the LORD, just as his father David had done. ⁴ He removed the high places, smashed the sacred stones and cut down the Asherah poles. He broke into pieces the bronze snake Moses had made, for up to that time the Israelites had been burning incense to it. (It was called Nehushtan.)

2 Kings 18:1-4

Reflect and Respond

When the people of Nepal search for the divine, they can find a new deity to worship as close as the nearest preschool. You see, they have a tradition where young girls, called Kumari, go through a rigorous selection process as toddlers and then are named a goddess. Instead of simply achieving potty training like their peers, they actually are considered to be divine.

Little Sajani Shakya was selected to be the goddess of her hometown of Bhaktapur near Kathmandu. She was expected to live in a temple during her childhood, where Hindus and Buddhists alike would come to worship her and receive her blessing in response. As a Kumari, she would remain in the temple until she reached puberty, when she could return to her family and go on to lead a normal life. However, Sajani did something against the rules of the Kumari tradition. Not only did she not stay in the temple as expected but she travelled to the United States to promote a documentary that explored Nepal's traditions and political turmoil. When she returned, she was chastised for not having sought the approval of the local religious leaders and removed from her post.

The chief of a trust that manages the affairs of the local Kumari goddess tradition declared Sajani's actions wrong and impure and announced that she was dismissed. Dethroned. Pulled down from the status of god and returned to the life of a little girl. "We will search for a new Kumari and install her as the living goddess," the chief stated.[2]

If you ask me, one of the clearest signs that a god or goddess actually might not be divine is if you can fire them and hire a replacement. Having this kind of control over a so-called all-powerful god or goddess means that, in fact, the object of worship is not powerful at all. Only the One True God is worthy of our worship. Though God's people have always been called to worship God alone, this does not mean that we are immune to placing lesser objects on the throne of our hearts—either today or in ancient history.

As we saw yesterday, the kings of Israel and Judah struggled to guard their hearts. Although King David began his reign with a heart for worship and a desire to build a Temple where God's people could worship Him, David's son Solomon rebelled against God's Word and took many foreign wives. Instead of being set apart from the pagan ways of the people around him, Solomon adopted the religions of his wives as they brought their idols with them.

Read 1 Kings 11:4-5. Write below the names of the foreign gods that Solomon followed. *Ashtoreth & Molech*

Later, when Solomon's son Rehoboam was on the throne, God promised to take part of the kingdom away from their family and give it to another king. The kingdom was already divided, as we learned yesterday, because idols had polluted their hearts and left them with doubts that God was the only true God.

The heart of the king was very important to God because where the king worshiped, the people followed.

Read 1 Kings 11:33 and review God's explanation of why the kingdom was split apart. Write the reason below, along with the names of the three foreign gods that the people worshiped. *Ashtoreth, Chemos & not followed Gods ways, or done what Molech pleases God & not obeyed*

Did you notice that the same gods King Solomon followed (plus another) were now being followed by the people of Israel? The heart of the king was very important to God because where the king worshiped, the people followed. Remember that the king did not lead a democracy. Whatever he did, so did the people. Wherever he led, the people followed.

Would you agree that "as goes the heart of the leader, so the people's hearts will follow"? Explain your answer.

At face value, the fact that so many of God's leaders and people were tempted to worship idols may seem like a mystery to us. After all, God clearly spelled things out for them in the very first two commandments:

"You shall have no other gods before me.

"You shall not make for yourself an image in the form of anything in heaven above or
> *on the earth beneath or in the waters below. You shall not bow down to them or worship them; for I, the LORD your God, am a jealous God."*
> Exodus 20:3-5

Yet First and Second Kings are filled with rulers and people who fall again and again to the temptation to worship false gods and make idols for themselves. If we can see so clearly how they were going wrong, why couldn't they?

Perhaps they did. God certainly had spelled out the dangers and consequences of idol worship. Whether or not the people recognized how wrong their idol worship was, the fact remains that idols had great appeal for them. Specifically, idols had the appeal of power, pleasure, passion, and popularity.[3] Let's look at each one separately.

Power. While worshiping God required people to bow to His ultimate power and obey His authority, idols offered people the power to choose—to hire and fire their gods at will—and thus to be in control. Making sacrifices to an idol was an attempt to control its power and to influence its will. Praying to the living God, on the other hand, meant surrender: "Not my will, but yours be done."

If you struggle at all with being a control freak, then you might understand where these people were coming from. We like to have some control over things, don't we? If they had some power with their gods, then they might feel some sense of control over their situations. But life with God doesn't work that way at all. God offers everything we'll ever need, but that provision requires giving up power in order to trust the power of God at work in us.

Pleasure. Human beings are sensual creatures, and idols can be seen and touched in a way that an invisible God cannot. Instead of a religion that promised to help people gain control over their sensual appetites, idolatry encouraged people to act them out in cults of worship, even encouraging people to engage male and female prostitutes in temples as an act of worship (see 1 Kings 14:24).

Idols offered an immediate sense of pleasure that stands in contrast to the sometimes difficult task of waiting on God. In contrast to an invisible God who demanded self-denial, humility, modesty, and patience, idols could be seen and touched and offered a virtual free-for-all lifestyle—"if it feels good, go for it."

Passion. Idols were depicted as having human passions and emotions. They were given human-like characteristics, making them easier to understand than a holy God with so many mysterious qualities. But they also were believed to be fickle. There was no unconditional love to be had from an idol; it could choose to reject your prayer or sacrifice on a whim.

From our perspective, we wonder why the people so easily fell prey to the worship of idols, but they are not that unlike us. We, too, like to make God into our own image, projecting our own characteristics and qualities onto God. If we are honest, we must admit that it can be easy for us to put God in a box, expecting that if we do all the right things then God must bless us.

Popularity. Since idols were more of a reflection of human nature than true deities, they were more culturally suitable to the people's imaginations. People could choose whatever idol they liked based on their need for the day. There were fertility gods, gods of war and harvest, and gods for whatever need emerged. How much easier it was to base your worship on choice and be free to choose to worship other gods or not to worship at all.

We, too, experience the struggle to remain loyal to the Living God when the world is worshiping "idols" and it seems so fun and loose and "right now." We can have the best intentions, but when the whole world is going one way, it takes more than good intentions to swim upstream.

Of course, these four appealing qualities of idols hold true even today. Although there are no wooden or metal statues in most of our homes, we too long for things having the appeal of power, pleasure, passion, and popularity.

We would like to have the power to be in control of our own destinies and those of the people we love. Even our prayers to God sometimes reduce Him to the status of an idol when we try to control the outcome. We are a people who love pleasure, following our passions and emotions and often having a difficult time denying ourselves what brings self-gratification. As Paul said of the Philippians, "their god is their stomach" (Philippians 3:19). Often we move at the whim of our desire for pleasure, and it easily becomes an idol. Likewise, we are driven by popularity to imitate what those around us do and to follow our whims rather than have the dedication and discipline of worship.

Before we ridicule God's people for their inclination to worship idols, let's take a minute to examine our own hearts. How strong would we be in a culture of pervasive idol worship? How might we stand strong in our worship of God when everyone around us is choosing to worship lesser idols? Actually, we are not far removed from their experience. This world competes for our attention and allegiance daily, and sometimes it takes all we've got to keep our hearts focused on God alone.

Which one of these idol-worshiping characteristics tempts you most often: power, pleasure, passion or popularity? Why?

I like a plan

What do you think are some of the most common idols of our day? To answer this question, think about commercials you've seen, conversations you've heard about activities and priorities, or actions and attitudes you've observed in the workplace, mall, or gym.

latest & greatest fads or styles

When Hezekiah came into power, he was the thirteenth king to reign over Judah since the split of the two kingdoms. While things were going better in the king department for Judah than for Israel, who had had a steady stream of bad kings, Judah still struggled with a rollercoaster of leadership from bad to good and back again. Hezekiah's grandfather Jotham had been the fourth good king in a succession of good kings. But Jotham's son Ahaz changed all of that.

Read 2 Kings 16:1-4. How do these verses describe King Ahaz?

didn't live in a Godly way

In addition to not striving to maintain the "set apart" status of God's people by worshiping God alone, King Ahaz adopted the most detestable practices of the pagan religions in the surrounding area, including sacrificing his own child to a foreign god. He also sent his priest to study the worship of foreign gods and then remodeled God's Temple to try to be like the pagan worshipers around them. In Ahaz we see some of the most important reasons why God detests idol worship. The prophet Jeremiah described it this way:

> *"My people have committed two sins:*
> *They have forsaken me,*
> *the spring of living water,*
> *and have dug their own cisterns,*
> *broken cisterns that cannot hold water."*
> Jeremiah 2:13

Substituting or supplementing anything for God's place in our lives not only turns us *away* from the God who is our help but also turns us *toward* things that "cannot hold water." When we turn toward sources that cannot supply our needs, we are left thirsty, dying for the Source that God alone can be for us.

What things have you turned to in the past to "quench your thirst" and meet your needs, only to find that they cannot hold water?

Ahaz was so desperate for help that he murdered his own son in sacrifice to an idol that was not real and could not help him. The nation of Judah was in a bad place. And into this bad situation came Hezekiah.

Instead of following the practices of his father, Hezekiah was more like his grandfather, Jotham. Sometimes we have to look farther up the family tree than one generation—or perhaps outside of the tree altogether—to find traditions of healing and blessing. Hezekiah wisely chose not to follow in his father's footsteps.

Turn back to 2 Kings 18:4 (page 143), and circle the verbs that describe what Hezekiah did to the sites of idol worship in his kingdom. Then write the verbs below: *removed, smashed, cut down, broke*

Extra Insight

Ahaz, the twelfth king of Judah, ascended the throne at age twenty and reigned sixteen years. He is known for his idolatry and contempt of the true God. Many of the prophecies of Isaiah are directed against him. Ahaz sacrificed his own children to idols, introduced Syrian gods into Jerusalem, altered the temple after the Syrian model, and eventually closed the temple altogether.[4]

Hezekiah certainly was serious about ridding his kingdom of idol worship!

If we are serious about worshiping God alone, one of the most important spiritual practices we can practice is self-examination. Each of us has things in our lives that act as substitutes or supplements for God's position of power. Sometimes we make a willful choice to put something above God, and other times something gradually usurps God's place of priority in our lives before we know it has happened. Often it's not a matter of choosing a destructive behavior or a life of sin. Most of us truly want to please God in the moment and with our lives. Allowing God to take the top spot in our lives means letting work, family, friends, stuff, and hobbies—all good things—scoot down the list. When anything becomes our number one priority before God, it becomes an idol.

What are the idols in your life? Answer the following questions, asking God to reveal the idols that are hard to see in your own life:

What do you worry about? *health issues, enough money*

What keeps you living a life that is busier and more hurried than you would like?

When you are most upset, what behaviors do you run to for comfort? *watch movies, talk to girl friends, read books*

What are you angry about now? What are you angry with God about?

What keeps you from feeling content?

These things do not need to have a hold on you. They may have become idols, but they have no power when you declare that God alone is Lord of your life. All the things that you run to instead of running to God don't care about you or your life. But God, who wants you to run to Him, cares about it all. He cares about your fears, your anger, your worry, your passions, your struggles, your hopes, your family, your time—He cares about all of you.

It's time to fire your idols! Tell them to step down. You don't have to do it alone. God will work in you and with you. He loves each step we take closer to Him, and He alone has the desire, power, and love to help you remove every obstacle that stands in the way.

Talk with God

Thank You, Lord, for forgiving me when I have replaced You with idols. Right now I am firing the idols that have taken Your rightful place in my life. Be the Lord of my life. I surrender all to You. Amen.

Act on It

Review your answers to the previous questions designed to help you identify the idols in your life. What do they reveal about your heart? What idols do they uncover? Make some notes in the margin. Now, hand over your idols to God in prayer. Like Hezekiah, commit to remove, smash, cut down, and break into pieces anything that stands between you and God.

You also might find it valuable to take some time today to discuss this exercise with a trusted friend, inviting accountability or prayer support.

Day 3: Worship the Giver

⁴ From Mount Hor they set out by the way to the Red Sea, to go around the land of Edom; but the people became impatient on the way. ⁵ The people spoke against God and against Moses, "Why have you brought us up out of Egypt to die in the wilderness? For there is no food and no water, and we detest this miserable food." ⁶ Then the LORD sent poisonous serpents among the people, and they bit the people, so that many Israelites died. ⁷ The people came to Moses and said, "We have sinned by speaking against the LORD and against you; pray to the LORD to take away the serpents from us." So Moses prayed for the people. ⁸ And the LORD said to Moses, "Make a poisonous serpent, and set it on a pole; and everyone who is bitten shall look at it and live." ⁹ So Moses made a serpent of bronze, and put it upon a pole; and whenever a serpent bit someone, that person would look at the serpent of bronze and live.

Numbers 21:4-9 NRSV

[Hezekiah] removed the high places, smashed the sacred stones and cut down the Asherah poles. He broke into pieces the bronze snake Moses had made, for up to that time the Israelites had been burning incense to it. (It was called Nehushtan.)

2 Kings 18:4

¹⁴ And just as Moses lifted up the serpent in the wilderness, so must the Son of Man be lifted up, ¹⁵ that whoever believes in him may have eternal life.

John 3:14-15

149

Reflect and Respond

As strange Old Testament stories go, the story of Moses and the people and the poisonous serpents ranks up there near the top of the list. The least strange part of the story is that God's people complained. That's kind of their thing, right? And if we're honest, it's ours, too. Have you seen the hashtag trend #firstworldproblems? This is to say, "I'm complaining even though I know I have no business complaining about such things." Somehow complaining is wired into our humanness, as if we just can't help it. To be sure, the Israelites did not have the ease of the developed world, yet they still had a knack for complaining when things weren't going their way or didn't make sense to them.

While following Moses from Egypt through the wilderness on their way to the Promised Land, God's people have developed a terrible habit of whining and complaining. There's something about openly complaining together that almost gives a community a mob mentality. Permission to openly complain rallies even the most distant people around a common enemy and often opens the door for people to think of more and more reasons to grumble. On the journey from Egypt, when God's people are complaining about the lack of water and food, God provides for their needs; but it never seems to be enough.

Finally, there seems to be a tipping point in the squabbling masses.

Reread Number 21:5 (page 149). What are the people's complaints?

no food + water + detest what food is given

The people actually complain that God has brought them out of Egypt. What an insult to God who went to a good deal of trouble to free them from their oppressors! In the same breath, they declare their lack of faith by predicting that they will die in the wilderness. Finally, they once again demean the gifts of God by saying that they detest the food He has given them. First, they complain that there is no food and water, but then they must remember that there actually is food—they just don't like it. This downward spiral of grievances and insults means that the people are now lashing out at God who loves them and who is in the process of delivering them from their worst nightmare to their best future. We get a clue at the motive for their discontent in the previous verse.

What does Numbers 21:4 tell us about the people?

The people became impatient when the journey was farther and longer than they desired. God was not working on their timetable. My guess is that, in one way or another, each of us can relate. We've already named a few times this week that most of us like to be in control. We like to know what's coming and how to prepare. We like to have an idea so that our expectations don't get too far off course.

Have you ever become impatient while waiting for God's plans and purposes to be realized in your life? Share your thoughts below:

What happens next is God's intervention. In fact, His intervention slithers into the camp in the form of poisonous serpents! People are bitten by the snakes, and many of them die. You read that right—God sends snakes to punish the people for their ridiculous complaining. You can bet that they weren't complaining about being miserable anymore; they were complaining about the snakes! And just like that, they are repentant and desperate for God's help.

Reread Numbers 21:7 (page 149). What did the people do and say?

Admitted they were wrong + ask Moses to pray for them to take away the serpents

They recognize that God has been helping them all along but they have been too ungrateful to realize it. You know, sometimes we don't realize how good we have it until something truly terrible happens, and here a camp full of poisonous serpents really does the trick!

Has there been a time in your life when tragic circumstances have made you realize how good you have it? If so, briefly describe that time and what you learned from it. *Hurricane Harvey*

Since the people left Egypt, God has rescued them in some dramatic ways—parting the Red Sea, producing water from a rock, raining manna from heaven. But this time God's rescue comes in an even more unusual manner—bizarre, even. God tells Moses to fashion a bronze snake, just like the snakes in the camp, and to lift it up on a pole. If the people will raise their eyes to it, they will be healed. The thing that wreaked havoc in their camp will be the symbol of their need for God—the very cure for what had plagued them.

While an unusual cure, it certainly seems like a great way to get people to take their eyes off their troubles and lift them up to the heavens.

Has God ever answered your cry for help with an unusual intervention? If so, how did this intervention shift your gaze from your own troubles to God?

When the episode with the snakes ends, the people of God continue on their way. They pack the bronze snake with their things and take it with them through the desert. We know this by reading between the lines of a verse found in Second Kings about Hezekiah, the king of Judah we are studying this week.

Reread 2 Kings 18:4 (page 149) to find out what became of the bronze snake that Moses had made in the desert. *it became an idol + Israelites were burning incense to it*

What had the people been doing with the bronze snake?
burning incense to it

What do you think is significant about the fact that they gave it a name?
it had become an idol

What did King Hezekiah do to the bronze snake? *broke it into pieces*

Just to recap: the Israelites complained; God sent snakes to expose their complaining; they repented; and God relented and told Moses to make a bronze snake on a stick so that when they looked up at it, they would worship God. That bronze snake doesn't get a whole lot of attention in the whole scope of the Bible, but if you pay close enough attention, you'll see that it carries some layers of meaning. From the time of Moses to the time of Hezekiah (some seven centuries between), the bronze snake had been carried around. Through the wilderness and into the Promised Land, from the time of King Saul and King David all the way to King Hezekiah (and that is a very long time!), the people had carried around that idol and held on to it like a security blanket.

Perhaps for years the bronze snake had been lifted up as a symbol to remind the people of the miracle of healing that God had worked for them. "Here's the snake," they might have said. "Look up at it and worship God. Remember His great gift of healing." But over the years a curious thing happened. The snake, once a gift, became an idol. When people looked at it, they forgot that the power to heal comes from God, and they began burning incense and praying to the snake instead. They even gave it a name! *Nehushtan.* It wasn't just a plain statue anymore. When they named it, it became a true object of worship. What started out as a gift from God, meant to point them to worship Him, became an idol. Instead of worshiping the Giver, the people began to worship the gift.

We are a people created to worship. In Romans 12:1, we are called to present ourselves as living sacrifices to God, to worship with our whole selves. That means to give all of ourselves to God, holding nothing back in our worship. Human history has shown that we will always find something to become the priority and focus of our lives. Unfortunately, as people who follow God, we are

Extra Insight
Though one interpretation suggests that Hezekiah scornfully named the serpent Nahushtan, meaning "a piece of brass," another points out that Nahushtan was not a common noun and, therefore, was the special name given by the people to this particular bronze serpent.[5]

As people who follow God, we are just as prone as those who do not know God to substitute or supplement other things in the place that God wants to have in our hearts.

just as prone as those who do not know God to substitute or supplement other things in the place that God wants to have in our hearts. We struggle to keep our eyes fixed on God, surrendering every bit of ourselves to Him instead of holding on to just a little bit for security.

Read 1 John 5:21 in the margin. In light of the fact that this verse was written to followers of Jesus, what does it reveal about the temptation of idol worship for us as Christians?

Dear children, keep yourselves from idols.
1 John 5:21

When Hezekiah became king, he was known as a crusader against idolatry. As we learned yesterday, he went around the kingdom ridding it of all the places and objects people used to worship false gods, some of those that even his own father, King Ahaz, had established. While Hezekiah's grandfather and great-grandfather had been "good kings" who worshiped God, they tolerated the presence of the places and objects of idol worship. Hezekiah, however, was a reformer. He knew that as long as the shrines and temples to idols were left standing, people would be tempted to worship there. So he made it his mission to make sure the kingdom was rid of idols by removing the high places, smashing the sacred stones, and cutting down the Asherah poles. I wonder if Hezekiah was surprised to find, among the things being worshiped as gods, the bronze snake—an ancient gift from God turned idol.

Here is the heart of the matter: Only God can fill the place in the center of our hearts that was meant for Him. Anything else is simply a counterfeit.

Only God can fill the place in the center of our hearts that was meant for Him. Anything else is simply a counterfeit.

Read James 1:17 in the margin. According to this verse, what is a gift from God? *every good & perfect gift*

This verse actually proclaims that *everything* we have is a gift from God, and that while the gifts in our lives come and go, God does not. He does not change. He is always there.

When you thank God for the gifts He has given you, what are the first ones that come to your mind? *family & friends - people in my life, good health, everything I have, my church family*

Every good and perfect gift is from above, coming down from the Father of the heavenly lights, who does not change like shifting shadows.
James 1:17

You may not think you're a gift-worshiper, but there are a handful of gifts we are often tempted to elevate in our lives, giving us an obstructed view of God. Let's take a brief look at four of these gifts.

1. People. People are gifts from God in our lives. They are meant to be treasured and loved. But if we try to control them or their futures, or if we continually worry or are anxious about them, as if we are responsible for them, then they have become idols in our lives. I struggle with this when it comes to my family. I want to say that I give them completely to God and that I never seek to be in control. But the truth is that it is difficult for me to let go of control and trust God. Sometimes I allow myself to get ahead of God and make decisions before waiting on God's will for our family. Can you relate?

2. Traditions. Traditions are gifts from God in our lives. Our families carry out traditions that bring meaning and connectedness through generations. We have holiday traditions, bedtime rituals or traditions, vacation traditions, and on and on. We also have traditions related to what it means to be the church and how we worship God—such as whether we use hymnals or praise and worship songs, whether we incorporate liturgy or follow a more casual order of worship. These traditions are particularly close to our hearts because they bring us close to God. But sometimes traditions can become idols. "We've always done it this way" can indicate a form of idol worship when we focus more on earthly things than on humbly looking to God for guidance.

3. Possessions. Cars, clothes, technology, hobby gear—stuff can accumulate in our lives and, before we know it, our closets are bursting at the hinges. Let's face it: many of us have a *need* for stuff! It can be difficult to loosen our grip on our stuff and change our perspective, but we must remember that we are stewards of our possessions, not owners. When we worship God alone, we recognize that everything we have and everything we are rightfully belongs to him. The things God has given us are meant to be held with open hands, not clinched fists. When we gain material possessions, we should ask ourselves: *How can this be used to glorify God? How can I share it with others? What will I do if someone needs it more than I do?*

4. Self. Ultimately, idolatry is the sin of putting ourselves before God. This is a blatant choice to put our wishes, dreams, and desires over what God has for us. Ed Stetzer describes it well:

> So my idols are much more personal than a piece of stone or a block of wood. Anything from my past or present that shapes my identity or fills my thoughts with something other than God, especially on a regular, ongoing, irresistible basis, is an idol. Idolatry does not count the cost of worshipping anything but God. And although few of us could ever imagine worshipping a picture of ourselves, the reality is—we are either worshipping God or some form of ourselves. When we are driven by physical and emotional appetites rather than being led by the Spirit of God, we are worshipping the idol of ourselves.[6]

Even our very selves are gifts from God. We are made in God's image, and God has called us good. But we have to remember to worship the Giver, not the gifts. A life with God requires that God is higher than our wants, wishes, and wisdom.

Besides people, traditions, possessions, and self, what are some other gifts from God that we might idolize or worship?

experiences?

Is there a gift from God that has obstructed your view of Him—something that has caused you to worship the gift instead of the Giver? Share your thoughts below.

> We must learn to surrender what we hold too tightly so that we can embrace God fully again.

Hezekiah's lesson for us is simple: we must learn to surrender what we hold too tightly so that we can embrace God fully again. How do we do this? Here are three simple ideas:

1. *Stewardship*: acknowledging that we only borrow these gifts from God for a short time, and we are to use them to serve Him.
2. *Gratitude*: letting our gifts remind us to thank God, the source of every good and perfect gift, and remembering that our attention and affections belong to Him.
3. *Worship*: praising God above all things. As our love for Him increases, our temptation to pay too much attention to the people and things in our lives decreases.

Loosening our grip means practicing stewardship. It is like a master gardener who tills and tends her garden into something beautiful, something that blooms for only a short time. The blooms are a symbol of the work, but even the work itself—tending and nurturing—can be worship.

Loosening our grip also means developing a heart of gratitude, remembering that what we have comes from and belongs to God. When we remember this, we are less prone to selfishness and greed and more open to praise and worship that are freely given for all of God's good gifts.

Finally, loosening our grip means putting God first; it means worship. When we lift our hearts and eyes to God in worship, looking above and beyond all the worries and struggles of this world, we let go of our need to be the center of our universe and put God in God's rightful place.

Recall a specific time when stewardship, gratitude, or worship rekindled your love for God, and describe it briefly below:

Because worship, in particular, is such a powerful resolution for the upside-down world of idolatry, tomorrow we will focus on true worship that turns our hearts fully to God. Jesus Himself reminds us of the saving power of worship in a conversation with a man named Nicodemus. As Jesus is explaining to Nicodemus that He is the source of eternal life, He recalls the bronze snake and its saving powers: "And just as Moses lifted up the serpent in the wilderness, so must the Son of Man be lifted up, that whoever believes in him may have eternal life" (John 3:14-15).

Jesus is the only One with the power to restore, heal, and save. Lifting Him up, placing Him above all else in our lives, is the antidote for sin. Just as the bronze serpent had been the antivenom for the venom of the poisonous snakes, so Jesus' death overcame death. Lifted up on the cross, Jesus took on the sins of the world and defeated sin.

The Israelites made an idol out of the bronze snake, forgetting that it was meant to point them to God. The snake had no power; there was no reason to praise this bronze statue. Jesus, on the other hand, is worthy of our worship! While earthly idols compete to take our attention, Jesus is the One—the only One—who is worthy of our praise. May we live our lives as an act of worship to Him!

Talk with God

Forgive me, Lord, for allowing idols in my life, which take my eyes off of You. Examine my heart and blot out anything that keeps You from being first in my life. Help me to practice stewardship, gratitude, and worship instead of selfishness, greed, or fear. Amen.

Act on It

Spend some time in worship today, just you and God. Play or sing one of your favorite worship songs and tell God why you love Him.

Day 4: The Real Deal

Read God's Word

¹ Hezekiah sent word to all Israel and Judah, and wrote letters also to Ephraim and Manasseh, that they should come to the house of the LORD at Jerusalem, to keep the passover to the LORD the God of Israel. ² For the king and his officials and all the assembly in Jerusalem had taken counsel to keep the passover in the second month ³ (for they could not keep it at its proper time because the priests had not sanctified themselves in sufficient number, nor had the people assembled in Jerusalem).

⁴ The plan seemed right to the king and all the assembly. ⁵ So they decreed to make a proclamation throughout all Israel, from Beer-sheba to Dan, that the people should come and keep the passover to the LORD the God of Israel, at Jerusalem; for they had not kept it in great numbers as prescribed. ⁶ So couriers went throughout all Israel and Judah with letters from the king and his officials, as the king had commanded, saying, "O people of Israel, return to the LORD, the God of Abraham, Isaac, and Israel, so that he may turn again to the remnant of you who have escaped from the hand of the kings of Assyria. ⁷ Do not be like your ancestors and your kindred, who were faithless to the LORD God of their ancestors, so that he made them a desolation, as you see. ⁸ Do not now be stiff-necked as your ancestors were, but yield yourselves to the LORD and come to his sanctuary, which he has sanctified forever, and serve the LORD your God, so that his fierce anger may turn away from you. ⁹ For as you return to the LORD, your kindred and your children will find compassion with their captors, and return to this land. For the LORD your God is gracious and merciful, and will not turn away his face from you, if you return to him."

¹⁰ The couriers went from town to town in Ephraim and Manasseh, as far as Zebulun, but people scorned and ridiculed them. ¹¹ Nevertheless, some from Asher, Manasseh and Zebulun humbled themselves and went to Jerusalem. ¹² Also in Judah the hand of God was on the people to give them unity of mind to carry out what the king and his officials had ordered, following the word of the LORD.

¹³ Many people came together in Jerusalem to keep the festival of unleavened bread in the second month, a very large assembly. ¹⁴ They set to work and removed the altars that were in Jerusalem, and all the altars for offering incense they took away and threw into the Wadi Kidron. ¹⁵ They slaughtered the passover lamb on the fourteenth day of the second month. The priests and the Levites were ashamed, and they sanctified themselves and brought burnt offerings into the house of the LORD. . . . ¹⁸ Hezekiah prayed for them, saying, "The good LORD pardon all ¹⁹ who set their hearts to seek God, the LORD the God of their ancestors,

even though not in accordance with the sanctuary's rules of cleanness." ²⁰ *The LORD heard Hezekiah, and healed the people.* ²¹ *The people of Israel who were present at Jerusalem kept the festival of unleavened bread seven days with great gladness; and the Levites and the priests praised the LORD day by day, accompanied by loud instruments for the LORD. . . .*

²³ *The whole assembly then agreed to celebrate the festival seven more days; so for another seven days they celebrated joyfully. . . .* ²⁶ *There was great joy in Jerusalem, for since the time of Solomon son of King David of Israel there had been nothing like this in Jerusalem.* ²⁷ *Then the priests and the Levites stood up and blessed the people, and their voice was heard; their prayer came to his holy dwelling in heaven.*

2 Chronicles 30:1-15; 18-21; 23, 26-27 NRSV

Reflect and Respond

I'll never forget an unscheduled visit I had to a small factory overseas. I was on a mission trip with a church group, and a family we met through a local church invited us to visit their home. They also eagerly invited us to see the clothing factory that was their family business. As we walked around the room, which was the size of a school gymnasium, we were introduced to women who were sewing away on coats and jackets. Many of them, we were told, were single mothers, and the family who began the business was helping to lift their struggling families above poverty level. They greeted us joyfully and were proud to show us their work. When we reached the very last station in the room, we watched a woman using an embroidery machine making a symbol on the back of each coat: "Adidas" it now read in distinct white lettering, with the familiar logo underneath.

It took me a minute to register that, although this family was nice and their intentions were good, they were creating knock-off goods—counterfeits of a brand name. The selling of counterfeit goods has become big business in recent years. From handbags to accessories, jewelry to designer jeans, products that look like "the real thing" are often sold for a steal both to knowing customers who are looking to sport a brand name for a cheap price and to unsuspecting ones who are duped into believing that what they've bought is the real thing.

It has been said that the best way to learn to recognize a counterfeit is to become familiar with the real thing. Those "Adidas" jackets may have appeared real from a distance, but if held side-by-side with jackets from the true brand, it would have been easy to distinguish the differences.

Have you ever come into contact with a counterfeit of some kind? How did you know?

> The best way to learn to recognize a counterfeit is to become familiar with the real thing.

So far we've talked about the wrong choices that God's people made by worshiping idols. These counterfeit gods were offered as sources of hope and help, but they were not real and could not help the people at all. Imagine the despair people felt when the gods they had worshiped were knock-offs, unable to provide help or relief to them.

King Hezekiah was committed to stopping the idolatry practiced by his subjects. He had watched so much wasted time and energy be given to the sin of idolatry. Hezekiah's own father, Ahaz, had even sacrificed one of his sons (2 Kings 16:3)—Hezekiah's brother—to a false god. No wonder this reformer king made it his life's work to strip away the idolatry that plagued his kingdom.

Just as with counterfeit goods, the best way to recognize and rid the kingdom of counterfeit gods was to spend time with the real thing. Hezekiah not only kicked out the counterfeits but brought people back to a real and beautiful practice of the worship of God Himself.

Though we've been reading Hezekiah's story in Second Kings, parts of his story also are told in Second Chronicles and Isaiah. In our Scripture for today from Second Chronicles, we read about Hezekiah's desire to bring all of God's people together to celebrate the Passover. This passage reveals some important points about true worship that can help us to avoid counterfeits and practice authentic worship.

1. True worship lifts God high so that we cannot be fooled by a counterfeit.

We see throughout Scripture that when God's people lift Him high in their lives—both as individuals and as a community—what follows is true, authentic worship. But when they do not, they are easily fooled by counterfeits. The story of King Hezekiah and the Passover celebration illustrates this beautifully.

As we've learned throughout the week, the people had allowed foreign gods to infiltrate their culture and their lives, and they had let their own religious devotion to the One True God slip. Worshiping God was no longer the priority of their lives; they had fallen away from the rituals, practices, and holy festivals that God had instructed them to keep.

Reread 2 Chronicles 30:1-5 (page 157). What was the proclamation that King Hezekiah made?

What does verse 5 tell us about the people's observance of Passover?

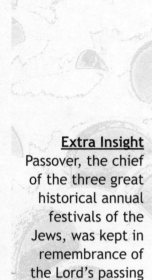

The celebration of Passover had not been observed as specified in Exodus 12 and 13 since the time of King Solomon. Naturally, as years passed without observing Passover, the story became less and less familiar in their homes and communities. They soon forgot the story of how God had rescued their people and had vowed to lead and care for them. When you forget your story, it's easy to fall prey to counterfeits. For years they had not observed any central acts of worship as instructed by God and carried out by their ancestors. By now, they didn't really know the difference between worshiping God and worshiping idols. True worship lifts God high and makes Him the priority in our lives—leaving no space for fake idols.

2. True worship recalls the mighty acts of God.

The celebration of Passover was not only a central act of worship; it also served as an important reminder to the people.

Read the Scriptures below. What claim was made in each of these instances of false idol worship?

Exodus 32:4

1 Kings 12:28 *2 gold calves as the gods who brought them out of Egypt*

Now read Exodus 13:8-10. What was the central reason for celebrating the Passover? *As a remembrance that God brought them out of Egypt*

God's people had developed a form of "memory loss" when it came to their history with God and the mighty acts He had performed. The memory loss happened because they did not regularly recall the events. Throughout the story of God and His people, we hear instructions to remember His acts, write them down, observe festivals of remembrance, and tell the stories of God's faithfulness. God knew how fickle and forgetful human beings can be, so He gave His people ways to help them remember. But as more and more time passed, the people became less intent on following God's instructions. Before long they had forgotten who they were and all that God had done for them.

We wonder how the people could fall for the false claims that golden calves delivered them from Egypt so soon after their miraculous exodus. It sounds so absurd to us. But this is an indication of how far they had strayed from true worship—and how quickly. They didn't remember because they had not practiced recalling God's faithfulness. When we fail to remember the mighty and good things God has done in our lives, it becomes easier and easier for us

Extra Insight
Passover, the chief of the three great historical annual festivals of the Jews, was kept in remembrance of the Lord's passing over the houses of the Israelites when the firstborn of all the Egyptians were destroyed. It is a type of the great deliverance from sin and death accomplished by Christ's death on the cross.[7]

to be tempted and fooled by counterfeits. We practice true worship when we remember God's mighty acts and praise His greatness.

3. True worship brings unity to God's people.

Hezekiah not only desired to reinstitute Passover and return the people to the right worship of God but he also had another desire. He wanted unity—for the two kingdoms to be the united people of God worshiping God in the Temple.

Look again at the verses in 2 Chronicles 30, and fill in the blanks:

Hezekiah sent word to all __*Israel*__ *and* __*Judah*__ . **(v. 1)**

So they decreed to make a proclamation throughout __*all Israel*__

_____ *, from Beer-sheba to Dan.* **(v. 5)**

Although Hezekiah was the king of Judah, he sent out invitations to participate in this Passover celebration to God's people in both Judah *and* Israel. He wanted to see the divided kingdoms come together in unity to worship God in the Temple in Jerusalem.

Reread verses 10 and 11 in today's Scripture passage (page 157). How did the people react? *people scorned & ridiculed them*

Although Hezekiah's invitation was genuine, most of the people of Israel mocked him, but a handful of those in Israel "humbled themselves and went to Jerusalem" (v. 11). Also those in Judah worked together in "unity of mind" (v. 12) to carry out what the king had requested.

Unity in worship was important to Hezekiah, and it is important to God even today. We can't fully worship God when we divide ourselves into competing groups before God, thinking ourselves more right or more worthy than others. Unity in worship today might not mean that all people are gathered in one place to worship God, but we can have unity of heart.

What are some ways that we need to be more unified (less divided) in worship today?

Sometimes after a tragedy we experience a unity in worship that draws us out of our normal routine. We gather together, despite our differences, to come before God because there is nothing else to do but affirm together that God is

God and we are not. When we practice true worship, we experience unity as the people of God.

4. True worship involves repentance and forgiveness.

When the people came together in Jerusalem to celebrate Passover, they did more than observe the festival. In the actions that they took, both the people and the priests showed evidence of true repentance.

Review verses 14 and 15 in today's Scripture passage (page 157). What did the people do? What did the priests do?

For the first time since Hezekiah became king, we see the people actually participating in the removal and destruction of altars used for idol worship. This was not part of the Passover ritual but a response that flowed from their sorrow and remorse for having neglected their God. Likewise, we read that the priests and the Levites were ashamed and repented for how far the people had strayed from God. Though slaughtering a Passover lamb was part of the festival ritual, they also sanctified themselves and brought burnt offerings to the Lord.

I love the prayer we hear from Hezekiah for his people: "May the LORD, who is good, pardon everyone who sets their heart on seeking God—the LORD, the God of their ancestors—even if they are not clean according to the rules of the sanctuary" (2 Chronicles 30:18-19). We read that the Lord heard Hezekiah and healed the people.

Repentance, which is recognizing that we have fallen short of the glory of God and need His forgiveness, is a healing act—one that is at the heart of our worship of God. Repentance is literally turning our backs to lesser things and turning toward God. We turn away from our sin, idol worship, and selfishness toward the light, grace, and forgiveness of God. He is always full of grace and forgiveness when we come to Him in repentance. He holds no record of wrongs and doesn't have to give us a lecture. He is full of grace and love. When we practice true worship, we come to God in repentance and receive His forgiveness.

5. True worship is an act through which we lose ourselves and our agendas.

The Passover celebration was intended to last seven days. But an interesting thing happened when the people gathered there in Jerusalem reached the seven-day mark.

Reread verses 21 and 23 in today's passage (page 158). What did the people decide to do? *have the festival another 7 days*

The people not only decided to keep going for another seven days but reached this decision unanimously! No one was ready to stop celebrating and worshiping God!

What is the length of an average worship service in your church? Can you imagine if people were so enthralled in worship that they spontaneously decided to double their time in worship that day? Probably not a common occurrence! But in this instance, the people were so grateful to God for what He was doing in them that they chose to stay an extra seven days, putting aside their daily lives and routines.

Have you ever been so lost in worship that you wanted to remain longer than the allotted time? If so, describe the experience briefly:

Sometimes in worship music lifts me to a place where I want to linger in the presence of God. I don't care how many times we've sung the same words; I just want to keep singing! In those moments, I feel God's nearness and assurance that there is nothing on this earth better than the love of God.

When we give ourselves in true worship, we lose ourselves and our agendas.

6. True worship involves both tradition and innovation.

A careful reading of our passage from 2 Chronicles 30 reveals that there were several details unique to this particular Passover celebration. First, it was held in a different month than usual because the priests did not feel ready to begin the celebration at the traditional time (vv. 2-3). Second, it lasted longer than usual—fourteen days, rather than seven—as we've just discussed. And third, it involved a king interceding before God, almost like a priest, for the people. But the marks of the traditional Passover were there too: the sacrifice of a lamb, a meal recalling the steps God's people took to leave Egypt, and all the traditional prayers and celebrations God's people had observed years before.

It was important for God's people to keep the most sacred parts of the tradition while at the same time acknowledging the things that would be unique in the time of this particular Passover. You might say that their celebration involved both tradition and innovation. Likewise, it is important for us to take both of these things into account when we worship today. The essentials are given to us in Scripture—prayers, praise, offerings, teaching, and expressions of encouragement to one another. But the nonessentials (sadly, the things churches argue most about) are open for innovation based on the community's make-up, the time in history, and the relevance of the particular aspect of worship. We have to remember that true worship holds together thousands of years of tradition as well as modern expressions of love for God.

What has stayed the same about worship over the years in your experience? (What traditions have continued?)

What has changed? (What innovations have been introduced?)

True worship isn't interrupted when we don't like the song choice or when the service gets changed to a different time to be more welcoming for young families in the area. We practice the traditions of our heritage, but we recognize that we worship God in a new and different context. When we practice true worship, we incorporate both tradition and innovation.

7. True worship is heard and cherished by God.

We've already seen that King Hezekiah cried out to the Lord on behalf of the people, and God heard his prayer (vv. 18-20). As the account comes to a close, we read that the priests and Levites—who themselves had repented of their sins of neglect and had been forgiven—cried out to the Lord as well.

According to verse 27 of today's passage (page 158), what happened when the priests and Levites prayed?

We're told that, like King Hezekiah, their voice was heard. I love the image evoked by the words "their prayer came to his holy dwelling in heaven" (v. 27). Just imagine for a moment their prayer wafting its way into God's presence, being graciously and lovingly received by a loving Father who loves His children.

Friend, God loves to hear our prayers and our worship. It touches His heart when we call out to Him with praise, remembering what He has done for us.

True worship humbles us as we remember how God has loved us and acted on our behalf. It draws us together in unity with those who love God. It brings us healing and joy. When we practice true worship, we touch the heart of the Creator of the universe and remember again that there is no substitute—no counterfeit—that can ever take His place.

> When we practice true worship, we touch the heart of the Creator of the universe and remember again that there is no substitute—no counterfeit—that can ever take His place.

Talk with God

God, I love You. I want to worship You fully with my whole heart and life. Help me to remember all that You have done for me. Help me to remember the redemption story—that You claim each of us as Your own, rescuing us from our sin and making a way for us to be with You forever. Receive my worship even now. Amen.

Act on It

Write an encouraging letter to your pastor. Express your thanks for teaching you who God is and what a life with God means. Be sure to say thank you also for working so hard on Sundays to create an atmosphere of worship that leads you into the presence of God.

Day 5: The Perfect King

Read God's Word

5 Hezekiah trusted in the LORD, the God of Israel. There was no one like him among all the kings of Judah, either before him or after him. 6 He held fast to the LORD and did not stop following him; he kept the commands the LORD had given Moses. 7 And the LORD was with him; he was successful in whatever he undertook. He rebelled against the king of Assyria and did not serve him. 8 From watchtower to fortified city, he defeated the Philistines, as far as Gaza and its territory.

2 Kings 18:5-8

1 In those days Hezekiah became ill and was at the point of death. The prophet Isaiah son of Amoz went to him and said, "This is what the LORD says: Put your house in order, because you are going to die; you will not recover."

2 Hezekiah turned his face to the wall and prayed to the Lord, 3 "Remember, LORD, how I have walked before you faithfully and with wholehearted devotion and have done what is good in your eyes." And Hezekiah wept bitterly.

4 Then the word of the LORD came to Isaiah: 5 "Go and tell Hezekiah, 'This is what the LORD, the God of your father David, says: I have heard your prayer and seen your tears; I will add fifteen years to your life. 6 And I will deliver you and this city from the hand of the king of Assyria. I will defend this city.

7 "'This is the LORD's sign to you that the LORD will do what he has promised: 8 I will make the shadow cast by the sun go back the ten steps it has gone down on the stairway of Ahaz.'" So the sunlight went back the ten steps it had gone down.

Isaiah 38:1-8

¹ At that time Marduk-Baladan son of Baladan king of Babylon sent Hezekiah letters and a gift, because he had heard of his illness and recovery. ² Hezekiah received the envoys gladly and showed them what was in his storehouses—the silver, the gold, the spices, the fine olive oil—his entire armory and everything found among his treasures. There was nothing in his palace or in all his kingdom that Hezekiah did not show them.

³ Then Isaiah the prophet went to King Hezekiah and asked, "What did those men say, and where did they come from?"

"From a distant land," Hezekiah replied. "They came to me from Babylon."

⁴ The prophet asked, "What did they see in your palace?"

"They saw everything in my palace," Hezekiah said. "There is nothing among my treasures that I did not show them."

⁵ Then Isaiah said to Hezekiah, "Hear the word of the LORD Almighty: ⁶ The time will surely come when everything in your palace, and all that your predecessors have stored up until this day, will be carried off to Babylon. Nothing will be left, says the Lord. ⁷ And some of your descendants, your own flesh and blood who will be born to you, will be taken away, and they will become eunuchs in the palace of the king of Babylon."

⁸ "The word of the LORD you have spoken is good," Hezekiah replied. For he thought, "There will be peace and security in my lifetime."

Isaiah 39:1-8

God testified concerning him: "I have found David son of Jesse, a man after my own heart; he will do everything I want him to do."
Acts 13:22

"Remember, LORD, how I have walked before you faithfully and with wholehearted devotion and have done what is good in your eyes."
Isaiah 38:3

Reflect and Respond

After a long line of corrupt kings, Hezekiah comes on the scene and leads with his heart for God. He isn't the self-serving, power-mongering king characteristic of years past. Instead, Hezekiah is described as the greatest king in generations, possibly the king most unreservedly given to the worship of God since King David himself. "He did what was right in the eyes of the LORD, just as his father David had done" (2 Kings 18:3). Hezekiah and David are similarly described in Scripture in terms of their "heart" for God. Like the famous worship song, Hezekiah really did bring his people back to the heart of worship when they had spent so many long years estranged from God.

Read Acts 13:22 and Isaiah 38:3 in the margin. What similarities do you find between David and Hezekiah in these verses?

Both of these great leaders belonged wholeheartedly to God. And yet they were still human. They still made mistakes. They still struggled with pride. But even after their struggles, the direction of their hearts was always rerouted to follow God again.

How would you describe what it means to belong to God wholeheartedly? What might this look like in *your* life?

We hear Hezekiah's claim to wholehearted love for God in his cry for healing when he becomes gravely ill. Afraid for his life, he calls out to God for healing.

Review Isaiah 38:3 (page 165), and and rewrite Hezekiah's prayer in your own words:

In his book *Called to Be Holy*, John Oswalt recounts the great acts of Hezekiah and his desire for God to hear him in his hour of need:

> Hezekiah not only replicated the works of his more faithful ancestors, he went beyond them. Unlike Asa and Jehoshaphat, he destroyed the high places and brought about the kind of centralization of worship which had been envisioned in the Torah. Second Chronicles also tells about refurbishing the Temple and the reorganization of the priests. Thus it comes as no surprise when we hear Hezekiah, in a moment of personal crisis, having been told his death is imminent, cry out, "Remember O Lord how I have walked before you in true faithfulness and with a perfect heart, and have done what is good in your eyes" (2 K 20:3). He had indeed lived a life of manifest obedience flowing out of a life center that was wholly given over to God. And God seems to confirm the truth of that claim in his response of giving Hezekiah a reprieve of another 15 years.[8]

God promises not only to heal Hezekiah but also to protect Hezekiah's people from Assyria, a nation that has been bullying and threatening the people of Judah throughout Hezekiah's reign. In 2 Kings 18, we see Assyria's king taunting the people with these words after claiming that Assyria will conquer them:

> *"Do not listen to Hezekiah, for he is misleading you when he says, 'The LORD will deliver us.' Has the god of any nation ever delivered his land from the hand of the king of Assyria? Where are the gods of Hamath and Arpad? Where are the gods of Sepharvaim, Hena and Ivvah? Have they rescued Samaria from my*

hand? Who of all the gods of these countries has been able to save his land from me? How then can the LORD *deliver Jerusalem from my hand?"*

2 Kings 18:32-35

Here we find again the theme of idol worship versus worship of our true and powerful God. The king of Assyria underestimates the God of Hezekiah, because every other god he has come up against has been false. Remember that God's people are divided into two kingdoms, and that the kingdom of Israel has had only bad kings and has worshiped idols since the division of the kingdoms. It's no wonder the Assyrian king would try to dissuade them from following Hezekiah; they are certainly a people prone to deception. To be sure, he would love to take over the kingdom of Israel, which we'll see as we continue in the story.

When Hezekiah gets well, word of his supernatural healing spreads to other nations. The son of the king of Babylon sends representatives to deliver letters and gifts to Hezekiah—get-well gifts from a king to a king! And here's where we get the sense that Hezekiah isn't, after all, the perfect king. When the envoys from Babylon arrive, Hezekiah does more than show them around.

Reread Isaiah 39:2 (page 166). What does Hezekiah show them? Be specific.

Hezekiah doesn't just show them some of his riches; he shows them *everything*: "the silver, the gold, the spices, the fine olive oil—his entire armory and everything found among his treasures. There was nothing in his palace or in all his kingdom that Hezekiah did not show them" (Isaiah 39:2).

When they leave, it is the prophet Isaiah who recognizes that this was not a wise move. He comes in like the friend who sees what's going on when your judgment is clouded. (Do you have a friend like this, someone who has a pulse on the situation when you fail to see it?) Another king has seen the riches of the kingdom, and Isaiah knows it is only a matter of time before that king desires to possess them. Hezekiah is so proud of what he has that it causes him to be foolish with national security and put his people at risk. After so much emphasis on Hezekiah's great leadership, we get this picture of a man who was so proud of his kingdom that he wanted to show it off, completely disregarding the consequences of allowing another king to know all the secret treasures of his kingdom. Isaiah speaks into Hezekiah's carelessness a word of doom. He might as well have said to Hezekiah, "Well, you just gave away your kingdom, man—not the best choice ever!"

Instead of the kingdom falling right away, though, Isaiah tells Hezekiah that the kingdom will remain his until the next generation, when it will be taken away. Hezekiah's response is astoundingly short-sighted.

Look back at Isaiah 39:8 (page 166), and write Hezekiah's response in your own words:

Here's my paraphrase: "Thank goodness! At least there will be peace as long as I'm alive!" Hezekiah knows there will be peace and security in his lifetime, so he doesn't worry much about what will happen in the generations to come. Talk about short-sighted leadership! A good leader thinks about much more than his or her own comfort and security. Yet how often we observe leaders being short-sighted in their decisions or actions, knowing that although the ramifications of their choices won't be hidden for long, at least it will be the next generation who will have to deal with them.

If we're honest, we must admit that we're often guilty of the same kind of short-sighted choices. If a decision doesn't have an immediate impact on our lives, then we often disregard its importance. This makes me think of living in the age of social media. We're often quick to post words, opinions, and pictures as if this public declaration has no impact on future relationships or plans. Yet we know that with every post we are creating a virtual scrapbook or digital thumbprint that testifies to our character, values, and integrity. It's a short-sided view.

Well, the next generation saw the words of Isaiah come true.

Read 2 Chronicles 33:9-11. Was Hezekiah's son Manassah a good king? What happened to the people and King Manassah as a result?

He wasn't only captured and thrown in a dungeon; they put a ring in his nose and shackles on his feet! He was no longer a powerful king but a humiliated slave. Here Manassah is experiencing the fulfillment of what the prophet Isaiah had told Hezekiah would happen. Mercifully, Manassah cries out in distress to God.

Read 2 Chronicles 33:12-13. How did Manassah approach God, and what was God's response?

I love that it says Manassah "humbled himself greatly" and "the LORD was moved by his entreaty" (vv. 12-13). Once again we see that God is moved by our sincere humility and repentance. God not only listened; He mercifully brought Manassah back to his kingdom. And we're told that as a result, "Manasseh knew that the LORD is God" (v. 13).

When have you experienced or witnessed the mercy of God, leaving you in awe of who God is?

This brings us to a critical point in our study today. The leaders of God's people—even those who were wholeheartedly His—were imperfect leaders at best. Hezekiah was known as the best king in generations, but his foolhearted pride caused him to show the secrets of the kingdom to the enemy. When he was told of the consequences, he didn't even think beyond his own security and comfort. Despite all of the good that he did, he was far from perfect.

In all of these stories from First and Second Kings we are studying, there are good kings and there are bad kings; but one truth surfaces again and again, and it is this: there is no perfect king among them.

God's people would continue to long for a perfect King, the One about whom the prophet Isaiah spoke these beautiful words:

> *For to us a child is born,*
> *to us a son is given,*
> *and the government will be on his shoulders.*
> *And he will be called*
> *Wonderful Counselor, Mighty God,*
> *Everlasting Father, Prince of Peace.*
> *Of the greatness of his government and peace*
> *there will be no end.*
> *He will reign on David's throne*
> *and over his kingdom,*
> *establishing and upholding it*
> *with justice and righteousness*
> *from that time on and forever.*
>
> Isaiah 9:6-7

This is the kind of ruler God's people waited for patiently for centuries, the one King who would not disappoint, who would not rule in His best interests but would govern with justice and righteousness and peace.

When our leaders are strong and good, we are grateful. But we would do well not to expect perfection from them. After all, they are human. The only One who belongs on the throne of our hearts is the King who will never disappoint and never fail. He alone is the perfect King, and He is worthy of our worship.

Talk with God

Lord, I ask that our leaders would seek Your heart. Help me too, Lord, in any areas where I might have leadership to lead by seeking Your will, Your strength, and Your wisdom in all things. Amen.

Act on It

Write a psalm of praise to the only perfect King who governs with justice and righteousness and peace. As you write, invite Him to sit on the throne of your heart and give Him your worship.

Week 5
Video Viewer Guide

"Why have you brought us up out of Egypt to die in the wilderness? For there is no food and no water, and we ___detest___ this miserable food."

Numbers 21:5 NRSV

*Then the L*ORD *sent poisonous serpents among the people, and they bit the people, so that many Israelites died. The people came to Moses and said, "We have sinned by speaking against the L*ORD *and against you; pray to the L*ORD *to take away the serpents from us." So Moses prayed for the people. And the L*ORD *said to Moses, "Make a poisonous ___serpent___, and set it on a pole; and everyone who is bitten shall ___look___ at it and live." So Moses made a serpent of bronze, and put it upon a pole; and whenever a serpent bit someone, that person would look at the serpent of bronze and live.*

Numbers 21:6-9 NRSV

And as Moses lifted up the serpent in the wilderness, even so must the ___Son___ of ___Man___ be lifted up, that whoever believes in Him should not perish but have eternal life.

John 3:14-15 NKJV

Jesus' death at the hand of sinners is somehow the ___antivenom___ for sin.

In the third year of Hoshea son of Elah king of Israel, Hezekiah son of Ahaz king of Judah began to reign. He was twenty-five years old when he became king, and he reigned in Jerusalem twenty-nine years. His mother's name was Abijah daughter of Zechariah. He did what was __right__ *in the eyes of the LORD, just as his father David had done. He* __removed__ *the high places, smashed the sacred stones and cut down the Asherah poles.*

2 Kings 18:1-4a NIV

Worshiping God alone means __identifying__ and __turning away__ from the things we had given our hearts to in the past.

He broke into pieces the bronze snake Moses had made, for up to that time the Israelites had been burning __incense__ *to it. (It was called Nehushtan.)*

2 Kings 18:4b NIV

Anything that __fills__ our __thoughts__ more than God does—especially if those thoughts are filled with anxiety and worry—that's usually something that has become an idol for us.

The __gifts__ that we hold in our hands can become our __idols__ so easily.

Worship of God—the practice of shifting our focus from the __inward__ to __upward__.

Week 6
Josiah
Set Apart by Discovering God's Word

Have you ever heard the song "The Word" by Sara Groves? If not, I encourage you to listen to it online. The song talks about our pursuit of anything and everything in order to get to know God's Word better—devotionals, books, mountain top experiences—when all the while the Bible sits right there on the shelf, just waiting to be opened.

It's true, isn't it? Instead of looking to the Scriptures, we often spend our time looking for resources *about* the Scriptures. We seek the Bible scholars and experts to tell us about the Bible instead of diving in and inviting God to speak to us through His Word. Don't get me wrong; there's nothing wrong with looking to those more qualified than us to study the Scriptures. Bible commentaries, devotionals, Bible studies, and other helpful resources can help us understand the Scriptures and what they mean for our lives, but they should never become a *replacement* or *substitute* for the Bible itself.

The spiritual practice of Scripture reading cultivates a passion for discovering the treasures found within the pages of the Bible. As you explore God's love letter written to you and discover the promises, encouragement, hope, and guidance that are there for you on every page, you will want to read it more and more. And as you regularly choose to meet God in His Word, inviting the Holy Spirit to speak to you, you will develop the habit of looking to the Scriptures first, before reaching for another book written about them.

This week I challenge you to make the Bible your go-to book. What I mean by that is to seek God through His Word first without depending on a guide. Of course, I don't mean that I want you to quit this Bible study before we get to the end! What I mean is that I want you to spend at least five minutes each day reading God's Word before opening this study or another book. Of, if you want to open this book and read and meditate on the Scripture passage found at the beginning of the daily reading, that's okay too. The idea is to focus on God's Word alone for five minutes. Just *soak* in the Scripture before moving on to the day's lesson—or before opening any other devotional book or study aid. As you read and reflect on Scripture in this way, invite God to speak to you. He will!

Day 1: Recovering the Story

Read God's Word

¹ Josiah was eight years old when he became king, and he reigned in Jerusalem thirty-one years. His mother's name was Jedidah daughter of Adaiah; she was from Bozkath. ² He did what was right in the eyes of the LORD and followed completely the ways of his father David, not turning aside to the right or to the left.

³ In the eighteenth year of his reign, King Josiah sent the secretary, Shaphan son of Azaliah, the son of Meshullam, to the temple of the LORD. He said: ⁴ "Go up to Hilkiah the high priest and have him get ready the money that has been brought into the temple of the LORD, which the doorkeepers have collected from the people. ⁵ Have them entrust it to the men appointed to supervise the work on the temple. And have these men pay the workers who repair the temple of the LORD— ⁶ the carpenters, the builders and the masons. Also have them purchase timber and dressed stone to repair the temple. ⁷ But they need not account for the money entrusted to them, because they are honest in their dealings."

⁸ Hilkiah the high priest said to Shaphan the secretary, "I have found the Book of the Law in the temple of the LORD." He gave it to Shaphan, who read it. ⁹ Then Shaphan the secretary went to the king and reported to him: "Your officials have paid out the money that was in the temple of the LORD and have entrusted it to the workers and supervisors at the temple." ¹⁰ Then Shaphan the secretary informed the king, "Hilkiah the priest has given me a book." And Shaphan read from it in the presence of the king.

¹¹ When the king heard the words of the Book of the Law, he tore his robes. ¹² He gave these orders to Hilkiah the priest, Ahikam son of Shaphan, Akbor son of Micaiah, Shaphan the secretary and Asaiah the king's attendant: ¹³ "Go and inquire of the LORD for me and for the people and for all Judah about what is written in this book that has been found. Great is the LORD's anger that burns against us because those who have gone before us have not obeyed the words of this book; they have not acted in accordance with all that is written there concerning us."

2 Kings 22:1-13

Reflect and Respond

When I was in my early twenties, both of my paternal grandparents passed away in the same year. My grandmother had been fighting terminal cancer for some time when my grandfather became ill with pneumonia and unexpectedly died first. Many of us wondered if he went knowing that he didn't really want

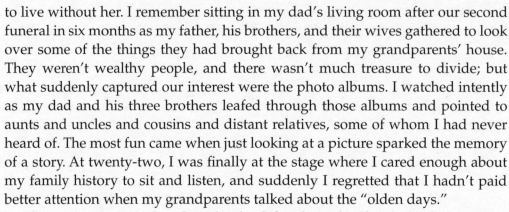

to live without her. I remember sitting in my dad's living room after our second funeral in six months as my father, his brothers, and their wives gathered to look over some of the things they had brought back from my grandparents' house. They weren't wealthy people, and there wasn't much treasure to divide; but what suddenly captured our interest were the photo albums. I watched intently as my dad and his three brothers leafed through those albums and pointed to aunts and uncles and cousins and distant relatives, some of whom I had never heard of. The most fun came when just looking at a picture sparked the memory of a story. At twenty-two, I was finally at the stage where I cared enough about my family history to sit and listen, and suddenly I regretted that I hadn't paid better attention when my grandparents talked about the "olden days."

The stories contained in those books defined our family's past: the struggles of the Depression and the antics of so many brothers and sisters growing up together in dusty West Texas.

What didn't occur to me until years later was that the stories didn't just tell our past but our present and future as well. What had happened in those black and white photos had formed and influenced all of us, even generations later. The lessons my grandparents learned were taught to their boys, who taught them to my cousins and me. Looking into those albums was like discovering a hidden history that had been lurking beneath the surface of my life. For the first time I was paying attention to the stories that helped to write *my* story.

As we will learn today, Josiah made a far deeper discovery, and this discovery transformed him and his people. He was the king who had the dubious distinction of being known as the last good king of Judah, and his discovery is a large part of what earned him that reputation.

After Hezekiah's reign ended, his son Manassah ruled for fifty-five years. Manassah was succeeded by his son Amon, who has one of the worst track records of any king mentioned in the Books of First and Second Kings. Many of the "bad" kings before him were syncretists, meaning that they tried to combine the worship of God and the worship of false gods by bringing idols into the Temple and setting them up as equals to God. But Amon actually wanted nothing at all to do with God. We read in 2 Kings 21, "He abandoned the LORD, the God of his ancestors, and did not walk in the way of the LORD" (v. 22 NRSV). He lasted only two years.

When Amon died, his son Josiah was only eight years old. Josiah had been six when his dad had become king, and suddenly, at the age most of us are taking our first piano lessons or playing on our first community sports team, he was sitting on a throne. He would remain there for thirty-one years, and his reign would have a bigger impact on his kingdom in Judah than most of the kings before him.

God's people had gone through the ups and downs of many rulers—some who built shrines to false idols and some who tore them down. Josiah stood squarely in the "righteous and upstanding" category—one of the few who deserve that distinction. How did he know how to reign? He couldn't follow the example of his father or his grandfather. Perhaps he knew stories about his great-grandfather Hezekiah. Perhaps he had good advisors teaching him God's ways as he grew up in the seat of power.

What we do know is that in the eighteenth year of his reign, Josiah decided to make things right in God's house of worship, the Temple built by his ancestor Solomon, and suddenly he got more than he bargained for.

The Temple had been in disrepair and needed work. After many years of bad kings who had neglected the upkeep of the Temple and had abused the very place that they were supposed to keep holy, defiling it with false worship, a Temple renovation was overdue. Ironically, Hezekiah—the last good king before Josiah—had a lot to do with why the Temple was in such a bad state.

Read 2 Kings 18:15-16 in the margin. What do these verses tell us that Hezekiah did? *he gave all the silver + gold to the King of Assyria*

When Hezekiah felt threatened by the possibility of attack by the Assyrians, he emptied the money in the Temple treasury and tried to buy them off. When that didn't seem to be enough, he then stripped the gold from the doors and doorposts of the temple itself and gave it to the Assyrian king.

Having been a person in the pew and then a leader and pastor in multiple churches over the years, I can see that what happened to the Temple in Josiah's day still happens today in the church. When God's people lose touch with their love for Him and their identity in Him, the church often falls into disrepair in many ways. Like Hezekiah, people may make poor decisions based in fear. Others simply forget that the people of God are called to be set apart and the community of faith is called to be different than any other community on earth. The outcome often is that gossip or conflict or power struggles begin to define God's people more than the fruit of the Spirit: love, joy, peace, patience, kindness, goodness, faithfulness, gentleness, and self-control (Galatians 5:22-23).

Look up the following Scriptures, reading for desired characteristics of the church. List them in the space provided:

Hebrews 10:24-25

Romans 12:10-13

So Hezekiah gave him all the silver that was found in the temple of the Lord and in the treasuries of the royal palace. At this time Hezekiah king of Judah stripped off the gold with which he had covered the doors and doorposts of the temple of the Lord, and gave it to the king of Assyria.
2 Kings 18:15-16

When God's people lose touch with their love for Him and their identity in Him, the church often falls into disrepair in many ways.

Colossians 3:16

Acts 2:42-47

How would you explain how the church is to be different than the world?

When Josiah commits to repair the place where God's people are called to worship, He also is making a commitment to return God's people to

- the culture of worship and community that they have been missing in that place,
- the cleansing or purifying power of the sacrifices and holy days they once celebrated there, and
- the connection they've been missing to the presence of God in the Temple.

Josiah knows that the place where God's people worship is much more than a building needing repair.

Tell what each of these important aspects of the church has meant to you personally:

Culture of worship and community

Cleansing power

Connection to God

Reviving God's people by repairing God's Temple was a good idea, but God knew that it wouldn't be enough for lasting transformation. This brings us to the exciting part of the story!

When the High Priest had received the final instructions about Temple repair from Josiah's secretary Shapan, he told him some interesting news. The tone of his announcement may seem casual, but his words have earth-shattering significance for the entire nation.

Reread 2 Kings 22:8 (page 175). What did the High Priest say and do?

he found the book of the law & gave it to Shapan

I wonder if this High Priest had recently discovered the book or had been guarding it for a while, waiting for the presence of a king who could be trusted with such treasure. Maybe he even knew about the book when Josiah's father was king but knew better than to show an evil king this great hidden gem. In any case, when Josiah showed himself to be a God-following king by repairing the Temple, it no doubt gained him the trust of the High Priest.

When Shaphan the secretary shares the news with Josiah, his tone is pretty unremarkable. First he tells about the funding for the repair of the Temple, and then, almost as an afterthought, he tells the king about the book: "'Hilkiah the priest has given me a book.' And Shaphan read from it in the presence of the king" (2 Kings 22:10). Josiah's reaction, however, is anything but casual.

Reread 2 Kings 22:11 (page 175). How does Josiah respond?

Josiah tears his clothes and weeps, knowing that the words he is hearing from this book—one that hasn't been read by God's people in generations—mean that he and his people have been utterly and willfully disobedient. If it was not apparent before this moment, the words of this book make it clear that God's people are far from being the holy, set-apart people God intends them to be.

Can you recall a moment when you suddenly became aware of how far you were from God's desires for you? If so, describe it briefly.

Josiah heard the story of God's people as if for the first time. It changed what he thought about how his people were supposed to be, and it changed how he ruled. Because he took that moment to heart, the kingdom would experience one of the greatest revivals recorded—a return to being God's people not only in name but also in actions.

The Scriptures can awaken us not only to the need to repent but also to a feeling, a desire, or even a longing that we hadn't yet put words to. I can remember many times when a word from Scripture not only named for me what I was going through but also spoke into my situation and revealed God's promises to me. When we've been away from God's Word for a time, reading Scripture can feel like an awakening or a new beginning.

Recall the moment you described above. How did you respond to your realization? How did your thoughts and actions change?

Extra Insight
Josiah was aided by the prophet Jeremiah in spreading the knowledge and worship of God throughout the kingdom. Jeremiah also wrote a funeral lament or song for Josiah upon his death.[1]

The story we are studying this week is about a people who don't know the truth behind the history of their people, the truth about what they've been through and about how they can trust God because of how far He has brought them. Josiah's people had lost their identity in the story of God.

There's some irony in this strange tale and how it relates to us today. One of the occupational hazards of being a preacher is that when we study the Bible, we think the things that interest us surely will interest everyone else. So naturally while I was working my way through this story, I tried to talk to a few people about Josiah's experience and the rediscovery of the buried treasure that was God's Word hidden away in the Temple. Although the people I talked to were mostly seasoned churchgoers and faithful Sunday school attendees, most of them had blank stares when I mentioned Josiah and the hidden book. When I asked if they were familiar with the story, they all said that they had never heard a sermon preached or a lesson taught on Josiah's story. In a sense it's as if the story about the Bible being hidden away is itself hidden away from many of God's people today.

I wonder how different we are from Josiah's people. Though our Bibles are not locked behind the doors of a Temple, are we a people who have lost our story? Do we have a firm grasp on the book that God has given us? Perhaps we need to reclaim God's story—in our own lives, our families, and the church.

In what ways do you think we are a people who have lost our story?

What are some ways we can reclaim God's story in our lives, our families, and the church? Brainstorm some ideas below.

During this last week of our study together, you have the opportunity to rediscover your love for God's story. No matter if you have been a devoted Bible reader for decades or if you are rediscovering the habit of digging into God's Word, you are invited to open up the Scriptures and uncover the treasures God has for you there!

Talk with God

Thank You, Lord, for speaking to me personally through Your holy book. Thank You for the gift of getting to know You better through Your Word. Help me to fall in love—again or for the first time—with the Scriptures. Amen.

> Though our Bibles are not locked behind the doors of a Temple, are we a people who have lost our story?

Act on It

Set aside a block of time this week to read the Gospel of Mark from beginning to end, as if you are reading a short story or novel. (Allow 1–1 ½ hours.) Or break your reading into three segments of 20–30 minutes each (Mark 1–5, 6–10, and 11–16), and read each segment at a different time. Pay attention to the action, characters, stories, and drama. Imagine yourself there in every scene. What does the message of the Gospel of Mark mean for your life with Jesus today?

Day 2: Working on What Works on Us

Read God's Word

11 *When the king heard the words of the Book of the Law, he tore his robes.* 12 *He gave these orders to Hilkiah the priest, Ahikam son of Shaphan, Akbor son of Micaiah, Shaphan the secretary and Asaiah the king's attendant:* 13 *"Go and inquire of the LORD for me and for the people and for all Judah about what is written in this book that has been found. Great is the LORD's anger that burns against us because those who have gone before us have not obeyed the words of this book; they have not acted in accordance with all that is written there concerning us."*

14 *Hilkiah the priest, Ahikam, Akbor, Shaphan and Asaiah went to speak to the prophet Huldah, who was the wife of Shallum son of Tikvah, the son of Harhas, keeper of the wardrobe. She lived in Jerusalem, in the New Quarter.*

15 *She said to them, "This is what the LORD, the God of Israel, says: Tell the man who sent you to me,* 16 *'This is what the LORD says: I am going to bring disaster on this place and its people, according to everything written in the book the king of Judah has read.* 17 *Because they have forsaken me and burned incense to other gods and aroused my anger by all the idols their hands have made, my anger will burn against this place and will not be quenched.'* 18 *Tell the king of Judah, who sent you to inquire of the LORD, 'This is what the LORD, the God of Israel, says concerning the words you heard:* 19 *Because your heart was responsive and you humbled yourself before the LORD when you heard what I have spoken against this place and its people—that they would become a curse and be laid waste—and because you tore your robes and wept in my presence, I also have heard you, declares the LORD.* 20 *Therefore I will gather you to your ancestors, and you will be buried in peace. Your eyes will not see all the disaster I am going to bring on this place.'"*

So they took her answer back to the king.

2 Kings 22:11-20

181

Reflect and Respond

I looked up from my desk to see one of our church members standing in the door of my office. His face was red with rage. "That man does *not* belong in our church!" he spat out. "They should never have hired him." As he threw himself down into the chair on the other side of my desk, he slammed his Bible on my desk. "God's Word says 'Thou shalt not steal.' What are people going to think when they walk into our church and see a thief, a liar, and a criminal with our church's logo on his uniform pocket?"

I knew immediately who he was talking about. Several weeks before, our church secretary had discovered that a man was coming into the church early in the morning each day to wash up in one of the bathrooms at the very back of the building. Further observation told us that he was sleeping in his car in the back parking lot each night. One of the other pastors invited him to lunch and learned his story. He had a criminal record for theft and had done time in prison. When he was released, he moved in with a girlfriend, but his criminal record made it almost impossible to get a job. She eventually threw him out, and here he was, literally, on the church's doorstep.

The church trustees and personnel committee put their heads together and decided they would help him get on his feet by giving him a job as a night custodian and giving him enough advanced pay to put down a deposit on an efficiency apartment nearby. One of the men in the church even began talking to him about a day-job in his construction business. But not everyone agreed with the decision. E-mails circulated and phone calls were made denouncing the decision.

The detractors were right that this man had sinned and had been caught. He had lived a life far beneath the gospel. He deserved every label they gave him. They could easily point to chapter and verse in God's Word and tell exactly how he had violated God's rules. But as the man in my office sat enraged across from me, tapping his finger on his Bible, I wondered if he had stopped to ask God to help guide his own attitudes and actions in this situation.

Finding truth in God's Word is an easy task. Open to any page, close your eyes, and let your finger fall on any verse, and there you have God's truth revealed to us. But letting that truth work its way into our hearts and shine a spotlight on our own actions and attitudes is a much harder assignment.

Have you ever found yourself or witnessed someone else using Scripture to condemn or look down on the actions of someone? If so, write about it briefly.

Extra Insight
"Second Kings does not pick up [Josiah's] story until eighteen years into [his] reign. However, 2 Chronicles 34:3 lets us know that Josiah became familiar with Yahweh, the God of David, when he was sixteen years old, and when he was twenty he began to purge the nation of foreign gods."[2]

When has God's Word shone a spotlight on your own actions or attitudes? Describe a time when you were convicted about something in your life by what you read in Scripture.

When Josiah sends his secretary to check on the renovations in the Temple, he can't possibly expect the news he receives in return. The book of the law that has been lost and forgotten, hidden away in the recesses of the Temple for years, has been discovered, and now Josiah is hearing the ancient words read aloud. His response is impassioned and immediate. He tears his robes in grief and immediately begins to find out what he can do to right the devastating wrongs revealed by that book. Take note that Josiah takes the words he hears personally. Josiah doesn't use the words he hears to point a finger at others, to deflect responsibility, or to judge the actions of past kings or people.

Reread 2 Kings 22:13 below, and circle the words *me* and *us*.

> *Go and inquire of the LORD for me and for the people and for all Judah about what is written in this book that has been found. Great is the LORD's anger that burns against us because those who have gone before us have not obeyed the words of this book; they have not acted in accordance with all that is written there concerning us.*
>
> 2 Kings 22:13

Though Josiah is honest in saying that the reason they are in such deep trouble is the fault of the people in the past who sinned against God, the personal pronouns *me* and *us* show his sense of ownership and personal responsibility for righting the wrongs that have been committed.

Josiah immediately seeks the wise counsel of a female prophet named Huldah. Her response confirms his fears that the wrongful actions of his people for generations have deeply offended God. There will be consequences.

Review 2 Kings 22:15-20 (page 181) and answer these questions:

What will happen to the people of Judah and why? (vv. 15-17)

What is God's promise to Josiah? (v. 20)

Why does God make this promise? What has God noticed about Josiah's heart? (v. 19)

Extra Insight
"As a prophetess in the reign of King Josiah, [Hulda] could be found sitting in the central part of the city ready to receive and counsel any who wished to inquire of Jehovah.... Huldah's standing and reputation are attested to in that she was consulted, rather than Jeremiah, when the lost book of the law was found, and that her word was accepted by all as a divinely revealed one."[3]

183

The discovery of the Word of God was a very personal moment for Josiah. It should be for us, too. Since you're part of a Bible study (and you've made it to the last week!), I know you have an earnest desire to know more of God's Word. When we engage in Bible study, it pleases God! He loved us enough to go to the trouble of revealing Himself to us in Scripture, and He is honored when we spend time and energy learning more about Him through the study of the Bible.

How can we make sure that we, like Josiah, are taking God's Word personally, letting it work its way into the innermost places that need God's attention for conviction and healing? Write a few thoughts below:

In his book *Shaped by the Word: The Power of Scripture in Spiritual Formation*, Robert Mulholland distinguishes between two different types of reading Scripture: informational reading and formational reading. Both are good and necessary, since we need to learn the information in the Bible in order to let it form us. But formational reading is a way of letting Scripture work on our hearts, not just live as facts and verses in our heads. I'd like to summarize some of the differences between these two methods of reading Scripture, which Mulholland discusses in his book.[4]

First, there is the difference of what I will call volume versus value. With informational reading, you might seek to read as much of the Bible as possible as quickly as possible. Perhaps you read a passage of Scripture in record time and at the end realize you haven't taken in as much of what you read as you would like, but still you have completed the reading or assignment. Formational reading, on the other hand, is not concerned with volume. You may find yourself reading one passage, one sentence, or even one word over and over again as you consider its meaning and application. You may not move forward as quickly but instead go deeper and deeper into the text.

A second difference has to do with mastering the text versus allowing it to master us. With informational reading, "we seek to master the text. We seek to grasp it, to get our minds around it, to bring it under our control."[5] Our control means that once we understand a text, once we find an interpretation we agree with, we stick to that and don't explore other possibilities. When we encounter another interpretation or reading of that text, we use our own gathered information to argue against it. In contrast, formational reading does not seek to master the text but allows the text to master us. Mulholland explains, "We come to the text with an openness to hear, to receive, to respond, to be a servant of the Word rather than a master of the text."[6]

Finally, there is what might be described as an outside versus inside difference. Informational reading causes us to distance ourselves, standing on the outside and looking in with a problem-solving approach. We read in order to find out something that will work for us, similar to using a manual for a piece of equipment. But with formational reading, we are on the inside, so to speak, inviting the text to work in us and shape us. Mulholland writes, "Instead of being an object to control and manipulate for our own insight and purpose—the text becomes the subject of the reading relationship, we are the object shaped by the text."[7] Instead of a problem to solve, the text becomes a source for us to connect with the Mystery that is God.

When and how do you use an informational approach to reading Scripture? (Think volume, control/comprehension, and problem-solving.)

When and how do you use a formational approach to reading Scripture? (Think value or meaning, openness to hear and receive, and source for connection.)

In what ways is God's Word currently working within you to form who you are becoming?

Opening ourselves to see the text as something that works within us rather than something we work on doesn't come naturally to most of us. It's often a change of approach that happens gradually, a discipline we have to develop. A wise older friend once said to me, "When I read something that stands at odds between me and the Bible, I don't ask *What's wrong with the Bible?* but *What's wrong with me?*"

Being set apart by discovering God's Word means inviting God to use the Scriptures to work in us, speak into our lives, and shape us into who God wants us to be. That's the spiritual practice part—intentionally giving ourselves to being formed by God. Hebrews 4:12 is an often-quoted passage about the pointed effect that Scripture can have in making us look closely at our own lives.

Look up Hebrews 4:12 and write it below: *For the word of God is alive and powerful. It is sharper than the sharpest two-edged sword, cutting between soul & spirit, between joint and marrow. It exposes our innermost thoughts and desires.*

The next verse takes the sword of God's Word to an even more intimate place when it tells us, "Nothing in all creation is hidden from God's sight.

Everything is uncovered and laid bare before the eyes of him to whom we must give account" (Hebrews 4:13).

The Greek word used for "laid bare" here is one that would have been used by gladiators in the ring. When the fight ended, the defeated gladiator would have been laid across the knee of the victor with his throat exposed—laid bare—for the death blow of the knife. In association with the animal sacrifices made in the Temple, the phrase "laid bare" described the position of the sacrifice on the altar—its head pulled back and its throat exposed for the sacrificial knife.

This is our position before the Word of God. As Mulholland describes it, it is "a position of total, absolute, unconditional vulnerability."[8]

Does this make you gulp as you think of the things in your life that are "laid bare" to a God before whom nothing is hidden? Keep reading! The very next sentences in the Book of Hebrews talk about Jesus as our "great high priest" who has faced every temptation we face, who stood in our place, and who empathizes with our human condition (Hebrews 4:14-15).

> *Let us then approach God's throne of grace with confidence, so that we may receive mercy and find grace to help us in our time of need.*
> *Hebrews 4:16*

Read Hebrews 4:16 in the margin. What are we invited to do?

Because of His great love for us, we are invited not to run away in fear but to come closer! Mercy. Grace. Help in our time of need. That's what we find in God's Word. That's what Josiah found there, too. Instead of just working to understand the text that had been discovered, Josiah was humble enough to let the text work on him.

The point of Bible study is not to get through the Bible. It's to let the Bible get through you. My prayer is that you will find yourself reading more and more "formationally" as you approach God's Word with confidence, certain of the grace, mercy, and help in time of need that you are sure to find.

> The point of Bible study is not to get through the Bible. It's to let the Bible get through you.

Talk with God

Lord, I want the Bible to get through me, shaping me and forming me into who You want me to be. Help me to read Your Word with the expectation that it will work within me, forming and fashioning me according to Your will for me. Amen.

Act on It

Memorize a favorite psalm or another passage of Scripture this week. Let the words get through you and begin to work within you. Remember that the task is not simply to conquer memorization but to let the words speak into your life.

Day 3: I Love Your Law

[1] Josiah was eight years old when he became king, and he reigned in Jerusalem thirty-one years. [2] He did what was right in the eyes of the LORD and followed the ways of his father David, not turning aside to the right or to the left. . . .

[8] In the eighteenth year of Josiah's reign, to purify the land and the temple, he sent Shaphan son of Azaliah and Maaseiah the ruler of the city, with Joah son of Joahaz, the recorder, to repair the temple of the LORD his God.

[9] They went to Hilkiah the high priest and gave him the money that had been brought into the temple of God, which the Levites who were the gatekeepers had collected from the people of Manasseh, Ephraim and the entire remnant of Israel and from all the people of Judah and Benjamin and the inhabitants of Jerusalem. [10] Then they entrusted it to the men appointed to supervise the work on the LORD's temple. These men paid the workers who repaired and restored the temple. . . .

[14] While they were bringing out the money that had been taken into the temple of the Lord, Hilkiah the priest found the Book of the Law of the LORD that had been given through Moses. [15] Hilkiah said to Shaphan the secretary, "I have found the Book of the Law in the temple of the LORD." He gave it to Shaphan.

[16] Then Shaphan took the book to the king and reported to him: "Your officials are doing everything that has been committed to them. [17] They have paid out the money that was in the temple of the LORD and have entrusted it to the supervisors and workers." [18] Then Shaphan the secretary informed the king, "Hilkiah the priest has given me a book." And Shaphan read from it in the presence of the king.

[19] When the king heard the words of the Law, he tore his robes. [20] He gave these orders to Hilkiah, Ahikam son of Shaphan, Abdon son of Micah, Shaphan the secretary and Asaiah the king's attendant: [21] "Go and inquire of the LORD for me and for the remnant in Israel and Judah about what is written in this book that has been found. Great is the LORD's anger that is poured out on us because those who have gone before us have not kept the word of the LORD; they have not acted in accordance with all that is written in this book."

2 Chronicles 34:1-2; 8-10; 14-21

Reflect and Respond

Author and pastor Eugene Peterson tells a story about going to an Orthodox Jewish synagogue in the region of Galilee early one morning while visiting there. Even though it was not too long after sunrise, a group of about fifteen boys ranging in age from twelve to seventeen were gathered, reading the Bible with several older men.

The boys were reading from a large scroll, handling it reverently and proudly. As one of them read, Peterson made this astounding realization:

> He only seemed to read for he had memorized it, the entire Torah, the first five books of the Bible. We later learned that all the boys had memorized it in its entirety—knew it by heart from beginning to end. And they were so unselfconscious about what they were doing, so boyish, so obviously comfortable and joyful in what they were doing.[9]

The people of God have always had a love affair with His Word, given to us as a gift. But we didn't initiate that love affair. As we read in First John, "We love because He first loved us" (4:19).

God is not a distant deity, watching over us with indifference or disdain. He cares enough to come near to us in every way possible. He has been intimately involved with His creation from the beginning. Instead of leaving us to wonder if He is there or if He cares enough about us to pay attention or have an opinion about our everyday lives, He gave us His Word to help us know His heart.

Today's reading is from 2 Chronicles, but it reflects the same story we've been reading this week in 2 Kings 22-23, Josiah's discovery of the lost Word of God in the Temple. The portion of Scripture that was discovered during Josiah's reign is thought to have been a part of the book of Deuteronomy. Let's consider three reasons that scholars recognize the book of Deuteronomy here.

1. Curses for wrongful actions. Josiah was already taking measures of reform around the kingdom prior to the discovery of the lost Word of God (see 2 Chronicles 34:1-7 for a more detailed account of the many years these reforms took place). Even so, the reading of the Word of God caused him deep distress. What did he read there that made him tear his clothes and launch even greater reform? Chapters 27 and 28 in the Book of Deuteronomy contain a "curse" section that would have directly applied to the wrongful actions of God's people and caused Josiah deep concern as a leader.

Read Deuteronomy 27:14-16. List two of the things people do that bring curses on them.

Why do you think Josiah was worried when he heard this?

God is not a distant deity, watching over us with indifference or disdain. He cares enough to come near to us in every way possible.

2. Renewal of covenant. Josiah's first response, upon the book's discovery, was to hold a ceremony of the renewal of the covenant. Deuteronomy gives an account of renewal of covenant in Chapter 29.

Read Deuteronomy 29:12-13. Why does God have Moses and the people renew the covenant?

The covenant God made with His people had never been nullified, but it had been neglected and hidden by years of disobedience. Yet God gave a way to renew the covenant, to begin again.

3. Celebration of Passover. After renewing the covenant, Josiah's next response was to gather the people to celebrate Passover, much like Hezekiah did. Deuteronomy is explicit in its instructions for God's people to celebrate Passover.

Read Deuteronomy 16:1-8. What are some of the instructions about Passover given in these verses?

What event in the life of God's people is this supposed to help them remember?

When we read the words of Deuteronomy, we are reading the words that were read to Josiah, fresh from their discovery in the Temple! We are reading the words memorized and recited by young Jewish boys for generations. These are precious words, words of life given to us by a God who loves us and wants us to know Him and the ways He has created for us to flourish in this life.

Josiah clearly takes the words he hears to heart. First they convict him. He sees how differently the people are living from what is outlined in Scripture. Then they cause him to act. He does everything in his power to move himself and his people toward full obedience to God's Word.

Recall a time when you were convicted by what you read in the Bible. How did it move you to greater obedience?

Notice that Josiah doesn't wallow in guilt or despair. He knows immediately that God will want Him to act in obedience and will honor the people's obedience with blessings, not curses.

Extra Insight
Though generations before the people would have known how to prepare the Passover by heart because they had done it so many times, Josiah and his people would have had to scour the Scriptures like recipe books to make sure they did everything just right. One source notes that "references to following Levitical procedures established by David or Solomon . . . reflect Josiah's desire to do everything in a God-pleasing manner."[10]

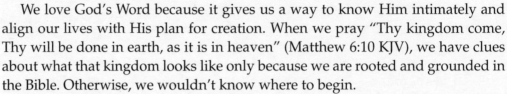

We love God's Word because it gives us a way to know Him intimately and align our lives with His plan for creation. When we pray "Thy kingdom come, Thy will be done in earth, as it is in heaven" (Matthew 6:10 KJV), we have clues about what that kingdom looks like only because we are rooted and grounded in the Bible. Otherwise, we wouldn't know where to begin.

Josiah's strong reaction to the discovery of Scripture may seem obvious to us. After all, what else would a king do if given a segment of Holy Scripture, right? Surely any king in his position would do the same. Actually, in the very next generation, Josiah's son Jehoiakim is offered to us as a contrasting figure. While Josiah restored the Word to its place of public prominence and thus restored God's people to right relationship with Him, Jehoiakim destroys the Word.

Here's how it happens. The prophet Jeremiah begins to write down the prophecies God is giving him with the help of his scribe Baruch. God instructs him to write with the hope that the people will hear the words and turn from their wicked ways to God and receive forgiveness. Once his scroll is completed—now the Book of Jeremiah in the Old Testament—Jeremiah asks Baruch to take it to the Temple and read it aloud. While Baruch is reading it, a man named Micaiah overhears him. This man is the grandson of Shaphan, the one who read the newly discovered book to Josiah! The story seems almost set up for the same kind of act of renewal that happened a generation before. Micaiah reports the reading to the Temple officials, and they tell him:

> *"Bring the scroll from which you have read to the people and come." So Baruch son of Neriah went to them with the scroll in his hand. They said to him, "Sit down, please, and read it to us."*
>
> *. . .*
>
> *So Baruch read it to them. When they heard all these words, they looked at each other in fear and said to Baruch, "We must report all these words to the king." Then they asked Baruch, "Tell us, how did you come to write all this? Did Jeremiah dictate it?"*
>
> *. . .*
>
> *"Yes," Baruch replied, "he dictated all these words to me, and I wrote them in ink on the scroll."*
>
> *. . .*
>
> *Then the officials said to Baruch, "You and Jeremiah, go and hide. Don't let anyone know where you are."*
>
> Jeremiah 36:14b-19

Do you see that the officials react in fear? They know in advance that the king, although he is the son of Josiah, is a bad man. They fear for Baruch and Jeremiah's lives and send them into hiding. Then they send for the king. Let's pick up the story in verse 20:

After they put the scroll in the room of Elishama the secretary, they went to the king in the courtyard and reported everything to him. The king sent Jehudi to get the scroll, and Jehudi brought it from the room of Elishama the secretary and read it to the king and all the officials standing beside him. It was the ninth month and the king was sitting in the winter apartment, with a fire burning in the firepot in front of him. Whenever Jehudi had read three or four columns of the scroll, the king cut them off with a scribe's knife and threw them into the firepot, until the entire scroll was burned in the fire. The king and all his attendants who heard all these words showed no fear, nor did they tear their clothes. Even though Elnathan, Delaiah and Gemariah urged the king not to burn the scroll, he would not listen to them. Instead, the king commanded Jerahmeel, a son of the king, Seraiah son of Azriel and Shelemiah son of Abdeel to arrest Baruch the scribe and Jeremiah the prophet. But the LORD had hidden them.

Jeremiah 36:20-26

Can you picture the scene? The scribe is reading from the scroll; the king is reaching over to tear off the words and throw them in the fire. Whereas Josiah tore at his clothes when he heard God's Word read, knowing that his people were in the wrong, Jehoiakim instead tears apart and destroys God's Word.

Though Josiah had a deep respect for the Word of God and did everything he could to follow it, his son Jehoiakim shows disdain for God's Word by his reluctance to either listen to it or follow its teachings. Last week we looked at the way a hunger for power can turn someone away from God. Jehoiakim's heart was more concerned with his power than what the Scriptures might mean for his people.

Psalm 119, the longest Psalm and the longest chapter in the Bible, is dedicated to the love of God's law. With 176 verses, Psalm 119 has more verses than fourteen Old Testament books and seventeen New Testament books! The love we are to have for God's Word is so important that it is the topic of the longest book in God's Word.

Read a few of these verses from Psalm 119, and write their message in your own words. If possible, write as if they are written to you. I've done the first one as an example, inserting my own name.

119:2   **Jessica, you will be happy if you seek God's decrees, if you seek Him with your whole heart.**

119:9-16

119:33-37

119:97-104

When Eugene Peterson encountered the group of young boys reciting the law in their synagogue, they were reciting passages from the first five books, or Torah, which they had memorized in its entirety. The last book of those first five is the book of Deuteronomy, which is believed to be the hidden scroll read by Josiah. Peterson makes this beautiful observation: "They were just boys, but boys who had discovered with delight how the Bible works in them, revealing a living God for their living, these Scriptures being digested within them as they came together every morning."[11]

There are times in my own journey with God that I feel excited about reading His Word. I open it with the attitude of one opening a love letter or a long-lost document that will reveal some exciting treasure. But there also are times when reading seems like more of a duty than a passion. It's then that I pray again for God to renew that love in me, and in time He always does.

God's Word is a treasure written for us. In it, God has hope, instruction, illumination, mercy, grace, and great wisdom for your life. It is a giant love story recorded for us to understand God's great love for you and for me. As you open it today, look for Him to communicate His heart, His message for you, and His blueprint for the Kingdom to come on earth as it is in heaven.

Talk with God

Lord, Your word is beautiful, containing treasures meant to enrich and edify my walk with You. Give me a passion to meet You in the Scriptures. Amen.

Act on It

Take one of the verses from Psalm 119 that you rewrote above, and write it on an index card. Tape it to your bathroom mirror or place it somewhere you will see it often to remind you of your desire to seek God through His Word.

Day 4: Together in the Word

[1] Then the king called together all the elders of Judah and Jerusalem. [2] He went up to the temple of the LORD with the people of Judah, the inhabitants of Jerusalem, the priests and the prophets—all the people from the least to the greatest. He read in their hearing all the words of the Book of the Covenant, which had been found in the temple of the LORD. [3] The king stood by the pillar and renewed the covenant in the presence of the LORD—to follow the LORD and keep his commands, statutes and decrees with all his heart and all his soul, thus

confirming the words of the covenant written in this book. Then all the people pledged themselves to the covenant.

⁴ The king ordered Hilkiah the high priest, the priests next in rank and the doorkeepers to remove from the temple of the LORD all the articles made for Baal and Asherah and all the starry hosts. He burned them outside Jerusalem in the fields of the Kidron Valley and took the ashes to Bethel. ⁵ He did away with the idolatrous priests appointed by the kings of Judah to burn incense on the high places of the towns of Judah and on those around Jerusalem—those who burned incense to Baal, to the sun and moon, to the constellations and to all the starry hosts. ⁶ He took the Asherah pole from the temple of the LORD to the Kidron Valley outside Jerusalem and burned it there. He ground it to powder and scattered the dust over the graves of the common people. ⁷ He also tore down the quarters of the male shrine prostitutes that were in the temple of the LORD, the quarters where women did weaving for Asherah. . . .

²¹ The king gave this order to all the people: "Celebrate the Passover to the LORD your God, as it is written in this Book of the Covenant." ²² Neither in the days of the judges who led Israel nor in the days of the kings of Israel and the kings of Judah had any such Passover been observed. ²³ But in the eighteenth year of King Josiah, this Passover was celebrated to the LORD in Jerusalem.

2 Kings 23:1-7; 21-23

Reflect and Respond

Every Thursday night in the dusty church library hidden behind the church offices, I gathered to lead a group of teenagers in studying the Bible. Because this was a remarkable group of young people, I rejected the curriculum written for teens that I found on our church shelves and instead selected an adult Bible study. I explained to them that this meant they had to approach it with a grown-up commitment: a lot of reading each week, a faithfulness to attend, and a promise to take the Word and one another seriously. While I was stern with my explanation of the requirements to participate, part of me wondered if I was doing the right thing by expecting this kind of commitment from fourteen to seventeen-year-olds.

To my surprise, they exceeded every one of my expectations. Sure, there were weeks when they didn't get all of their reading done—just as happens with all of us. There were weeks they complained that they were missing their favorite TV show, which happened to fall at the same time as the study. They struggled with understanding how parts of the Bible applied to them and wondered why they should read it at all. But every week there was some moment of epiphany, an "aha moment" that this was an ancient book with a message that spoke to the

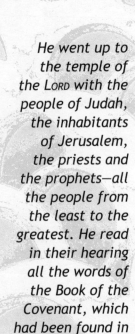

very things they were experiencing in their everyday lives. Every week one of them would see something in Scripture that I had not seen before, and the way God showed up when we were together reminded me of just why this book has brought awe and amazement to God's people for as long as we have called ourselves His.

One of my favorite things about Bible study is how God reveals things to us when we're together that we would not realize on our own. There is something communal about the nature of God's Word. We are not meant to read and interpret the Bible alone. In fact, there is a real danger that when we do so, we will stick to our own preconceived understandings and interpretations of God. Reading Scripture in community pushes us to understand it in light of the whole people of God, pushing our understanding beyond our boundaries.

How has studying God's Word with others pushed you beyond your own understanding of Scripture and of God?

Josiah understood the communal nature of God's Word. He was a monarch, a ruler, a decision-maker. He easily could have kept the book on a shelf in his throne room or taken it to the priests of the Temple and read it with them, determining that the group of leaders should read this holy book privately and make decisions on behalf of the kingdom. Instead, "He went up to the temple of the LORD with the people of Judah" (2 Kings 23:2).

Read all of 2 Kings 23:2 in the margin. When it says "the people of Judah," the passage is very specific. Who was included?

What did Josiah do when the people were together?

Why is it important to read Scripture together? There are so many reasons that it's hard to name them all. Let's consider just a few.

1. *As I've mentioned, reading the Bible together challenges and encourages us to grow outside of our own initial interpretation of Scripture.* When we read in community, we are able to help answer one another's questions as well as cause one another to ask more questions. Sometimes when we hear the questions or thoughts from others about a passage of Scripture, it helps us to better understand it and apply it more fully in our lives.

2. *Community gives us a source of accountability and guidance.* We all lead full lives, and it can become easy to skip daily reading of Scripture when things get

He went up to the temple of the LORD with the people of Judah, the inhabitants of Jerusalem, the priests and the prophets—all the people from the least to the greatest. He read in their hearing all the words of the Book of the Covenant, which had been found in the temple of the LORD.
2 Kings 23:2

busy. If we know that we are coming together with others to read and study together, we are more likely to stay accountable to a consistent plan for reading God's Word. Community also enriches the experience. Just as exercising is often easier and more enjoyable when meeting with a group of friends, so it can be with reading and studying the Bible. And let's face it: without a commitment to meet with others, we can find a million excuses to skip exercise—or Bible study! As we train ourselves to set a regular pattern of Scripture reading, the community helps to keep us on track.

3. In community we become aware of connecting what we're learning from God's Word with how we're growing in Him. Sometimes community with others makes us painfully aware of how much we still need to grow—not only spiritually but also relationally. Community can spark feelings ranging from compassion to irritation for those with whom we are studying. We must remember that our relationships in community are not separate from what we're learning in God's Word; they are reflections of our growth in discipleship.

4. Studying together reminds us that Bible study is not a dry, intellectual exercise but a fun, life-giving event! Community brings joy, laughter, and fun—helping us through sadness, grief, and struggle. Integrating our life in the Word with our real life events and emotions is a great way to remember that God wants to be part of every aspect of our lives.

5. Finally, when we study in community, we experience God's presence in unique and wonderful ways. Because we are made in the image of God and carry God's very Spirit within us, we are bearers of His image and presence to one another. As we interact and share how God is speaking to us through His Word, we spread the love and encouragement of God one to another. We know that whenever we gather together with the purpose of seeking God, He promises to meet us there.

Of these five reasons for studying the Bible together, which one resonates most strongly with your own experience? Why?

I love how Eugene Peterson talks about the community of God reading the Word of God together. Instead of *community* describing only the people in the sanctuary, worship hall, classroom, or wherever people might be reading and studying together, he says that the reading of Scripture makes community extend beyond the time and space that can be seen or touched. He writes:

> It is obedient, participatory listening to Holy Scripture in
> the company of the holy community through time (our two
> thousand years of responding to this text) and in space (our
> friends in Christ all over the world). High-church Anglicans,

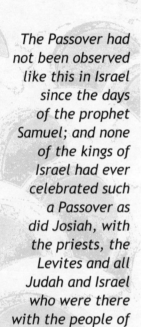

revivalistic Baptists, hands-in-the-air praising charismatics, and Quakers sitting in a bare room in silence are all required to read and live this text liturgically, participating in the holy community's reading of Holy Scripture.[12]

In other words, there is a huge and holy "cloud of witnesses" that is part of our community of reading Scripture. Recognizing that the people of God stretch across time and space reminds us that God's purposes and concerns are bigger than our ordinary, everyday lives. Remembering that God still cares about our day-to-day experiences, even as He is bigger than time or space, gives us a renewed gratitude that He loves us.

How has reading and studying God's Word with others increased your awareness or appreciation of the reality that God loves you?

The Passover had not been observed like this in Israel since the days of the prophet Samuel; and none of the kings of Israel had ever celebrated such a Passover as did Josiah, with the priests, the Levites and all Judah and Israel who were there with the people of Jerusalem.
2 Chronicles 35:18

Josiah didn't stop at reading the Scripture together with others. He also called the people to worship God together. Specifically, they were to celebrate the Passover together. While the Passover was observed in Hezekiah's day as well, we are told that this Passover celebration called by Josiah was special: "Neither in the days of the judges who led Israel nor in the days of the kings of Israel and the kings of Judah had any such Passover been observed" (2 Kings 23:22).

Read 2 Chronicles 35:18 in the margin. According to the last part of this verse, what in particular set this Passover celebration apart from those of the former kings of Israel?

The entire chapter of 2 Chronicles 35 is devoted to describing Josiah's Passover celebration. But a defining characteristic of this celebration was that *all* of the people who heard God's Word—priests, Levites, and all those from Judah and Israel who were there—were moved to worship together.

Think about this: reading Scripture together leads us to worship God, and worship gives us a chance to read Scripture together. It's a beautiful continuous cycle!

When I am out of town and miss worshiping with my church body on Sundays, I truly *miss* it. I often visit other churches, but they are not my home congregation. There's something special about worshiping in the company of those with whom we regularly read and study the Word of God. Have you found this to be true in your own life?

How does reading or hearing the Word of God in community move you to worship? Think about the worship service(s) and Bible study group(s) you attend.

What is special to you about worshiping with your home church? Why?

We've seen that Josiah spent a great deal of time and energy ridding the kingdom of things that were bad for his people. In 2 Kings 23:4-20 we read of all the places that idol worship had run amuck, which Josiah turned his full attention to stopping. Reading Scripture certainly helped to root out the things that were damaging to the people. But it convicted Josiah of more than the things they needed to *stop* doing together; it also convicted him of the things they needed to *start* doing together. Reading the Word of God together inspired them to renew their covenant with God and motivated them to worship by celebrating the Passover together. To put it simply, it drew them closer to God.

How has reading and studying the Scripture with others inspired you to renew your relationship and commitment to God?

In what ways has it renewed your practice or experience of worship?

As we learn from Josiah and his people, God's Word is best read and understood in community. The Bible is not meant to be read alone. When you read and have questions, let it drive you into community to find answers. When you read and are convicted of ways you need to change and grow, let it drive you into community to seek help and accountability. When you read and stand in awe of the greatness of God, let it drive you into community to worship and praise Him with others.

At the end of his story, Josiah gets an incredible commendation in Scripture.

Read 2 Kings 23:25 in the margin. How was King Josiah set apart from all the other kings before and after him?

> The Bible is best read and understood in community.

> *Neither before nor after Josiah was there a king like him who turned to the LORD as he did—with all his heart and with all his soul and with all his strength, in accordance with all the Law of Moses.*
> *2 Kings 23:25*

Perhaps the reason Josiah turned to the Lord with all his heart, soul, and strength "in accordance with the law of Moses" is that he read the law of Moses—the Word of God—with God's people. I hope the same will be true of us. My prayer is that you and your group are experiencing the deep connections that occur when God's people come together regularly to read the Scriptures, draw closer to God, and practice being a people of the Word. Wonderful things happen when we gather before God to discover His Word together!

Talk with God

Thank You, God, for my community of believers. Thank You for those who have taught me about Your Word, shared wisdom from Your Word, or exposed truth found in Your Word. Renew our commitment to seek You personally and corporately through Scripture reading. I'm so grateful that You have promised to meet us there! Amen.

Act on It

Send a text, e-mail, or letter to women in your Bible study community (group) this week, thanking them for walking with you as you discover God's Word together. (You might ask your group leader to provide e-mail addresses.)

Day 5: Set Apart for the Gospel

Read God's Word

¹ Paul, a servant of Christ Jesus, called to be an apostle and set apart for the gospel of God— ² the gospel he promised beforehand through his prophets in the Holy Scriptures ³ regarding his Son, who as to his earthly life was a descendant of David, ⁴ and who through the Spirit of holiness was appointed the Son of God in power by his resurrection from the dead: Jesus Christ our Lord. ⁵ Through him we received grace and apostleship to call all the Gentiles to the obedience that comes from faith for his name's sake. ⁶ And you also are among those Gentiles who are called to belong to Jesus Christ.

⁷ To all in Rome who are loved by God and called to be his holy people:
Grace and peace to you from God our Father and from the Lord Jesus Christ.

Romans 1:1-7

Reflect and Respond

We made it! We've arrived at the last day of our study together. I hope that during the last six weeks you have experienced encouragement, grown in wisdom, felt connected to God and others, and understood yourself as a chosen and blessed child of God.

Throughout these weeks together we've learned that God has set us apart from the world around us. This call to be set apart is not an act of withdrawal or a sign that we are better than anyone else. We are called to be set apart by giving all of ourselves—heart, soul, mind, and strength—to God.

Paul makes his identity and purpose clear in the very first sentence of his letter to the Romans: "Paul, a servant of Christ Jesus, called to be an apostle and set apart for the gospel of God." An apostle is one who is sent out for a purpose. So, Paul is saying that he is a servant who is set apart from those around him by the good news of Jesus Christ and sent out to share this good news with others. He is so passionate about proclaiming this identity that he can't even wait one sentence to get it out there! Being set apart is a lovely calling, one that means we will be different intentionally, not out of spite for the world around us but out of love for them.

Read the first verse of the Book of Romans aloud, replacing Paul's name with your own name:

_____, a servant of Christ Jesus, called to be an apostle and set apart for the gospel of God.

It may seem awkward to describe yourself in those words, but you are all of those things. You are called to serve Jesus. You are called to be set apart from the common and accepted practices of the world around you. You are being sent to share the good news of God with those around you and around the world.

What does it mean for you to live as someone who is "set apart" for the gospel?

How can you do this even as you continue to live and work and play in a world that is not surrendered to the plan and purposes of God?

The stories of First and Second Kings have given us some clues about spiritual practices we can participate in if we want to be wholly God's. Let's review each

199

of these practices briefly as we bring our study to a close and prepare to walk out the holy habits we have been exploring together.

Set apart by being consecrated. Solomon showed us what it was like to move from living an ordinary life to being royalty, consecrated and set apart for God. He had extreme ups and downs as he discovered what it means to be set apart. He had to learn that although a coronation happens to you, a consecration is something you participate in. He had to give himself to God, choosing to be used by God in his kingship.

We may never experience coronation, but we are to intentionally step into a different life when we join ourselves to Christ's royal family. Being set apart by God means that we are different in our practices, our faith, and what we love and worship. It means being marked by the same holiness that characterizes God Himself. This means you are consecrated to serve and love Him and to be a light in the darkness for others to see. That's the beauty of a set apart life. As you give each moment, each part of yourself, back to God, you are consecrating the life He has given you to Him.

What is one step you would like to take related to the practice of being consecrated—of giving yourself fully to God?

Set apart by listening. Elijah demonstrated that prayer involves not only talking but also listening. If we want to be set apart for God, we need to spend time saturating ourselves in His presence in quiet, absorbing His truth and peace. Elijah had to learn to discern the voice of God through the strong wind, earthquake, and fire. He had to train his heart to hear God—the still small voice —that would speak at just the right time. Likewise, we must train our hearts to know the voice of God as well. Remember that God speaks to us through Scripture, through the Holy Spirit, through saints, and through our common sense.

We live in a culture of noise, where music and media surround us all the time. We wrap noise around us like a blanket, and too often it insulates us from truly hearing each other and hearing God. The spiritual practice of listening to God requires paying attention, turning down the world's volume, and training our hearts to know God's voice.

What is one step you would like to take related to the practice of listening to God?

Set apart by mentoring. Elijah and Elisha showed us that it's possible to grow in faith only if we link ourselves to those around us who have already learned and practiced the ways of discipleship. We look to mentors who are strong in the faith and imitate what they do. Participating in mentoring relationships enables us to see the practices and attitudes of Jesus in flesh and blood human beings as we receive help and guidance from those we trust. Then we become a chain of faith, with mentors going before us and those we are mentoring coming behind us. We receive a heritage of faithfulness and we pass on that legacy to those who follow us. That's how the Christian faith works.

Jesus started with just twelve disciples, and now over two billion people around the world today profess faith in Christ. That chain of faith can be traced back through each generation; and believe it or not, you have a place in that chain! You are one of the links of faith.

What is one step you would like to take related to the practice of mentoring?

Set apart by practicing humility. Elisha and Naaman's story revealed that it's not favoritism that causes God to bless the humble over the proud. Rather, humility is the only state in which we give up our illusion of control and come before God with desperate and dedicated hearts. Naaman had it all and could order up anything he might want. But only when he truly needed help from others was he able to see his deeper need. It was the spiritual practice of humbling himself, of obeying what God asked of him through the prophet Elisha, that finally brought healing to Naaman. We don't always choose the moments—big or small—that humble us. But we can choose how we respond to them.

What is one step you would like to take related to practicing humility?

Set apart by worshiping God. Hezekiah reminded us that we are all likely to fall into the trap of giving our hearts to something less than God. Casting out our idols means cleansing our lives of those things we put before God and then coming to Him regularly in joyful worship.

Remember that bronze snake? It was meant to be a symbol, a reminder to look to God. A good thing became an idol when God's people focused their gaze on the statue instead of looking up to God. They began to worship a created thing instead of the Creator. That's why Hezekiah smashed it and called the people to worship God alone and to clear out all the idols.

The spiritual practice of worshiping God dethrones our idols, because there's simply no room for anyone or anything else in our line of sight when God is in the center.

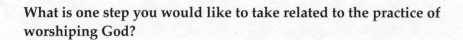

What is one step you would like to take related to the practice of worshiping God?

Set apart by discovering God's Word. Josiah ended our study by giving us a picture of what it means to discover the Word of God all over again. His passion for the buried treasure discovered in God's Word reminds us that we all need to return to our thirst for the living water found in Scripture.

Our Bibles aren't meant to sit on the shelf collecting dust. Instead, they are meant to be opened and explored, as if we are looking for buried treasure. The spiritual practice of Scripture reading requires a devotion to the Word itself, not simply to books about the Bible.

None of us is really supposed to be an expert on God's Word. We're supposed to be learners, disciples—always open to what the Word has to teach us. As we practice Scripture reading, our goal is not to master God's Word but to invite God's Word to master us.

What is one step you would like to take related to the practice of discovering God's Word?

Of all the spiritual practices we have explored, which are you most comfortable with and why?

Which of these spiritual practices challenges you the most and why?

Complete each of the following statements:

Something surprising I've learned from this study is . . .

Something I've learned about myself is . . .

Something I've learned about God is . . .

Because of what I've learned, I want to live differently by . . .

My prayer for you is that this study has given you renewed courage to live differently, to live a set apart life. The spiritual practices we have explored together are a wellspring of life that God can use to make your life unlike the world around you, unlike anyone else you've ever known, and even unlike the way you've lived in the past. These practices are tools to help you seek and connect with God as He continues to lead you in a set apart life. There's no "magic" in the practices, but the Holy Spirit can use them to shape you, form you, and reveal a word of truth to you.

As we've learned from the history of the kings and prophets we've studied, staying close to God matters. And spiritual practices can help us to do that. It is our holy habits that help to keep us from becoming full of ourselves, over-scheduled, and dependent on our own resources. They put us in the path of grace where God meets us and speaks into our lives.

May God bless you as you seek to be set apart. I challenge and encourage you to surrender your all to God, listen for His voice, link up with mentors who connect you to a long history of discipleship, bow in humble service, worship His holy name, and discover the treasure of His Word. Although the stories you've read happened long ago, God is still looking for those today He can set apart for His gospel as powerful change agents in the world. May you be one who listens to and answers that call!

Talk with God

Thank You, Lord, for the gift of spiritual practices that keep me close to You. Guard my heart against idols and the lesser things of this world. Set me apart for a life that is fully devoted to You. Take my whole life as an act of worship and praise to You, my faithful and loving Creator. I love You, Lord. Amen.

Act on It

Review your responses about the steps you would like to take related to the spiritual practices we have studied. As you look at your schedule for the next several weeks, consider when and how you will devote time to taking these steps. How can you work the practices into your regular routine? What can you do to ensure that you will follow through with your plan? Share your thoughts with a friend from your group or an accountability partner.

Week 6
Video Viewer Guide

We need to be more than just casual _observers_ of what someone else says is in God's Word. We need to _____ with God's Word ourselves.

_37_ % of people read the Bible once a week or more

Average American household has _4.7_ Bibles

> The high priest Hilkiah said to Shaphan the secretary, "I have found the _book_ of the _law_ in the house of the LORD." When Hilkiah gave the book to Shaphan, he read it. Then Shaphan the secretary came to the king, and reported to the king, "Your servants have emptied out the money that was found in the house, and have delivered it into the hand of the workers who have oversight of the house of the LORD." Shaphan the secretary informed the king, "The priest Hilkiah has given me a book." Shaphan then read it aloud to the king.
> . . .
> When the king heard the words of the book of the law, he _tore_ his clothes.
>
> 2 Kings 22: 8-11 NRSV

> The king went up to the house of the LORD, and with him went all the people of Judah, all the inhabitants of Jerusalem, the priests, the prophets, and all the people, both small and great; he read in their hearing all the words of the book of the covenant that had been found in the house of the LORD. The king stood by the pillar and made a covenant before the LORD, to follow the LORD, keeping his commandments, his decrees, and his statutes, with all his heart and all his soul, to perform the words of this covenant that were written in this book. All the people _joined_ in the _covenant_.
>
> 2 Kings 23:2-3 NRSV

We are not supposed to be experts on God's Word.

We're always to be *learners*, disciples—always open to what it has to *teach* us.

When we want to share God's word with other people, we don't have to be *experts*.

God uses us to help each other fall even more deeply in love with God's *Word*.

God wants us to be *matchmakers*

The spiritual practice of opening God's Word for *yourself* . . . is one that will help you immeasurably as you *grow* in your faith.

Notes

Week 1
1. Mark Haughwout, *Chronicles and Kings*, A Comparison. Hebrew University Jerusalem, 2002.
2. John N. Oswalt, *Called to be Holy* (Nappanee, Indiana: Evangel Publishing House, 1999), 4.
3. William Loader. "First Thoughts on Year B Epistle Passages from the Lectionary, Epiphany 7." Accessed March 10, 2015. http://wwwstaff.murdoch.edu.au /~loader/BEpEpiphany7.htm.
4. Oswalt, 55.
5. Claude Mariottini. "Forced Labor Under Solomon." Posted February 18, 2014. http://claudemariottini.com/2014/02/18/forced-labor-under-solomon/.

Week 2
1. William LaSor, David Hubbard, and Frederic Bush, *Old Testament Survey* (Grand Rapids: Eerdmans, 1996), 202.
2. Debra Scoggins Ballentine. "Baal," *Bible Odyessey*. Accessed March 12, 2015. http://www.bibleodyssey.org/en/people/related-articles/baal.
3. Warren Wiersbe, *Be Responsible* (Colorado Springs: Cook Communications Ministries, 2002), 129.
4. Gerritt Scott Dawson, *Part 4: Responding to Our Call, Companions in Christ Participant Book* (Nashville: Upper Room Books, 2006), 220.
5. J. Hampton Keathley, III. "The Major Prophets." Accessed March 12, 2015. https://bible.org/seriespage/major-prophets.
6. "Life and Ministry of Watchman Nee," www.watchmannee.org.
7. Warren Wiersbe, 130.
8. Ibid.
9. Keep Believing Ministries. "Elijah and the Ravens." Posted March 7, 2006. http://www.keepbelieving.com/sermon/elijah-and-the-ravens/.
10. Ronald S. Wallace, *Readings in 1 Kings* (Edinburgh: Scottish Academic Press, 1995), 123.
11. Bryant G. Wood. "What Do Mt. Horeb, The Mountain of God, Mt. Paran and Mt. Seir Have to Do with Mt. Sinai?" *Associates for Biblical Research.* Posted November 17, 2008. http://www.biblearchaeology.org/post/2008/11/What -Do-Mt-Horeb2c-The-Mountain-of-God2c-Mt-Paran-and-Mt-Seir-Have-to-Do -with-Mt-Sinai.aspx#Article.
12. Dorothee Soelle, *The Silent Cry: Mysticism and Resistance* (Minneapolis: Fortress Press, 2001), 74.

Week 3
1. *Oxford Dictionaries Online*, s.v. "Mantle," accessed March13, 2015, http://www. oxforddictionaries.com/us/definition/american_english/mantle.

2. J. Hampton Keathley, III. "Taking Up Your Mantle." *Studies in the Life of Elijah.* Posted June 4, 2004. https://bible.org/seriespage/17-taking-your-mantle-1-kings-1919-21.

3. *ATS Bible Dictionary Online,* s.v. "Jethro," accessed March 13, 2015, http://biblehub.com/topical/j/jethro.htm.

4. W. Dennis Tucker Jr. "Commentary on 2 Kings 2:1-12." Workingpreacher.org. Posted February 22, 2009. http://www.workingpreacher.org/preaching.aspx?commentary_id=242.

5. *ATS Bible Dictionary Online,* "Elisha," accessed March 13, 2015, http://biblehub.com/topical/e/elisha.htm.

6. *Dictonary of Bible Themes Online*, s.v. "5188: Tearing of Clothes," accessed March 13, 2015, https://www.biblegateway.com/resources/dictionary-of-bible-themes/5188-tearing-clothes.

7. *Baker's Evangelical Dictionary of Biblical Theology Online*, "Elijah," accessed March 14, 2015, http://www.biblestudytools.com/dictionary/elijah/.

8. Ibid.

9. Robert Coleman, *The Master Plan of Evangelism, 2nd edition* (Grand Rapids, Baker Revell, 2010), 33.

10. Barbara Quick, *Under Her Wing: The Mentors Who Changed Our Lives* (Oakland: New Harbinger, 2000), 91–92.

Week 4

1. Carly Simon Music. "You're So Vain–The Washington Post." Accessed March 15, 2015. http://www.carlysimon.com/You're_So_Vain.html.

2. Rebecca Konyndyk DeYoung, *Vainglory: The Forgotten Vice* (Grand Rapids, Eerdmans, 2014), 37.

3. Ibid., 25.

4. Ibid., 84.

5. Rick Warren, *The Purpose Driven Life* (Grand Rapids, Zondervan, 2002), 148.

6. DeYoung, 25.

7. *Easton's Bible Dictionary Online*, s.v. "Naaman," accessed March 15, 2015, http://www.biblestudytools.com/dictionary/naaman/.

8. Donald E. Demaray, *Experiencing Healing and Wholeness: A Journey in Faith* (Indianapolis , Light and Life, 1999), 178–179.

9. Ibid., 230.

10. *Easton's Bible Dictionary Online*, s.v. "Thorn in the flesh," accessed March 15, 2015, https://www.biblegateway.com/resources/dictionaries/dict_meaning.php?source=1&wid=T0003643.

11. Andrew Murray, *Humility: The Beauty of Holiness* (New York, Randolph & Co., 1895), 14.

12. Ibid., 16.

13. *Holman Bible Dictionary Online*, s.v. "Gehazi," accessed March 15, 2015. http://www.studylight.org/dictionaries/hbd/view.cgi?n=2230.

14. John Pollock, *Amazing Grace: John Newton's Story* (San Francisco: Harper and Rowe, 1981), 182.

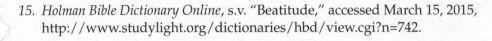

15. *Holman Bible Dictionary Online*, s.v. "Beatitude," accessed March 15, 2015, http://www.studylight.org/dictionaries/hbd/view.cgi?n=742.

Week 5

1. *ATS Bible Dictionary Online*, s.v. "Jeroboam," accessed March 16, 2015, http://biblehub.com/topical/j/jeroboam.htm.
2. "Nepali living goddess fired after U.S. visit," Reuters: July 4, 2007, http://uk.reuters.com/article/2007/07/04/oukoe-uk-nepal-child-goddess-idUKDEL21775220070704.
3. *Life Application Bible* (Grand Rapids: Zondervan, 1991), 575.
4. *ATS Bible Dictionary Online*, s.v. "Ahaz," accessed March 16, 2015, http://biblehub.com/topical/a/ahaz.htm.
5. *International Standard Bible Encyclopedia Online*, s.v. "Nehustan," accessed March 16, 2015, http://biblehub.com/topical/n/nehushtan.htm.
6. Ed Stetzer, *Idolatry Is Alive Today: Why Modern Church Leaders Still Fight an Old Battle*, *Christianity Today* (online edition), October 8, 2014, http://www.christianitytoday.com/edstetzer/2014/october/idolatry-is-alive-today-why-modern-church-leaders-still-fig.html.
7. *Easton's Bible Dictionary Online*, s.v. "Passover," accessed March 16, 2015, http://www.biblestudytools.com/dictionary/passover/.
8. Oswalt, 62.

Week 6

1. *Smith's Bible Dictionary Online* and *Easton's Bible Dictionary Online*, s.v. "Josiah," accessed March 17, 2015, http://biblehub.com/topical/j/josiah.htm.
2. "Josiah: Rediscovering the Word," Dr. Jerald Daffe, *Evangelical Sunday School Lesson Commentary*, http://www.biblestudytools.com/bible-study/topical-studies/josiah-rediscovering-the-word-11636193.html.
3. *All the Women of the Bible Dicitionary*, s.v. "Hulda," accessed March 17, 2015, https://www.biblegateway.com/resources/all-women-bible/Huldah.
4. M. Robert Mulholland, *Shaped by the Word: The Power of Scripture in Spiritual Formation* (Nashville, Upper Room, 1985), 49–54.
5. Ibid., 50.
6. Ibid., 54.
7. Ibid., 55.
8. Ibid., 39.
9. Eugene Peterson, *Eat This Book: A Conversation in the Art of Spiritual Reading* (Grand Rapids: Eerdmans, 2009), 35.
10. Tremper Longman and David E. Garland, eds., *The Expositor's Bible Commentary: 1, 2 Chronicles*, (Grand Rapids: Zondervan, 2010), 320.
11. Peterson, 35.
12. Ibid., 76.